On the Frontlines

ON THE FRONTLINES

Exposing Satan's Tactics to Destroy a Generation

Nathan L. Street

FOREWORD BY
Alan Wimberley

RESOURCE *Publications* • Eugene, Oregon

ON THE FRONTLINES
Exposing Satan's Tactics to Destroy a Generation

Copyright © 2019 Nathan L. Street. All rights reserved. Except for brief quotations in critical publications or reviews, no part of this book may be reproduced in any manner without prior written permission from the publisher. Write: Permissions, Wipf and Stock Publishers, 199 W. 8th Ave., Suite 3, Eugene, OR 97401.

Resource Publications
An Imprint of Wipf and Stock Publishers
199 W. 8th Ave., Suite 3
Eugene, OR 97401

www.wipfandstock.com

PAPERBACK ISBN: 978-1-7252-5122-9
HARDCOVER ISBN: 978-1-7252-5123-6
EBOOK ISBN: 978-1-7252-5124-3

Scripture quotations from The Authorized (King James) Version. Rights in The Authorized Version in the United Kingdom are vested in the Crown. Reproduction by permission of the Crown's patentee, Cambridge University Press.

Manufactured in the U.S.A.   10/15/19

This book is dedicated first to the glory of my Lord, Savior, and soon-coming King, Jesus Christ in Whom all things are possible and to my wife, Shannon, without whose love, support, prayers, patience, encouragement, and understanding, this journey would have been impossible.

CONTENTS

Foreword by Alan Wimberley | ix
Acknowledgments | xv

1. Introduction | 1
2. The Poison: Relativism | 6
3. The Dirty Bomb: Secularism | 19
4. The Shield: Our Conscience | 70
5. The Wolf in Sheep's Clothing: Social Justice | 82
6. The Enemy Within: Secular Humanism | 98
7. Equivocating Command: Pluralism | 122
8. The Front Lines: Public Education or Public Indoctrination? | 134
9. The Secret Weapon: Prayer | 159

Bibliography | 167

FOREWORD

It was late on a Friday night and we were sitting around a campfire, grateful for the Texas autumn evening, telling stories and taking a break from the busy week we had just had. Sometime around 10:30 or so, I noticed movement just beyond the glow of our fire. Someone or something was walking just outside the light.

I pointed out to my friends that something peculiar was happening and, as we watched, a form stepped quietly into the light. It was a beautiful deer. A whitetail doe, seemingly unafraid of us. She was standing not more than ten feet from where I was sitting in my lawn chair. I stood from my chair and faced this visitor from the woods, wondering why she wasn't staying away from us.

Having been raised on a farm, and having been a deer hunter my entire life, I had a lot of experience observing the nature of deer and other wild animals. But one thing I'd never seen was an animal like this actually walking from the safety of the forest and head straight into the campsite of humans. That's not normal animal behavior.

Not knowing exactly what to do, I moved toward the adult doe and waved her away from our campsite. The hooves of a deer can be potentially dangerous and there's no way to predict how any animal will react when crossing paths with people, I decided we just needed to remind the deer that it's best to keep to the woods.

As I encouraged her to run, waving my arms and shooing her back out of the light of the fire, she slowly turned and trotted back into the night. We returned to our fire and started back with our stories, once again appreciating the peace of the October evening. About five minutes later, I looked and saw our guest appear again at the edge of our campsite, stepping once again into the light. This was past unusual. This was weird.

Deer are naturally afraid of us. Yet, she kept coming back to our campsite. Suddenly, I thought I knew why. After moving her back toward the woods, I told my friends to grab their flashlights and start carefully walking around the edges of our campsite, being careful where we stepped. Sure enough, not more than five feet into the darkness, opposite the place where the deer kept entering our site, was a small hollowed-out nest of grass.

And curled inside that small nest was a tiny, freshly-born baby deer. Taking care not to touch the nest, we watched this sleeping beauty. This was the reason for the unnatural bravery of the doe. This was the reason for the courage and the refusal to leave the area. Her baby lay just outside our site and she wasn't going to let her natural fear of man make her abandon her young child.

After taking a couple of pictures on our phones, we quietly picked up our gear, put out the campfire and left the deer alone. Mother and child reunited and the natural enemy retreats. That's what children do for us. They make us braver than we are. For the sake of our children, we are willing to face any enemy and take on any challenge.

What we do for generations of children matters. For centuries, those who taught, led and engaged with the young knew that what we passed on was important. And, for centuries, what was passed on to those generations was nobility. The significance of the classical elements in life. Education had always been founded on the beliefs that:

- people are created to be noble and fully human; to appreciate truth, beauty and goodness
- people are not naturally good
- therefore, it's the duty of adult generations to teach the young to be noble.

In the latter years of the nineteenth century, however, those who taught the young began shifting the focus of education toward a modern and progressive push. While nothing is wrong with being relevant, the belief systems that had anchored the "passing of the torch" of nobility were replaced by a new set of ideas about the young and the responsibilities toward them. These new ideas began changing the direction, and the purpose, of what was being passed on.

The primary focus became to prepare children for good jobs and to teach children to survive the current culture. Serving as the ever-changing cycle of curriculum revisions, modern and progressive education began chipping away at the trusted, reliable body of content that had been fixed for centuries.

And the new set of beliefs forming the foundation borrowed much from the Age of Romanticism, namely that people are naturally and basically good already and we shouldn't worry about things such as nobility. If education, once the center for moral thought, becomes, instead where nothing is certain or reliable, the classical elements are now threatened. Move forward more than one hundred years later.

We are afraid to speak of morality on campuses and in classrooms. Truth is no longer considered a fixed, objective reality for young generations as they grow up in a confusing culture. Now, it's who's truth, your truth, their truth.

We find our young being powerfully influenced by social media. Celebrities are becoming the voice of counsel for these generations. In the age of the megachurch, we are afraid of offending anyone and everyone. We don't know how to take a stand because we have traded discernment for tolerance, chosen relevance over the offensive nature of the gospel and shaved off the cutting edge of the cross.

While never criticizing the Bride of Christ, the body of believers throughout the world, it's difficult not to point out some truths about the organized church when pastors care more about the crowd and are willing to be silent to keep the numbers rising. The gospel can get lost in those generations if we replace that sharp message with a pleasant overture of comfortable language and nice feelings.

In a world that changes every day, those who follow Christ often find themselves in a confusing culture that demands their attention, challenges their faith and questions the objective truth found only in the Word of God. Countless answers are offered all around us. Yet, these often reduce scriptural teaching to nothing more than self-help, self-improvement and self-centered manuals. So much time is spent orbiting around the Word of God while never piercing the central axis of His message to man.

And the gospel is too often treated as nothing more than an entrance doorway to a community created to shape, coach and polish the believer to a shinier, prettier and more acceptable version of himself. Knowledge of the gospel is seen as an assumed truth, an apologetic allegiance or a tolerated requirement in a culture of tickled ears and applauding crowds searching for an easy way to be better.

Stepping into this current environment with a sharp word for all of us is Dr. Nathan Street. The opening paragraph of chapter two sets the foundation for the entire book. Dr. Street starts this chapter introducing several points regarding what he describes as a chaotic, and alarming, culture where generations are being affected and shaped dramatically different than ever before.

"On the Frontlines" is an unapologetic calling out by a new author, experienced in the things he speaks of from the viewpoint of a believer committed to generations of children and adolescents. Whether it's the school, the church, the home or the community at large, all of us need what Dr. Street is challenging us to do, and be, in this book.

Rather than merely providing an endorsement or a "jacket review", I'm honored to introduce Dr. Street to readers who will carefully consider the things he points to here. I know Nathan as one who is committed to the best we can do, and be, for those who need us the most; our children.

Having been his professor and doctoral chair, I've always appreciated the tremendous role Dr. Street has played in the lives of so many. And, with "*Frontlines*", one more opportunity to encourage and influence others for the sake of the gospel and younger generations is now a reality in his work.

Balancing between the descriptive and the prescriptive, this book doesn't hide from anyone. The best writers will always have those who won't agree with everything they propose. Within the pages of this book, the reader may not always agree with every point, idea or assertion made by this new author.

I believe, though, you'll find yourself more aligned with Dr. Street more often than not because he doesn't weigh himself down with complexities that can be negotiated and watered down as he proposes the simple return to the right things. With a clear call back to the scriptural anchor of prayer.

"*How can Christians defeat the attacks of the enemy outlined in this book? By prayer. I worry when Christians who have an honest concern about not doing enough state that all they can do is pray while a loved one is experiencing difficulty. To be fair, the human mind seeks to control sometimes uncontrollable situations and when that is impossible, one feels powerless. But this is exactly where God wishes to bring His people—to a place of powerlessness in themselves.*" This passage draws us back, but in a more insistent and genuine way, to the most powerful and the most effective.

As you read "*On the Frontlines*", you may want to focus only on the serious issues described here. Or you may get caught up in the weaknesses of the adult generations pointed out by Dr. Street. You may even find the stark, "no holds barred" style of the writing to be refreshing or offensive depending on your personal stance.

However, my encouragement is that you not land on any of these elements and judge from that limited angle. As I read, I see hope. I see an earnest call to stand up and be counted. We have to remember that the enemy is not omnipresent, omniscient or all powerful.

While the tools of the enemy can be used to cause much damage, that enemy has no power in the presence of God. And this book reminds us of that. Whether we are standing up for right, kneeling in prayer or walking steadfastly in the power and grace of our Father, this book pushes us to the frontlines of a battle that's worth fighting.

Our enemy is patient. Willing to wait for generations, the strategy employed was to begin with the minds of children. The enemy, being patient, teaches our children to tolerate everything. Sacrifice discernment and tolerate everything.

If these generations of children are not trained in discernment, and if they tolerate everything, they are more ready to not only tolerate but to readily accept everything. Once all things are tolerated and accepted, these things can even be celebrated in a culture that demands no discernment. In those generations, once they've grown and are now leading, much damage lies ahead in our future.

In education, we are seeing some tremendous efforts to return to the timeless, reliable and classical education that stood firm throughout the centuries of the past. This return is being led by those who have seen the dramatic shifts in our culture and how damaging they can be for coming generations of children. "On the Frontlines" is a call to a battle that must be fought; a war that must be waged. As in all things, it begins with love. As you read, let the Spirit of God minister to your heart through the words of Dr. Street's message.

What we do for generations of children matters. Join those on the frontlines. That work is worth it. Just as that mother deer showed unnatural courage on that quiet Texas evening, refusing to abandon her newborn, so must we not abandon our young generations to those things that would do them harm.

Alan Wimberley

Education Architect, Professor & Author
"Designed for Learning:
Transferring Wisdom to Digital Generations"
"Reshaping the Paradigms of Teaching and Learning:
What Happens Today is Education's Future"

ACKNOWLEDGMENTS

Where would I be without my parents? I would like to honor the Lord by honoring them with this book. My mother raised me in the nurture and admonition of the Lord my entire life. While my dad was not always saved, he ensured I lived in a safe environment, had food to eat, and was loved. He ensured my rearing was aligned with the moral and natural laws. I had a good home. It was not one with everything I could ever want but it was one where I was loved, cared for, and where I was in church no matter the circumstances. I will never forget hearing my mother pray for me and read scriptures to me daily. This is indelibly etched on my conscience forever. I am eternally grateful. I hope to be half as good as a parent myself.

I would like to thank the Randleman Church of God in Randleman, North Carolina for its support and guidance throughout my tenure there as member and music minister. Pastor Emeritus Troy Wilhelm has been my pastor for nearly 30 years and has greatly influenced my life for good. Pastor Wilhelm has been a role model and friend. I greatly appreciate him, his wife Wanda, their family and their service to the Lord. The Church of God (Cleveland, TN) has been my home church for the duration of my life. I am grateful for the courageous stance for the gospel of Jesus Christ undertaken by the Church of God. I am saved, sanctified, and baptized in the Holy Ghost because of the invaluable training I have received throughout the years under the banner of the Church of God.

I would also like to thank my mother-in-law, Judy Smith, for her love, care, and guidance throughout my marriage to Shannon. She has been a model of fortitude. Judy is a widow. She is the caregiver for my sister-in-law who suffered a traumatic brain injury as a toddler. Her life has been met with pain, heartache, and turmoil, but through it all, she has never wavered in her faith, trust, and love for the Lord.

Dr. P. Douglas Small is also a major influence in my life. He recruited me to speak at conferences he hosted throughout the region. It is because of these conferences I generated the bulk of the material I have presented in this book. Dr. Small gave me an opportunity and I am so grateful.

ACKNOWLEDGMENTS

I would like to acknowledge the school district where I work. While I will withhold the name for separation's sake, I am grateful for the job with which the Lord has blessed me. While it is challenging and seems to grow more challenging daily, I am grateful for the ability to work there. I am also very grateful for my positions working with Liberty University and Southern Wesleyan University. Both institutions are filled with wonderful, caring professors who truly love the Lord. I am honored and blessed to be counted among their faculty. Liberty University is special to me as it was where I earned my doctorate. The chair of my dissertation, Dr. Alan Wimberley, is more special to me than he can possibly know. I am grateful to him, particularly, for his leadership, guidance, support, and friendship. I aspire to be a teacher, mentor, and guide like him. My current instructional mentor, Dr. Charles Schneider, is such a good man and mentor. He has been such a tremendous asset to me. I am grateful to have him in my life as well.

Finally, I would like to acknowledge all of the Christian students and teachers in our public schools. It is becoming increasingly difficult and dangerous to be an open, practicing Christian in our public arenas. I hope to encourage those individuals to continue to live your faith out loud. While you will be met with resistance and hatred, your reward in eternity will be great. Endure the struggles and hardships because, in the end, it will be worth it all. Preach the gospel whether openly or through your walk with Christ. Do not be ashamed or afraid. We possess the gift of eternal life. It is incumbent upon us to share the gospel of Jesus Christ wherever we can. Fight the good fight. Finish the course. Keep the faith.

1. INTRODUCTION

I SEE IT NEARLY every day. The culture is devolving into a jumbled, chaotic quagmire of insanity. Events are occurring in the modern culture, causing many to respond often with such phrases as, "I never thought I would see the day . . ." Indeed, we are living in a day and age when good is considered evil and evil deeds and lifestyles are considered good. As Christians, we should never be surprised by this though. If we have thoroughly read Scripture, listened to anointed men and women deliver gospel messages, and remotely remained attentive to current events, it is blatantly obvious that what God said would happen is happening.

This book endeavors to expose the tactics Satan has utilized to destroy the culture and, he hopes, destroy an entire generation. Being a public-school employee, I maintain a unique perspective on the effects of this seismic cultural shift occurring in our society. A large proportion of millennials not only buy into the modern cultural dogma but they are becoming activist purveyors of its tenets. Through my thoughts in this book, I will make clear the real, objective truth behind the most commonly utilized tactics of Satan. That truth is that our culture has adopted a new religion—secular postmodernism that has transformed into fascist social justice. Make no mistake: this is no less than a religion and it should be treated as such.

Our culture is confused, blind, careless, selfish, and careening toward a cliff. As much as we would like to save it from disaster, the simple truth is that we will not. No amount of evangelism will rescue the entire culture from devolving into complete mindless secularism. This book is not designed to prevent that from happening. It is already well progressed. It is a cancer that is in stage four classification. However, this does not relieve the Christian of his or her responsibility to fulfill the Great Commission. On the contrary, it is a clarion call to preach the unadulterated gospel of Jesus Christ to as many as possible.

This book is designed to provide Christians with an awakening alarm. We must be vigilant in these last days. Where the enemy used to be subtle, he is more overt. Where he used to stealthily poison minds, he now splashes it across the airwaves. Sin is overt and ubiquitous in our culture and it seems as though Christians are either ignorant, careless, or worse: accepting.

In this book, I am quite critical of the church in general. The church has abdicated its responsibility as the conscience of the culture and ceded its God-given authority to the public schools, media, and government. The gospel of Jesus Christ has given way to the gospel of prosperity. Fire and brimstone have bowed to tolerance and equity. Sin is no longer perceived to be an issue for the pulpit. It is simply easier to accept sinful lifestyles than to preach against them and lose congregants. Churches have become nothing more than social gathering spots where people can come on a weekly basis to make themselves feel good about their lifestyles. More than ever before, it seems people are heaping to themselves teachers having itching ears.

This book is also a clarion call for the family. Too many parents subject children to parenting fads and faux science in an effort to keep up with the Joneses. Discipline is no longer exercised in the home. Family devotions are a thing of the past. Learning in the home is no longer a necessity. It is more important to ensure children get in the best preschool, school, and college. It is more important for them to learn a second language, musical skill, sport, or some other skill deemed important for life. These things have taken the place of God in the lives of even Christian children. The modern culture, through television, has become the new altar at which the family worships. Ensuring children play in this week's sports game is more important than ensuring children are in church. Staying home to watch the Super Bowl is more important that ensuring the family is in church on a Sunday night. Indeed, the culture and its benefits have supplanted God in the lives of so-called Christians.

What does one think would happen should the Lord return for His bride and the family has elected to stay home and watch football? Do we honestly think the Lord would wait until the last field goal to take those to heaven who have put a game with no eternal consequences before the worship of Him? This is not popular but true: the individual who chose football over God made his choice. He chose football as his god. Anything that comes before God is one's new god.

Make no mistake, parents, children see what is more important to you. From this, they learn that anything they wish to do or see is more important than worship of the one, true God. Do not be surprised when they choose cultural ills over godly interests and succumb to the evils described in this book. Do not be surprised when confronted with atheism and evolution,

1. INTRODUCTION

they choose to believe a lie. Do not be surprised when your son or daughter comes home with a baby out of wedlock. I mean, they have seen Mom and Dad watch it on television and apparently approve of it, right? They never learned that God is the Author of Creation so what an ungodly, perverse professor says is true, right? Mom and Dad chose to stay home, away from church whenever they felt like it so it must not be that important, right?

A part of me cannot, however, blame people for wanting to stay home from church. In most cases, church has become a self-help group. It is a place for motivational speeches, coffee, doughnuts, and a pat on the back. What are we really getting from that anyhow? Might as well stay home. Church used to be where one went to experience the awesome power of the Holy Spirit move in particularly expressive ways. It used to be where one could go to learn how to live a godlier life. It used to be a place where one could go to draw closer to the Lord in order to experience more of His presence in daily life. Sadly, none of that is very important to the modern church anymore.

The home and the church are the most critical elements of child-rearing that anyone could imagine. Because the home and church are so critical, it is crucial we, as a body of believers, understand the tactics the enemy has employed against the home and church. Some of these tactics are operational in the home and church. In the book, I will deal with relativism and how it is a poison to the mind, how it is pervasive in school curriculum and culture, how the government has even succumbed to many of its destructive forces, how the church is dealing with it, and how God expects us to resist it.

After there is a firm understanding of relativism, the reader needs to understand what I term as "the dirty bomb." Secularism is a dirty bomb because when it explodes, it scatters shrapnel as far and wide as possible. Inherent to our discussion on secularism is a brief treatment of the term, secularism's philosophical cousin (postmodernism), their evil stepchild (progressivism), the crazy but deadly aunt (feminism) and how abortion is her religion of choice, the so-called "Me Too" movement, universalism and how it is gaining acceptance in the church, antinomianism and the hyper-grace movement, evolution and its effects on children, atheism, and agnosticism.

The discussion will then progress to perhaps the most vile and pervasive new structure in public school discourse: social justice. Social justice is an evil, totalitarian belief system perpetrated on public schools and modern culture whose intended result is outright Communism. At the roots of the social justice movement is a topic often misunderstood: humanism. Humanism, in short, is the worship of self rather than the worship of God and how this self-worship is founded in satanism.

From there the discussion focuses on what I have termed as the "equivocating command," which proceeds from no clear leader. This is the modern belief in pluralism. Pluralism, in short, is the belief that there are multiple philosophical means to reaching God, whoever he/she/it is and whatever his/her/its name is. Pluralism has even infiltrated aspects of the church, primarily through the first church of Oprah and her so-called minister/pastor/evangelist friends.

I could not write a book about such matters without a treatise on the conscience. Is the conscience divinely inspired or is it the actual voice of God? What is the age of accountability? Is conscience a natural phenomenon or is it nurtured through the actions of parents, then our own actions? I present a case study on an actual situation I encountered regarding a transgendered child and relate it to how Proverbs 22:6 should be so critical to families. From there, I ask why we should "why," discuss the role of shame and guilt, and end with how sanctification is a rarely utilized term in our churches but is invaluable to eternity.

As the book progresses to a close, I discuss the role of the public school in the conveyance of Satan's tactics. Is public school public education or public indoctrination? I deal with the separation of church and state and how this relates to the establishment clause, Satan's desire to wrest control of our children as early as possible, how the silence of the church has not only allowed these evils but promulgated them, the psychological underpinnings of children's ministry, understanding our children as consumers of a digital world, why questioning God is not necessarily a bad thing, and an analysis of the law when it relates to Christianity in schools.

Finally, I end the book with a chapter on the most powerful secret weapon known to mankind: prayer. I explain why I call it a "secret" weapon, why we need it now more than ever, and end the chapter with a final entreaty to our Christian brothers and sisters.

Hopefully, the book will challenge you to activate your discernment and look for the signs of Satan's tactics at work in school curriculum, modern culture, television broadcasts, popular music, and even the church. There are times when the book is difficult to read because it challenges some sacred cows. It even challenged my own. In the end, I hope readers will understand that I wrote this book with a loving spirit in an attempt to call us all back to a fundamental, prayerful, holy, and sanctified life. Time is short. The Lord is soon coming. We must be ready.

2. THE POISON: RELATIVISM

THE WORLD IS IN chaos. School shootings—a horrific scenario—are nearly routine. When the world seeks a motive for such heinous acts, it typically discovers a history of violent behavior, lack of moral center, and a general noninterventionist strategy to parenting. Many school shooters almost appear to be completely devoid of emotion or sympathy. Many fail to realize school shootings are singular acts in a generally protracted timeline of consistent barrages of cultural devolution on the psyche and spirit of this generation. Students are presented with a social curriculum, a "hidden curriculum" so to speak, that is tolerant and accepting of every idea, concept, emotion, and action, no matter how aberrant. In fact, traditional, conservative, Christian ideals are typically considered by such curriculum as socially unacceptable, antiquated, and irrelevant. Ironically, the purveyors of tolerance, acceptance, and social justice are customarily the very individuals who censor and excoriate conservative values in a conspicuous demonstration of prejudice and animus.

Relative Justice

Modern media is no longer concerned with masking its abject hypocrisy; even justifying such hypocrisy in an effort to buttress the notion of what they incorrectly conceive as justice. It is typically a justice spawned in their own preconceived notions of how a socialistic, atheistic, progressive utopia would be superior to whatever is considered the converse of such ideology. Justice is, in fact, no longer considered the act of measuring one's actions against an immutable standard but is, instead, contingent upon one's background information, demographics, intent, and feelings. Recently, the Supreme Court of the United States ruled in favor of upholding President Donald Trump's travel ban as constitutional in a narrow five to four ruling.

In the dissent, Justice Sonia Sotomayor excoriated the decision by highlighting supposed intent on behalf of the president "motivated by hostility and animus toward the Muslim faith."[1] Edmonson further explained Justice Sotomayor's perspective as a Latina required her to consider, as she once stated, "personal experiences affect the facts that judges choose to see." She further iterated, while continuing to explain her decision to dissent, how President Trump had failed to repudiate any of his previous comments on Islam.

Whether one agrees with President Trump's particular stance on this issue is, frankly, irrelevant. The United States judicial system, much like biblical justice, is built on "rule of law." The Constitution of the United States is considered the standard by which all people and actions must be measured in such cases. Notice how Justice Sotomayor underscored how she perceived the president's intent as hostile toward Muslims. Again, whether President Trump harbors antipathy toward Muslims or not is irrelevant. The Constitution of the United States does not regulate one's personal feelings. It does, however, regulate one's actions should those personal feelings result in such behavior.

Sotomayor's dissent must be considered in light of her own statement whereby she insinuated her own rulings would be colored by litigants' personal experiences. This is contrary to the justice system of the United States as framed by the Constitution whereby the president possesses the authority to initiate a travel ban, regardless of personal feelings. This is the reason the nation's justice system is characterized by a blindfolded woman holding a scale. One's intent, motivations, demographics, and personal experiences should never be considered when determining a legal course of action. To do otherwise is the very definition of prejudice. The application of law must not be contingent upon personal qualifying characteristics nor should that law be considered in light of modernity. The Constitution must be interpreted as it was originally framed in strict constructionism.

In fact, the Supreme Court of the United States should never be considered political operatives; however, one can only consider them as such in the modern era because of the socio-political indoctrination that they make evident in nearly every ruling. Let us consider an alternative scenario. Let us imagine that the act of abortion, currently legal in the United States, was considered in the Supreme Court once again. Five justices voted to overturn the law, making it illegal to obtain an abortion again. The chief justice then presented the majority opinion citing his own deeply held

---

1. C. Edmonson, "Sonia Sotomayor Delivers Sharp Defense in Travel Ban Case," *The New York Times*, June 26, 2018.

religious beliefs that life begins at conception and that following the model of his own rearing that such an act is tantamount to murder.

We should be certain that should this scenario occur, the progressives in the nation would accuse the majority of adjudicating, based on their own religious beliefs, rather than the law. One may ask how this could possibly be any different from the methods Justice Sotomayor admittedly employs when coloring her own judgments with litigants' and her own personal experiences. In short, it is the height of hypocrisy and it is prevalent in modern society. It is also the context by which social justice is envisioned.

A House Without a Foundation

A deeply dangerous precedent has been long-established in modern society and the result will be disastrous. In fact, we are already witnessing the vile effects of such a precedent. That precedent is, essentially, no precedent at all. Open hypocrisy, outright lying, and prejudicial treatment in the name of social justice is acceptable today because of cultural relativism. Relativism entails the belief that one's moral convictions may not necessarily be the convictions of another but that each perspective is valid. Among the central tenets of relativism is that there can be no objective, absolute truth but that there are many truths completely dependent upon the perspectives, intents, emotions, and experiences of the individual. Mahatma Gandhi once wrote, "Nobody in this world possesses absolute truth. This is God's attribute alone. Relative truth is all we know. Therefore, we can only follow the truth as we know it. Such pursuit of truth cannot lead anyone astray."[2] That was quite an absolute statement from someone who is preaching absolute truth is untenable.

Gandhi's statement could, perhaps, not be more dangerous or stupid. If Gandhi's statement is indeed true, which would, ironically, be contrary to the point of the statement itself, then Adolf Hitler followed truth as he knew it and, in so doing, he could not have been led astray. The debate would be, however, that Hitler was evil and his truth was injurious to others. Still, how could one who does not possess absolute truth, judge Hitler's truth as invalid?

Qualifying truth as not being injurious to others inherently assigns an absolute—truth does not injure—hence the argument spirals into asinine

2. Mahatma Gandhi, *Collected Works of Mahatma Gandhi* (New Delhi: Publications Division, Ministry of Information and Broadcasting, Govt. of India, 1969).

circular reasoning expeditions from which one will never recover. Regrettably, many in modern society are hopelessly mired in endless circular reasoning expeditions, painfully attempting to justify and reason a concept like relativism that is inherently illogical in order to pacify their own resistance to conducting a life in harmony with scriptural truth.

Jesus warned of such reliance on the unreliable. In Matthew 7:24-27, He commented that the action of not heeding His teachings is tantamount to building a house on the sand. He further illustrated that when rain, flood, and winds persisted against the house, it collapsed spectacularly. Conversely, those who heed the words of Christ are likened to wise men who built their house on a rock whereby the rains, floods, and winds cannot prevail. The assumed, but not overtly referenced, component of Jesus's illustration is the foundation. A foundation supported only by loose particulate will result in severe instability. Even modern building techniques require foundations to be built on bedrock. This requires the builder to dig through the loose particulate until he or she arrives at solid, immovable, unshakable rock. When the house is anchored in something as steadfast as bedrock, then winds, rains, and floods may, indeed, damage the house but the foundation will remain intact.

When considering our lives as the houses in Christ's illustration, we see that when we build our existence on something that possesses no absolute authority on which we can firmly establish a foundation, then the fall will be spectacular. The relativist may argue that they have firmly established their "house" in the belief that there is no objective truth and that he or she has many options. Again, this argument returns us to the circularly reasoned, illogical position that all truth is relative except the belief itself that all truth is relative. Such a position is oxymoronic and moronic all at the same time. Either all truth is relative or truth is absolute. There can be no compromise because either no truth is absolute or no truth is relative to those who respectively believe in either premise. Truth cannot be concurrently relative and absolute. This is a violation of the *law of noncontradiction,* which states A cannot be both A and B simultaneously. It is a basic law of logic.

We should build our spiritual and figurative house on a firm foundation, establishing our worldview, actions, and thoughts in a standard or concept that is superior and transcendent to ourselves. For the church and Christian, that standard is the Word of God. For the nation, that standard is the Constitution of the United States, which is, incidentally, originally constructed on many of the virtues and principles inherent in the Word of God. At times, one must tunnel through layers of particulate to get to the solid bedrock of truth on which to establish a firm foundation. In modern society, the once-reliable traditions, such as the media, have now become nothing more than biased, agenda-driven, tabloids.

With the advent of social media and other forms of digital media, the constant barrage of information and misinformation presents quite a quandary for those who seek the truth. The information presented can, and often is, completely false and designed to advance a specific agenda. At times, the information is laced with enough truth to be mostly accurate but is presented in a fashion so as to make the listener or reader make assumptions or decisions the presenters prefer. Regrettably, the majority of Americans choose to obtain their news from these sources and accept, at face value, the presentation with little to no additional research.

The result of little to no additional research leads one into deception. Paul wrote that there would be those who would believe a lie and ultimately be damned for rejection of truth.[3] That is no more evident than in the modern society. Most refuse to study further in order to show oneself approved unto God.[4] Too many pick up what is readily available and observable from the surface and establish their foundations there. They never dig deeper to the bedrock of truth in order to firmly establish their foundations. Digging to the bedrock requires much time and effort—something most, including Christians, refuse to expend.

There is no better example of this assertion than what one would find in most churches on Sunday mornings. The pastor has an hour, at best, to deliver what the Lord has laid on his or her heart for the congregation. If he or she preaches past twelve o'clock, there will be trouble. God must be willing to accomplish what He desires to accomplish during this hour because we are not going to give Him one second more. Imagine if that had been the case when Jesus told his followers to tarry in Jerusalem until they be endued with power from on high.[5] Sorry, Jesus, I just cannot wait past noon for this promise. I have places to go and people to see. On how many occasions have we failed to obtain a mighty blessing from the Lord because we lacked the patience or, frankly, the hunger for Him?

---

3. Thessalonians 2:11-12.
4. Timothy 2:15.
5. Luke 24:49.

2. THE POISON: RELATIVISM

Let there be no mistake—the social progressives and postmodernists in our culture are hell-bent on destroying the foundation of our faith. While the church and Christianity muddles along on the surface of the particulate, never reaching the bedrock of our faith, the radical progressives are below the surface, whittling away at our foundations.[6] Unfortunately, we either lack sufficient will or knowledge to tunnel to those same foundations in order to repair them. The foundations of family are routinely challenged by perverse lifestyles flagrantly displaying sinful practices for the world, while openly challenging anyone to disagree. Children are encouraged to explore their own gender identity, ranging in number to sometimes over twenty various possibilities.

Truth, we are told, is relative. Gender, we are told, is a concept of the mind and not actual. The definition of family, we are told, is not absolute but is fluid, encompassing any iteration of structure one sees fit. The practice of relativism is invading every aspect of modern life and is a tool the enemy, through the radical progressives, is utilizing as a jackhammer below the surface to destroy the foundations. All the while, the church continues to muddle along the surface, never reaching the bedrock of faith and truth. Worse yet, the church is deaf to the jackhammering below the surface because the enemy has coddled and eased the church into self-submission and slumber.

Perhaps even more alarming is how relativism has invaded the church. The days of "fire and brimstone preaching" are all but lost. That style has been replaced by "tickles and tulips," "coffee and doughnuts," and all manner of gimmicks. What happened to the unadulterated preaching of the Word of God? Are jets and limousines more important than the human soul? Are larger bank accounts more important than the lives of the next generation? Are nickels and noses on Sunday mornings more respected than the disciplining of a generation to reach the lost? Where is truth? Why is the church refusing to draw a line in the sand on sin? In short, the spirit of Thyatira has invaded the church.[7]

---

6. Ravi Zacharias, *Deliver Us From Evil: Restoring the Soul in a Disintegrating Culture* (Nashville, TN: Thomas Nelson, Inc., 1997).

7. Revelation 2:18-29.

Tolerance

The church has embraced relativism in the form of tolerance. Tolerance is a buzz word among the academically elite in modern society. To be tolerant is to be sophisticated, intelligent, and self-actualized. Let me be clear: we must tolerate our fellow humans. We should be patient with those who are enslaved by sin because Christ died for them just like He did for us. We, too, were once slaves to sin. However, we are never called by God to be tolerant of sin. Modern society has essentially deemed it taboo for anyone to be discerning or judgmental. To challenge a sinful practice is to be labeled a rube, unintelligent, lacking in character, unenlightened, and unsophisticated. Worse yet, challenging sin may result in one being labeled a bigot, homophobe, or hater.

The church, from the perspective of the postmodernist, should be inclusive, pluralistic, and open-minded. There is no appetite for civil discourse in the modern society. The 24-hour news cycle is fraught with one person after another trying to shout down another. The immediate response of the Left is to attack another personally. Generally, the conditioned response is, "Well, you're racist." This is a tactic the Left has learned from Vladimir Lenin who once stated, "We can and must write in a language that shows among the masses hate, revulsion, and scorn toward those who disagree with us."

I have often heard in church the phrases, "That is my conviction," "That is not my conviction," "Do not project your convictions on me." Similarly, I have often heard the phrase, even in my own family, "Do not let others' judgment define you," "Do not judge me," and "Who are you to judge me? You're not God. You do not have the right to judge me." Recently, a member of my own family made the following statement to my wife: "I respect the way you live your life; you need to respect the way I live mine."

Let me be clear: these collective statements are designed to appease an individual's own conscience about the sinful practices in which they have engaged while, simultaneously, attempting to shame the individual castigating the practices. The ultimate goal is to silence the confrontation. We live in a day and hour when people do not want to hear the truth about sin. I will not tolerate or respect a sinful lifestyle no matter if that lifestyle is led by family or not. Neither should we encourage that sin with our silence or overtly accept it simply because the individual is family. To do so is presenting a double standard, is hypocritical, and is paving the road to hell.

One needs not judge the actions of another individual. God has already judged those actions in His Word, and when someone illuminates that world of darkness, it is done in an effort of love to save a soul from eternal separation from God. To remain silent and tolerant while someone conducts a lifestyle of sin is to hate them, be complicit in their sinful practices, and sentence them to an eternity in hell.

The relativist worldview has led even Christians to accept sinful lifestyles. James 1:8 records, "A double-minded man is unstable in all his ways." The modern Christian is far too concerned with "fitting in," "not rocking the boat," and "going along to get along." Decades of this perspective has led the modern church to accept practices once universally deemed sinful, recategorizing them to be, at best, questionable, and, at worst, resoundingly acceptable. This is the exhibition of a double-minded and unstable worldview present in the modern church world.

For example, the church used to almost universally renounce alcohol consumption as sinful. Now, many churches either candidly question its categorization as sin or unconditionally accept it as defensible. The church used to universally repudiate homosexuality as an abomination. Now, many churches ordain openly gay and lesbian individuals as pastors, proclaiming it is a God-supported lifestyle. The church used to even go as far as to reject movie theater attendance as sinful. Now, parishioners and pastors not only attend movies, which, in and of itself is not necessarily sinful, but they attend rated-R movies that curse God, display sexual acts on a widescreen, and fill the ears with profanity-laced diatribes.

We could take this even further. One might be very offended should a couple walk into one's home, sit on the couch, and begin engaging in sexual intercourse; however, we have no problem with it happening in our living rooms if it happens to be on a television screen. The sin is relative. It is acceptable on the television but unacceptable happening in real-time on the couch. We wonder why our children choose to engage in such behaviors when parents set it before their own eyes at home. King David wrote, "I will set no wicked thing before my eyes."[8] Sadly, too many Christian homes have no issue with sin on the silver screen, even in the presence of their children.

We should be reminded that God is holy and no person will see the Lord without living a holy life.[9] What was once a sin is still sin. He is the Lord and He does not change.[10] Holiness is still the standard by which

---

8. Psalms 101:3.
9. Hebrews 12:14.
10. Malachi 3:6.

God expects us to ascribe. But the sin is relative. If my son or daughter comes out as gay, we must accept it because we do not want to lose our children. We really want to have a glass of wine with dinner like other enlightened individuals so we find methods for justifying the act. At least we are not getting inebriated like the Scriptures clearly reject, right? My pastor emeritus, Troy Wilhelm, best denounces such a silly excuse by stating, "If it takes ten beers to get one drunk and he or she only drinks one, he or she is one-tenth drunk." Imagine that ratio if it takes one far less than ten, like the majority of humans, to become inebriated. The writer of Proverbs 23:31 is clear when he cautions the reader to not gaze upon the wine when it moves itself aright. He is clearly discussing the molecule-moving process of fermentation.

Christians justify premarital sexual relationships while fully cognizant that the Scriptures clearly repudiate such actions as "fornication." What the church once called "shacking up," modern believers now refer to as "tax savings." So-called believers willingly "move in together," enjoying all the benefits of a marital relationship all the while remaining unwed in order to save money in taxes. First, the act of living together without the benefit of marriage is a sin. Second, employing the act with the expressed desire to beat the tax system is theft and is a sin. All the while, so-called believer family members and friends will support such actions, rejoice in bastardized pregnancies, and endorse the activities as acceptable. If one sin can be considered relative and our relativist philosophy is reasonable, logical, and sound, should not all sin, including murder and rape, also be relative? God forbid.

Think about the fairly prevalent bumper stickers that cajole motorists to "coexist" or be "tolerant." Those bumper stickers illustrate religious symbols from major faiths in the world, manipulated to conform to the letters in the word. The implication behind the message is that all religions are equal and should be considered valid. While this primarily speaks to pluralism, another method for destroying the foundation we will explore later, it is an accurate picture of how modern society views the truth—it is relative and different for each individual.

The world demands the church be tolerant of all lifestyles, actions, faiths, and ideals but then demonstrates abject intolerance to devout, fundamentalist Christians. One needs to look no further than how the homosexual agenda targets Christian bakers, florists, and photographers; the removal of the Ten Commandments from public squares; the constant attempt to remove God from the Pledge of Allegiance; and the constant

2. THE POISON: RELATIVISM

attempt to remove "In God We Trust" from coin and currency. The Christian God is not welcome. Jesus Christ is certainly not welcome. Mohammed, Buddha, and even Satan are all welcome because it demonstrates our heightened state of enlightenment and tolerance.

Ruth Benedict argued all cultures are relevant with no one culture more or less advanced than the other.[11] Normality, she explained, is culturally defined. Supposed problems, as defined by another culture, are conditioned on the society in which one resides. This relativistic example is a classic conjecture designed to validate all thought, ideals, actions, and culture. To be clear, this perspective validates the actions reported by United States servicemen and women in Afghanistan who say Afghan men enslave preteen boys, chain them to a bed, and subject them to horrific sexual deviancy when the men desire. Application of Benedict's logic and reasoning results in these acts being deemed equally advanced as Western thought and culture and thus, should be validated.

Louis Pojman defined relativism as the perspective that there are no objective moral principles. Valid moral principles are made thus by virtue of people's respective cultural acceptances. Purveyors of this thought assert one should be tolerant of all respective moral principles because of culturally-defined subjectivities. Pojman accurately challenged this notion by exposing the illogical, circular reasoning of such an assertion by positing, "If morality simply is relative to each culture, then if that culture in question does not have a principle of tolerance, its members have no obligation to be tolerant."[12]

One could also argue that relativistic postmodernists and secularists who supposedly value tolerance and then fail to demonstrate tolerance to Christian ideals, then they are, by their own principled reasoning, not fulfilling their doctrine of openminded acceptance and enlightenment. By applying the standards of cultural relativism, it is morally reprehensible to reform established cultures. By this standard, it was morally reprehensible to reform the slave-holding Southern states in the nineteenth century. It was also morally reprehensible to stop Hitler from achieving his mission of genocide and extermination of the Jews. Clearly, relativism, when

---

11. Ruth Benedict, "Anthropology and the Abnormal," *The Journal of General Psychology*, 10. 1934: 59-82.

12. Louis Pojman, "A Defense of Ethical Objectivism," in *Moral Philosophy, Fourth Edition*, ed. Pojman, Louis (Indianapolis, IN: Hackett Publishing, 2009), 42.

authentically applied, does not even withstand scrutiny by its own adherents. It is self-refuting and self-defeating.

The Spirit challenged the church at Thyatira because they "suffered Jezebel." Essentially, they tolerated the spirit of Jezebel in their midst. Jezebel proclaimed herself a prophetess. She was charismatic, cunning, and seductive with a message inclusive of idolatry. The "go along to get along" mentality of the modern church has resulted in the declination of its spiritual authority, promotion of sin in the camp, and rejection of holiness. The church has traded the power of Pentecost for a paltry pittance of temporary popularity. Refusal to call out the relativistic doctrine of Jezebel will result in the suffering of tribulation and sickness along with sinners.

Zacharias posited that when one's life has been dramatically altered by a culturally-induced, radical change, an equally radical antidote will be necessary to correct the damage.[13] The radical change necessary for modern society is Jesus Christ; however, this radical change will require a fearless believer to make a stand and proclaim, "Thus says the Word of God." The apostle Paul asked several questions in 2 Corinthians 6:14-17 that are worth repeating:

> Be ye not unequally yoked together with unbelievers: for what fellowship hath righteousness with unrighteousness? And what communion hath light with darkness? And what concord hath Christ with Belial? Or what part hath he that believeth with an infidel? And what agreement hath the temple of God with idols? For ye are the temple of the living God; as God hath said, I will dwell in them, and walk in them; and I will be their God, and they shall be my people. Wherefore come out from among them, and be ye separate, saith the Lord, and touch not the unclean thing; and I will receive you.

It Is So Because I Said It Is So

Even relativists cannot legitimately understand the hypocrisy of their own relativistic philosophies. A recent episode of Tucker Carlson on Fox News Channel featured Tucker debating an individual on the merits and tenets of transgenderism. In short, the transgender advocate supported individuals assigning the opposite sex to their own persona simply because they say it and believe it. While utilizing this very same logic, Tucker Carlson issued a very

13. Zacharias, 1997.

controversial statement by declaring himself African American. Of course, the leftist transgender advocate exclaimed, "It is not the same!" Tucker, in his feigned bewilderment surely expectant of such a claim, asked the advocate why this is not considered the same. The advocate had no response.

Relativists are simply hypocritical. They adhere to this wildly illogical philosophy but, when it best suits the situation, the very same standards to which they espouse no longer applies when it fails to meet the political narrative they wish to project. Michael Rectenwald, a former New York University professor, recounted his shift from "left of Marxism" to a more "right of center" philosophy when he was confronted with relativistic hypocrisy.[14] He came to realize logical positivism (the process of scientific theorizing based on empirical evidence) was "beyond the reach of society and culture" when "the trend was to consider all knowledge claims, including those of science, as driven by social and political interests."[15] Supplanting logical positivism was linguistic constructivism. Linguistic constructivism in this sense is the assertion that science is basically linguistic or symbolic. In short, it is the rejection of what is objectively epistemological in favor of subjective constructs. In other words, it is what I say it is no matter what evidence demonstrates otherwise.

Rectenwald brilliantly traced the roots of postmodernism to the monstrosity that is social justice, featuring this relativistic concept of *transgender theory*. In true radical linguistic constructionism fashion, transgender theory rejects all empirical evidence that is contrary to its subjective belief. Gender is determined by *beliefs* about empirical evidence and naming. Differences between men and women have nothing to do with biology and everything to do with social constructs.[16] Again, because one believes he is a female and says it, then by all intents and purposes, he is female. Radical transgender theory not only suffers clear mental instability, but it demands everyone else also accept one's delusion and either adhere to it or at least make-believe. The very act of rebuffing such nonsense while utilizing empirical evidence to the contrary (i.e., chromosomes, anatomy, physiology) is considered an affront to the transgender and gender studies community.

14. Michael Rectenwald, *Springtime for Snowflakes: "Social Justice" and Its Postmodern Parentage* (Nashville: New English Review Press, 2018).
15. Ibid, 80.
16. Heather Mac Donald, *The Diversity Delusion* (New York: St. Martin's Press, 2018).

Rectenwald underscored Harvard University's Office of BGLTQ Student Life insane stance that gender can change from day to day.[17] Refusal to believe in such garbage can be considered "an attack" on the snowflake population, causing them to seek refuge in "safe spaces." Literally, college millennials who ascribe to this relativistic nonsense believe that words equate to a physical attack. This is why many conservative speakers are barred from speaking on college campuses. If they do happen to speak, their lives are often threatened.[18] Rectenwald posited an excellent question when he asked, "Why would Hormone Replacement Therapy or Gender Reassignment Surgery procedures ever be necessary or advisable? Since, under transgender theory, believing is seeing, why would anyone ever need to change the secondary characteristics of sex?"[19] In short, belief trumps reality in the relativistic world. Of course, try to apply the basic relativistic belief that "truth is relative" to transgender theory and expect to be met with harsh criticism and violence. Would it not make sense that given the relativity of truth that transgender theory is not true? Oh yeah, I forgot. We are not dealing with sense here.

Light and dark, good and evil, Christ and Satan cannot coexist. They cannot be tolerant of one another—one will prevail. One cannot "ride the fence" as the old-time Pentecostals used to say. The choice is to cling to Christ and shun the world as Joseph did in Potiphar's house or to lie with the enemy.[20] With Christ, there are no shades of gray. A relative life will result in an eternity in hell. Christ calls His people to return to the standard of holiness; shunning evil, accepting righteousness, and living a glorified, abundant life. But how will the sinner hear without a preacher?[21] Where are the preachers? Who will stand for holiness and preach the unadulterated Word of the Living God? Our churches and pastors need a fresh Elijah anointing, causing them to stand in the face of evil, trust the Lord will meet the need, and declare the Word of God, whether it is politically correct or not.

---

17. Ibid, 107.
18. Heather Mac Donald, *The Diversity Delusion* (New York: St. Martin's Press, 2018).
19. Rectenwald, 107.
20. Genesis 39.
21. Romans 10:14.

3. THE DIRTY BOMB: SECULARISM

Secularism is an all-encompassing term. It is a dirty bomb that when detonated spreads death and destruction like wildfire. There are definitions of secularism that simply mean anything not religious or sacred. This is not the point of the chapter, however. The secularism that has been weaponized by the enemy to destroy a generation is much more insidious and overwhelming. The mission of progressive liberals in our nation is to eradicate Christianity from the public square. Notice, I specifically emphasized *Christianity*, for it is our faith that is disagreeable to a secular worldview. Have we as Christians ever asked *why* the Christian faith is so disagreeable to an "enlightened" secularist agenda? One will discover an areligious mention of "God" is acceptable because, in the secularist mind, God can be generalized to any religion.

Simply stated, Christianity is disagreeable to the progressive secularist because, in Christ, there is conviction of sin, power to save, and truth. One cannot be confronted with Christ and not make a choice. Furthermore, the progressive secularist is working to advance a very specific agenda that, when finalized, will result in what they consider to be a liberal utopia; however, the converse is true. Secularism will bring death and destruction. Christianity is the anathema to progressive secularism. With Christianity as the majority faith in the nation, the secularist cannot achieve his or her desired utopian paradise of socialism and communism. Jesus came to seek and to save that which was lost.[1] He came to deliver the captive.[2] The progressive secularist exists to enslave others to an ideology of groupthink in which anyone with a dissenting view is ostracized and maligned—where good is evil and evil is good.

Secularism is essentially an umbrella term for several ideologies discussed in this book. Among the most influential secularist ideologies are relativism, pluralism, atheism/agnosticism, postmodernism, humanism,

---

1. Luke 19:10.
2. Luke 4:18.

social justice/socialism, progressivism, antinomianism, feminism, and universalism. Of course, a thorough treatise on each topic separately could result in volumes. Because relativism, pluralism, social justice, and humanism are subtly pervasive in modern culture, those topics are highlighted for in-depth analysis. There will be a short, conceptual discussion on atheism and agnosticism as those ideologies are fairly well understood. All other ideologies will be investigated within the confines of a chapter on secularism.

Postmodernism

Postmodernism, like secularism, is an all-encompassing term utilized to describe the period in which modern culture now inhabits. Postmodernists admit their philosophy is difficult to define because defining anything comports a definitive, whereas the central tenet to postmodernism requires one to eschew any form of absolutism. To the postmodernist, there is no truth, Christianity does not dictate morality, traditions and customs are meant to be relegated to history, humankind is divine, nature is scientifically rather than spiritually comprised, and anyone who thinks otherwise is among the unenlightened. Radical postmodernists go so far as to indicate they believe nothing in this world is real but is the construct of language. How enlightening.

Hicks defined the belief structure of postmodernists as "liberated from the oppressive strictures of the past."[3] Of course, those "oppressive strictures" include the inconvenience of religion and truth. One must understand, if postmodernists can "eliminate truth" and the inherent truth of Jesus Christ, then he or she is free to be, say, and do anything he or she wishes.

Michel Foucault, one of the foremost postmodern philosophers, railed against the idea of "universal necessities" in human existence. He often postulated on the meaningless of reason and truth.[4] While a philosophical foundation of postmodernism in and of itself is not necessarily devious, the activism of such a philosophy is. The modern Left has co-opted the inane and meaningless philosophy in an attempt to radically alter society. Reason and power, the enemies of postmodernism, is

---

3. Stephen Hicks, *Explaining Postmodernism: Skepticism and Socialism from Rousseau to Foucault* (China: Ockham's Razor Publishing, 2018).

4. Michael Foucault, *Foucault Live (Interviews 1961-1984),* edited by Sylvere Lotringer, translated by Lysa Hochroth and John Johnston, (New York: Simiotext(e), 1988).

3. THE DIRTY BOMB: SECULARISM

most prevalent in Western civilization. The historically perceived seats of reason, power, and knowledge have resided with white, heterosexual, wealthy men. They have wielded "the whip of power" cruelly to repress women, the racially marginalized, poor, and gay.[5]

Jean-Francois Lyotard, a postmodernist philosopher, apparently had no problem with dictators like Hitler, Mussolini, Franco, and Saddam Hussein. In fact, Lyotard refers to such individuals as "victims" of American imperialism.[6] Today, one can easily witness this kind of thought process behind the statements of Representatives Ilhan Omar and Rashida Tlaib. Both are blatant anti-Semites who routinely blame the "plight" of their Muslim brothers and sisters on the supposed whip of power wielded by the Jews and Americans. This is the culture of victimology—the Left maintains its own power structure by intersectionality. It is a divide and conquer strategy rooted in postmodern ideology. Everyone must be cognizant of their own specific identity and the historical repression and victimhood status of which that identity consists. Not only should the "whip of power" be removed from those who have traditionally wielded it, but that whip must now be activated in retaliation. If the Left can convince people they are victims, then they can maintain control. It is nothing short of inciting hatred against one another based on skin color, creed, class, and other favored characteristics.

As a freshman in college, I had the distinct pleasure of clashing with a postmodernist professor for the first time. To preserve her identity, I will refer to her as Dr. Smith. Dr. Smith assigned several term papers by which we, as a class, were to express and defend a point of view on several sensitive topics like capital punishment and homosexuality. When writing the paper on homosexuality, I, of course, took the position that the act was a sin requiring Christ's forgiveness while including many Scripture references to affirm that position. Clearly, as a college freshman, my use of the English language in written form left much to be desired. Looking back on those first iterations of my attempt at conveying an idea, I can clearly see personal growth. Upon receiving the graded paper, I read through the comments Dr. Smith scribbled on the pages. When I arrived on the last page, I was met with a statement that, to this day, I vividly remember. Dr. Smith had assigned a grade of B. While, of course, my goal was an A, I was not displeased with the

---

5. Hicks, 2018.
6. Jean-Francois Lyotard, *Postmodern Fables,* translated by Georges Van Den Abbeele (Minneapolis, MN: University of Minnesota Press, 1997).

grade specifically; however, what displeased me greatly was the back-page comment that read, "Can you support your position with anything other than the Bible? You are a dogmatic absolutist."

A dogmatic absolutist? I considered this point for quite a while. Am I a dogmatic absolutist? I reread my feeble attempt at conveying a position and realized Dr. Smith's in-text scribbles only referenced my position and never once corrected grammar, spelling, syntax, or mechanics. She had, indeed, graded my position against her own, rather than the mechanics of my attempt. This is when I scheduled an appointment with her to confront her.

The first statement Dr. Smith made to me in her office that day was, "I want you to know I did not grade your paper based on your opinion." Really? How so, when all the comments related solely to the expressed opinion? Of course, I did call her out on that. She went on to express that she is concerned with my hardline stance on sensitive issues and that I should consider the real effect on people my perspective may yield. Furthermore, she wanted me to be able to support my arguments with more than just biblical references.

I am not naïve to think that I do everything without mistakes. I am quite open to criticism because it is from criticism we can grow and improve. One aspect of Dr. Smith's discussion I did take to heart, whether she intended this or not, was to include more support for my arguments other than scriptural references. In my estimation, she clearly intended for my argumentative papers to be devoid of scriptural references altogether; however, when making an argument, even to this day, I work to utilize the Scriptures to prove other referential material I include in my argumentative works. Clearly, I do not write material devoid of scriptural references because the scriptures, the very Word of God, should be central to our existence. A life led apart from the Word of God is a life wasted. Why would one not utilize a heavenly resource that after many millennia has yet to be disproved?

This is also a tactic of the enemy. Scientism is the view that the hard sciences alone possess the intellectual authority to contribute to epistemology.[7] Nothing can be known apart from the hard sciences. Therefore, utilizing any evidentiary concepts from theology or philosophy are moot and amount to a failing argument. Moreland appropriately describes real concepts that science fails to explain such as consciousness, aesthetics,

---

7. J.P. Moreland, *Scientism and Secularism* (Wheaton, Illinois: Crossway, 2018).

rationality, and the precision of basic natural laws.[8] Satan wishes to eradicate God's Word from the earth. This is why the Bible is often considered irrelevant when taking an argumentative approach to anything when secularism rules the day.

So, I responded to Dr. Smith with two simple statements. The first demonstrated my knowledge that when considering a preponderance of evidence, it is clear that she assigned a grade based on my personal opinion. Second, I made it clear that I am, indeed, a dogmatic absolutist because I believe in the Word of God and that it is infallible. It is the truth and one should never recoil from the truth. I would rather be a dogmatic absolutist than an unrepentant liberal.

This true illustration, however, perfectly underscores the postmodernist perspective and worldview. If one truly believes the Word of God is infallible, then he or she is labeled dogmatic. If one believes the Bible is the only truth, then he or she is labeled an absolutist. The postmodernist does not necessarily believe in either. Allow me to explain. It is possible the postmodernist will project him- or herself as a Christian. I am no judge of the heart, therefore, I am in no position to adjudicate one's sincerity of belief. I can, however, purport to be a judge of the fruit one bears because it is evident. One's life will produce fruit of some sort. Of false prophets and teachers, Christ told us we would know them by the fruits they bear.[9] Clearly, if fruit inspection works for false prophets and teachers, it would work for anyone.

Here is where we need to exercise caution. While the postmodernist perspective may allow for an adherent to proclaim Christianity, a true postmodernist will not believe in Scripture as entirely true. As a fundamentalist, I believe the entirety of the Word of God is true. While I may be labeled a rube or hillbilly for believing such, there has been no counterargument to prove otherwise. For example, Jesus died on the cross for our sins and rose again on the third day. Where is the evidence this did not happen? Simply stated, the evidence suggests that it did happen and I am not even weighing faith into the equation at this point.

Central to the postmodernist dogma (and yes, it is a dogma), is the idea that traditional sources of knowledge and expressions are no longer valid. Rather than identifying a singular source of truth, the postmodernist will not necessarily declare that there is no truth but that there is no need

---

8. Ibid.
9. Matthew 7:16.

to identify right from wrong, truth from lies, or good from evil. All those conditions are simply preconceived ideas, including science and empirical facts, concocted by those in authority, primarily white patriarchy, to define culture and society to fit the whims of the powerful. Furthermore, Americans are racist and bigoted, whether they realize it or not, including the very institutions espousing this doctrine as well as the purveyors of those ideals, even though they purport to be liberal, progressive, and enlightened.[10] This worldview will, indeed, lead to pluralism, relativism, agnosticism, socialism, and the such but is also closely related to progressivism and secularism. Whereas secularism is the father of such ideations, postmodernism would be considered the next generation.

Progressivism

Progressivism, a term often utilized in the modern political lexicon, is the vehicle by which postmodernism and secularism are activated. Progressivism and liberalism are often incorrectly utilized synonymously. In fact, liberalism, up until the modern era, was a term with which a conservative wished to be associated. For example, the term "liberal arts," when referencing a course of study at the college or university level, is the classical higher education course of study. It is the foundational study that is often neglected in higher education of the postmodern era. Inherent in these courses of study; literature, philosophy, mathematics, social science, physical science, and humanities, is the study of customary, time-honored ideas and topics. Proponents of classical liberalism such as James Madison, Thomas Paine, Thomas Hobbes, Adam Smith, and Thomas Jefferson advocated for limited government, the right to private property, laissez-faire economic philosophies, and the rule of law. Classical liberals believed in rule by the people, whereas classical conservatives supported monarchist rule. While generally socially liberal, classical liberalism would have been considered the more conservative philosophy if measured by modern definitions. Modern libertarianism is perhaps more aligned to classical liberalism than any other ideology of the twenty-first century.

To equate modern liberalism to progressivism is a misnomer of sorts. While modern liberalism is primarily accepting of modern progressive ideologies and most modern progressives identify with modern liberal

10. M. Shermer, "The Unfortunate Fallout of Campus Postmodernism: The Roots of the Current Campus Madness," *Scientific American* 317, no. 3 (2007): 90.

philosophies, they should not be considered synonymous. Progressivism, particularly modern progressivism, is far more nefarious than liberalism. Properly delineating the two ideologies is particularly difficult in the twenty-first century. A non-progressive liberal, while admittedly rare, would accept as normal and good the activities in opposition to Scripture. For example, a modern liberal would not take issue with homosexuality, abortion, pre-marital sexual relations, drug use, alcohol consumption, and other activities modern conservatives would define as vices. The liberal perspective could best be summed up as "live and let live" which is, ironically, a quote originating from the first World War. The irony will be defined shortly.

A modern liberal, devoid of progressive ideologies, would be perfectly happy living in sin and supporting others' sinful practices while not entirely rejecting opposing perspectives but expecting those other perspectives to refrain from impinging on their own chosen lifestyle. The modern liberal would be content to discuss your opposing viewpoints and part as a friend. This is not the practice of modern progressivism, however. While progressivism is primarily associated with liberalism, there are professed conservatives who prescribe to its tenets. In order to fully comprehend the enemy's radical utility of progressivism in the twenty-first century, we must first understand how progressive philosophy was established.

Classical liberals such as Thomas Jefferson and Thomas Hobbes wrote about freedom and liberty being God-given, natural rights. Philosophers like John Dewey, upon whose ideas much of the American educational construct was and is designed, often taught freedom was something to be achieved. He believed humans were socially constructed and devoid of natural rights because there existed no natural law.[11] One must fully understand the magnitude of such a belief and how it advanced progressivism to the modern monstrosity as is its current state.

Natural law is essentially the belief that a higher power—God, to most who proscribe to it—has determined truth and the law based upon principles inherent to creation. This law is reasoned and reasonable, immutable, and universally applicable. Morality is not a construct of the human psyche but is divinely inspired and inherent to every human, guiding him or her to choose good and eschew evil. Aristotle referred to natural law as the common order established by God and reflected in nature. Thomas Aquinas believed any

11. William A. Schambra and Thomas West, "The Progressive Movement and the Transformation of American Politics," Heritage.org, https://www.heritage.org/political-process/report/the-progressive-movement-and-the-transformation-american-politics (accessed August 5, 2019).

law in violation of the natural law is an unjust and perverse law.[12] All other laws must adhere to the natural law because it was established by God as a guide for living in a just human society.

There is evidence throughout Scriptures in which various writers underscore the natural law as essential. In the books of Judges, Chronicles, and Kings, there are many references to various leaders "doing what was right in their own sight." This is a direct reference to leaders ignoring the natural law of morality established by God. Paul made a direct reference to the law of nature when referencing how a man should appear in 1 Corinthians 11:14 by utilizing the phrase, "Doth not even nature itself teach you . . ." Aristotle, Aquinas, and various biblical transcribers all agree with natural law.

Considering Dewey's beliefs, it is these humble but odious beginnings of progressivism that essentially lead to moral relativism. Perhaps the most nefarious aspect of progressivism that is becoming blatantly apparent in the twenty-first century is statism. In essence, the state (or government) has all authority and moral imperative to interject into the lives of the citizenry to impose its will. Returning to John Dewey, he wrote, "The state has the responsibility for creating institutions under which individuals can effectively realize the potentialities that are theirs."[13] Schambra and West contended classical liberals, like the founders, envisioned a nation that protected individuals as opposed to the progressive ideal of a nation that created them.[14]

Hegel[15] and Burgess[16] even went as far as to declare the state as an expression of human divinity. Clearly, the march toward humanism that was driven by progressive ideology was in full effect. At the heart of progressivism is control: control of economy, religion, education, law, and ultimately, the individual. Equalizing the conditions of mankind by force is the ultimate goal of progressivism. President Woodrow Wilson, one of history's most flagrant progressives, sought to cede control of national autonomy

---

12. Thomas, *The Summa Theologica of St. Thomas Aquinas* (London: Burns Oates & Washbourne, 1912).

13. John Dewey, *Liberalism and Social Action* (New York: G.P. Putnam, 1935).

14. Schambra and West, 2019.

15. Georg Wilhelm Friedrich Hegel, "General Introduction to the Philosophy of History by Hegel," Marxists.org, https://www.marxists.org/reference/archive/hegel/works/hi/introduction.htm, (accessed February 10, 2016).

16. J.W. Burgess, *Political Science and Comparative Constitutional Law* (Boston, U.S.A., and London: Ginn & Co, 1890-91, 1923).

3. THE DIRTY BOMB: SECULARISM

to the then-League of Nations, now-United Nations, in order to equalize the world power structure. President Franklin Roosevelt sought to equalize all Americans through force by enacting the New Deal. President George W. Bush sought forced control over Americans through unconstitutional surveillance techniques codified in the Patriot Act.

President Barack Obama, perhaps the most progressive president in history, succeeded in forcing Americans to purchase a product: health insurance. The United States Supreme Court, in a dramatic overreach of constitutional authority, legalized gay marriage, forcing American magistrates to perform such unions, regardless of their personal religious objections. Until recently, such radical agendas were in full effect to force business owners to perform services for same-sex weddings, even though such actions were contrary to service-providers' deeply held religious beliefs—a direct affront to the First Amendment. In true progressive fashion, many of those seeking such services would rather force a service provider to perform services than to seek another willing party. Again, at the heart of progressivism is control and force.

Progressivism in modern society is a rather widely accepted state of conscience. Freedom of religion as well as freedom of speech are to be controlled at all times and, in their purest forms, are an anathema to the progressive agenda. Progressives worship at the altar of forced government, and if one does not adhere to that practice, he or she is to be castigated. It is a philosophy that is best summarized by the statement, "Do as I say, not as I do."

One needs to look no further than our own Congress. The United States Congress, primarily facilitated by progressives, passed a law requiring Americans to purchase health insurance of which they exempted themselves. Another idiom comes to mind: "What's good for the goose is good for the gander." If this government-controlled health insurance is good enough for the American people, then it is good enough for Congress. I have a friend who travels quite often to California for work. He has often iterated to me how many homeless can be found on the streets of some of California's largest cities. Those who are not homeless per se are relegated to living in inadequate housing. When investigating average incomes in America, some of the wealthiest people live in Southern California. After all, it is the heart of filmmaking and technology. Americans are often subjected to Hollywood actors, actresses, and tech billionaires preaching about fairness in the distribution of wealth, healthcare, and education; however, in their own backyards exists some of the highest concentrations of homeless and underprivileged. Where is Hollywood when it comes to helping the unfortunate and oppressed? Why, with all that money, power, and prestige, are there this many people on the streets in California?

The simple answer is the progressive worldview is one of exempting the elite while forcing everyone else to comply. Progressives, for the most part, are not interested in helping the downtrodden and oppressed. They are more interested in using them to advance a narrative that will result in a changed cultural or governmental practice whereby their elite status is maintained and everyone else is taxed into oblivion to support their own agenda and initiatives.

For another great example of the progressive hypocrisy, let us consider former Vice President Al Gore. Vice President Gore is an evangelist of the highest order, preaching the gospel of global warming (now climate change). Incidentally, the term "global warming" was not sufficient, given the many cold winters that have been occurring over the past decade; therefore, climate change was used in order to further deceive the populace. Authors such as Jason Samenow contend this change was not perpetrated in order to reverse course and hide the climate change myth but also cited evidence of how that change occurred.[17] The change occurred simply because global warming referred to rising temperatures when, in actuality, temperatures were variable. Last time I checked, temperatures do increase and decrease and have since the dawn of time, Mr. Samenow.

My mission is not to debate the qualifications of climate change or global warming, although I do believe it to be a concocted plan by progressives to ultimately control the populace. My mission is to highlight how the original climate change evangelist, Vice President Gore, extols the need to change global practices and charge the world a "carbon tax" in order to offset the damage humans have perpetrated on the earth. If these steps are not initiated, the world will be inhabitable due to rising temperatures, resulting in increased catastrophic weather events.

All right, I cannot let this go. Let us step back to high school biology for a moment. Plants produce oxygen. Humans inhale oxygen. Humans exhale carbon dioxide. Plants consume carbon dioxide. It is the system God instituted from the beginning of time and it will continue until He creates a new heaven and new earth. Any questions?

---

17. Jason Samenow, "Debunking the Claim 'They' Changed 'Global Warming' to 'Climate Change' Because Warming Stopped," January 29, 2018, *The Washington Post*.

3. THE DIRTY BOMB: SECULARISM

While I am on this topic, there is a sect of Christians called Dominionists who believe we are already in the new earth and that we must protect it. Often, Dominionists are social justice activists, radical environmentalists, and progressive in political ideology who do not necessarily believe in a rapture of any kind but that it is the duty of the Christian to control the government in order to establish theocratic rule on earth. Dominionism is not biblical and is often hijacked by the political Left to influence Evangelicals to vote for progressive agendas. Dominionists typically adhere to the climate change dogma and work with progressives to advance the narrative.

Going back to Vice President Gore, the Tennessee Center for Policy Research in 2007 reported the Gore family home utilized more energy than the average American home.[18] Furthermore, he has been exposed as deceptive when, in 2017, he stated in an interview with CNN's Jake Tapper that "he does not own a private jet" when, in fact, he has been spotted utilizing a chartered jet when he travels.[19] In fact, Mr. Gore proposed in the documentary, *An Inconvenient Truth*, that the world was "sitting on a time bomb." He posited that if the scientists were correct, the earth would essentially be destroyed in ten years. The documentary was released in 2006 (that is right, twelve years ago, and we are still here).

Vice President Gore, a progressive, is not necessarily interested in curbing any conception of a global warming disaster. His first interest is his pocketbook. Larry Bell reported that between 2008 and 2011, Gore and his investment partner David Blood (yes, they have an investment management group initiated from the funds raised through the global warming "crisis") profited $218 million.[20] His secondary interest stems from his interest in carbon credits that, if implemented in the United States, would result in untold billions. Ultimately, the carbon tax is a means to control the activities and actions of the populace in order to firmly establish the elite progressives, like Mr. Gore, who has no interest in changing his own lifestyle to adhere to his own dogma.

Make no mistake: the world as we know it is coming to an end. Our Lord will descend from heaven with a shout, resurrect the dead in Christ,

---

18. D. Johnson, "Al Gore's Personal Energy Use Is His Own 'Inconvenient Truth,'" *The Chattanoogan*, February 26, 2007.

19. A. Moore, "Al Gore Busted About Private Jet Use," DCStatesman.com. https://www.dcstatesman.com/al-gore-busted-private-jet-use/, (accessed July 29, 2019).

20. Larry Bell, "Blood and Gore: Making a Killing on Anti-Carbon Investment Hype," Forbes.com, https://www.forbes.com/sites/larrybell/2013/11/03/blood-and-gore-making-a-killing-on-anti-carbon-investment-hype/#dbc64ee32dc9, (accessed November 3, 2013).

collect we who are alive and remain, and soar through the heavens to walk on streets of gold.[21] When Christ has assembled His bride from off the earth, the world will plunge itself into a chaos and destruction the likes have never been witnessed in history.[22] The world will ultimately be destroyed by fire.[23]

There is an element within me; however, that partially believes global warming is not entirely mythical. While the root cause of human-caused global warming is entirely mythical, the Bible makes many references to a tangible place called hell, located most likely in the center of the earth[24] where scientists assert the earth's core is enlarging:[25] an assertion supported by Isaiah 5:14. With the enlarging core where hell is likely situated, perhaps this is the cause for increasing earth temperatures. If this is the case, it should only assure the Christian watching for the Lord's return that it is soon.

Progressivism is a tactic the enemy is utilizing to destroy a generation. Many modern youths join the movement to implement fundamental change to our society without fully understanding the change they wish to implement. Sadly, this same youth is being manipulated by the elitist progressives to further the mission to seize control of lives. Unfortunately, innocent marks for the progressive agenda fail to recognize the nefarious plot they are promulgating that will ultimately wreck their own future lives. Furthermore, the progressive agenda, fraught with its secularist antichrist sentiments, wants to suppress the libertarian (small "l;" not the party) ideals and freedoms Christ brings to those in captivity.[26] It is Satan who wishes to enslave, whereas Christ wishes to deliver. It is the progressive agenda to enslave and control—clearly, a satanic ordinance disposed to destroy a generation.

Feminism

I am aware that as a man, writing about feminism can be a disastrous venture; however, there are differences between legitimate, godly feminism and the monstrosity that secular humanist progressives have concocted in

21. Thessalonians 4:16-17; Revelation 21:21.
22. Daniel 12:1.
23. Peter 3:10.
24. Psalms 63:9.
25. Curiosity Team, "Earth's Core is Getting Bigger," Curosity.com, https://curiosity.com/topics/earths-core-is-getting-bigger-curiosity/, (accessed, April 19, 2016).
26. Luke 4:18.

3. THE DIRTY BOMB: SECULARISM

the modern era. In short, feminism is a position of advocacy for women's rights to be equal to men. There is no doubt that women are and should be considered equal to men. This is biblical, as Paul wrote in Romans 2:11 that God is not a respecter (i.e., gives preferential treatment of) persons. Women have every right to demand equal pay for equal work, equal treatment under the law, and equal consideration for leadership positions. In fact, some of the best supervisors to whom I have reported over the years have been women.

It is important to note that when God created Eve,[27] He did not take her from a bone in Adam's foot whereby Adam would keep her repressed and oppressed. Conversely, He did not take her from a bone in Adam's head whereby she would usurp authority over men simply because she was a woman. God created Eve from a rib in Adam's side so she would be a "help meet" or partner to Adam.[28] Subsequently, women and men should be partners in their relationship with neither engendering more respect with God over the other. In essence, each have their divine responsibilities to perform, and when one neglects those divine responsibilities, it disrupts the divine order God established.

Perhaps the most critical aspect of feminism that has gone awry in modern society is the blurring of lines between equality and difference. Women want equality with men, but in the process, this has become some illogical, ungodly fascination, with there being "no difference" between men and women. This perspective completely ignores reality, logic, and rationality. There are differences in men and women as it should be and as it was ordained by God from the beginning. Interestingly, it is the same radical secularist progressives that proclaim there should be no differences between genders that also preach we should all embrace diversity. It is a self-defeating narrative and an overt lesson in blatant hypocrisy that has nothing to do with advancing gender equality but everything to do with advancing an ungodly, areligious, anti-christian narrative intended to create disharmony between men and women, promote homosexuality, and ultimately gain control of people's lives.

Modern feminism argues that there is, in fact, no difference between men and women. To fully understand this concept, one must explore how the progressive manipulation of science has resulted in a proclamation that

---

27. Genesis 2:22.
28. Genesis 2:18.

the terms "sex" and "gender" are not synonymous.[29] Sex refers to the actual physical characteristic differences between male and female. Gender is considered a social and cultural construct designed to assign expectations to males and females based on traditional ideals for each. In other words, boys play with trucks and girls play with dolls. Frequently in the modern media, gender identity is thusly a personal understanding of oneself and his or her role in femininity or masculinity.

Modern secularist progressives will argue that encouraging conventional roles among males and females is not healthy. They propose children should be reared in an environment devoid of such socialization and acculturalization in order for them to develop the gender identity that will allow them to realize their full potential.[30] A term that has surfaced over the past several years related to unhealthy gender identification is "toxic masculinity." The term has been derived from the definition of gendered behavior whereby one is taught the conventional norms of "being a man" or "being a woman." Toxic masculinity, however, takes gender behavior further into a more nefarious and bigoted direction. In essence, manhood is measured by violence, sex, status, and aggression.[31] Femininity is measured by emotional vulnerability and not being hypersexual.

Clemens goes as far to make several references to mass shootings in her treatises on toxic masculinity, insinuating that childrearing whereby boys are encouraged to embrace conventional norms of masculinity, somehow encourages them, later as men, to behave in a severely aggressive manner.[32] This is the approach of the radical secular feminists of the modern era. The ultimate goal is to emasculate men in order to better gain the authority they wish to own.

What is so wrong about a woman in authority? Nothing at all. This is not the point. Feminism has devolved into a psychological illness whereby adherents simply despise anything masculine with the exception of other women who choose to behave in a masculine way which, of course, is, in their opinion, a conventional gender identity norm perpetrated by an unfair society. If a man or a woman aspires to authority and leadership

---

29. S. Barkan. *Sociology: Understanding and Changing the Social World* (Minneapolis, MN: Flat World Knowledge, Inc., 2011).

30. S. Barkan, 2011.

31. C. Clemens, "What We Mean When We Say 'Toxic Masculinity,'" Tolerance.org, https://www.tolerance.org/magazine/what-we-mean-when-we-say-toxic-masculinity, (accessed December 11, 2017).

32. Ibid.

3. THE DIRTY BOMB: SECULARISM

simply because they wish to one up the other gender by usurping authority, then their aspirations are misguided and spiteful. Sadly, progressive secular feminism has devolved into this pitiful state.

If men are either emasculated or too intimidated to aspire to authority, it makes it much easier for progressive secular feminists to control the narrative and control the populace. Even today, men are reticent to make statements about women or feminism, in general, because of the potential for pseudo-political incorrectness resulting in intentional misunderstanding whereby progressives can publicly humiliate and castigate men for taking such an approach. The media is rife with such. Abortion is considered a "woman's right to choose," and if any male politician takes a public stance against abortion, he is castigated not entirely for his beliefs but because he is a *man* ascribing to those beliefs. In modern society, the man should have no authority on what a woman "chooses to do with her own body."

While on the topic of abortion, let me be clear: it is a religion of progressive secular feminism in modern society. Judge Brett Kavanaugh was nominated to the Supreme Court following Justice Anthony Kennedy's retirement. Immediately upon Justice Kennedy's announcement, liberals in this nation began their assault on whomever President Trump was to nominate. To be clear, the assault began *before* anyone was nominated. Clearly, the name of the nominee didn't matter. It was an intimidation tactic by the Left, and more specifically, the progressive secular feminists to force the president or Congress to refrain from nominating or confirming a pro-life adherent.

What is it about abortion that is so critical to the radical progressive feminists? If one wants to see pure, unadulterated rage, allow one to attempt to criminalize or restrict abortion. Abortion advocates rest their entire political, social, and cultural persuasions on this one topic. There are many factors at play leading to such insane commitment to such an abomination; however, I will address the two most critical.

The first factor is that ultimately, modern society desires to live and act without restraint and without consequence. The progressive secular feminist essentially desires to have sexual relations with whomever she pleases, as many times, with no repercussions. Support for this statement can be provided by highlighting the continual debate and subsequent court cases revolving around the Affordable Care Act (i.e., Obamacare). The Affordable Care Act, mandating Americans purchase health insurance or employers provide it, stipulated contraceptive provisions. Famous court cases specifically regarding Catholic adherents' religious rejections for such measures ensued.

Political pundits like Rush Limbaugh spoke out against public funding of contraceptives specifically while accusing liberal activist Sandra Fluke of promiscuity being her motivation for demanding the service.[33] In the very same article, Fard cited Fluke's congressional testimony in advocating for such services because her fellow Georgetown University students have to "pay as much as $1,000 a year for birth control because health plans do not cover contraceptives for women." One thousand dollars per year?! Perhaps Rush Limbaugh, while incorrect in deriding Sandra Fluke, was ultimately correct in his overall assertion. How much sexual activity is occurring to warrant $1,000 per year in contraceptives? Again, this is ultimately an attempt at shock and intimidation, designed to force others to take responsibility for those who refuse to take responsibility for themselves.

In 2014, thirty-eight million women sought contraceptive care of which twenty million sought public assistance.[34] Of the twenty million, seventy-seven percent were of low-income and twenty-three percent were younger than twenty years of age.[35] Sonfield and Kost estimated the total cost of publicly-funded contraceptive care to be $2.37 billion.[36] The cost of contraceptive care, ultimately to assist people in making or reversing poor decisions, is simply unsustainable. Furthermore, it is unethical to continue to demand the American taxpayer fund fornication.

Is this not more advantageous than paying for unwanted children? This question stems directly from a severe lack of presence from the church. The church has traded its moral authority on such issues while ceding control of what should be biblically based contraceptive education to an immoral, areligious government. The school has relegated the teaching of personal responsibility in favor of a more politically correct, socially-just platform of assigning blame for one's condition on an "unjust system." Make no mistake: the church is to blame for sleeping through one of the most pivotal

33. M. Fard, "Sandra Fluke, Georgetown Student Called a 'Slut' by Rush Limbaugh, Speaks Out," *The Washington Post*, March 2, 2012.

34. A. Sonfield, K. Hasstedt and R.B. Gold, "Moving Forward: Family Planning in the Era of Health Reform," March 2014, Guttmacher Institute White Paper.

35. J. Frost, L. Frohwirth, and M. Zolna, September 2016, "Contraceptive Needs and Services, 2014 Update," Guttmacher Institute White Paper.

36. A. Sonfield, and K. Kost, "Public Costs from Unintended Pregnancies and the Role of Public Insurance Programs in Paying for Pregnancy and Infant Care: Estimates for 2008," October 2013, Guttmacher Institute White Paper.

times in world history, while allowing satanic influences to control the narrative, shape government, train children to live as haphazardly as they please, and destroy the moral fabric of our culture. Rest assured, judgment begins at the house of God.[37]

The second factor leading to such ardent commitment to abortion among radical progressive feminists is simply demonic influence. I realize some reading this will roll their eyes at this statement but allow me to explain. At the risk of potentially sounding zealous, I am convinced the religion of abortion is demonically motivated and is rooted in idolatry. Worship of the false god Moloch is well-referenced throughout the Scriptures. It was an Ammonite deity[38] whose worship was often adopted by Israelites. It appears as though Scripture, while forbidding worship of any idol or false god, distinctly and vehemently forbids the worship of Moloch and Baal specifically.[39]

One reason why worship of Moloch was specifically forbidden related to the horrific methods of sacrifice. Ultimately, worshippers would literally sacrifice their children to the fires of Moloch.[40] The location of the fire was most often in the abdomen of the metallic idol. Worship of Moloch was often performed in the valley of Hinnom,[41] which would later be called "Gehenna" (translated as "hell").

The spirit of Moloch is still alive and active in modern society through the child sacrifice our nation calls abortion. It is no coincidence the sacrifice to Moloch required burning children alive in fires formed in the idol's abdomen. Children are ripped from the abdomen of women in order to murder them for the sake of "a woman's right to choose." One needs to realize this was no simple idol worship. Worshippers had to stand in the presence of this idol, listening to the screams of their infants as they were literally burned alive in worship to a false god. But, for what reasons would a woman sacrifice to the ancient spirit of Moloch by way of abortion? Micah 6:7 reads, "Shall I give my firstborn for my transgression, the fruit of my body for the sin of my soul?"

Essentially, an abortion is the sacrifice of a baby for the transgression of fornication or adultery. Because people like Sandra Fluke, who demand

---

37. Peter 4:17.
38. Kings 11:7.
39. Leviticus 18:21; 20:2-5.
40. Kings 23:10; Isaiah 57:5; Jeremiah 19:5.
41. Jeremiah 32:35.

they be able to engage in sexual perversion with wild abandon and with no regard for the consequences, want to bear no responsibility for their actions, medical facilities around the world engage in infanticide and Moloch worship, further feeding the demonic influence that has gripped radical progressive women in the name of feminism.

Margaret Sanger, the founder of Planned Parenthood, is often referred to as a feminist icon by the progressive Left. In fact, Planned Parenthood has instituted an award named for Sanger to honor those who contributed to, lead, and excelled in "the reproductive health and rights movement."[42] The list of award recipients, stretching back to 1966, is a roll call of some of the most elitist, leftist, progressives to ever operate within the nation.

Most are aware of the atrocities perpetrated by Planned Parenthood as exposed in 2015. To be fair, there were congressional committees that found no evidence of "wrongdoing," of course, other than the mass murder of innocent children. The undercover videos produced by the Center for Medical Progress captured high-level Planned Parenthood employees discussing the selling of aborted human tissue and body parts for profit. Interestingly, no one from Planned Parenthood has been prosecuted; however, the individuals who exposed the atrocity were charged in a California court with fifteen counts of felony invasion of privacy. Sure, let us ignore Godzilla in the room while we bring out the bazookas for the pesky gnat flying around. The world calling evil good and good evil, anyone?

Planned Parenthood, while capable of providing some benefit to a local community, primarily exists to murder helpless, innocent babies. However, believe it or not, Planned Parenthood is historically even more nefarious in mission than many know. Margaret Sanger championed coercive eugenics.[43] Essentially, the founder of the modern Planned Parenthood was in favor of forcing women to undergo medical procedures in order to control the characteristics of the population. The mission: first, eradicate those with mental and physical disabilities and second, quarantine all "illiterates, paupers, unemployables, criminals, prostitutes, and dope-fiends" on

---

42. Planned Parenthood, "PPFA Margaret Sanger Award Winners," PlannedParenthood.org, https://www.plannedparenthood.org/about-us/newsroom/campaigns/ppfa-margaret-sanger-award-winners, (accessed March 1, 2019).

43. J.J. Conley, "Margaret Sanger was a eugenicist: Why are we still celebrating her?" AmericaMagazine.org, https://www.americamagazine.org/politics-society/2017/11/27/margaret-sanger-was-eugenicist-why-are-we-still-celebrating-her, (accessed November 27, 2017).

a government farm.⁴⁴ Sanger further suggested those collected and forced onto the government farm would only be allowed to reenter American society if they "volunteered" to be sterilized.

How racist was this supposed champion of women's and human rights? In a letter to Clarence Gamble, Sanger, a Darwinist, unsurprisingly, delineated the appropriate approach to possibly her most nefarious plot. It would be by religious indoctrination that Sanger wished to "exterminate the Negro population" and use the minister to make it more acceptable to the population. Sanger even recounted, with pride, her message to the women of the Ku Klux Klan in 1926.⁴⁵

Let me spell this out with a little more clarity: the same people who preach tolerance, acceptance, political correctness, multiculturalism, equity, and diversity are the very same people who worship at the feminist altar of one of the world's most horrendous eugenicists and racists. She was certainly not alone either. Presidents Theodore Roosevelt and Woodrow Wilson along with Supreme Court Justice Oliver Wendell Holmes all supported forced sterilization. Again, they are all champions of the progressive feminist Left. How much clearer can it be that the agenda of the progressives as well as modern feminists is not to advance the well-being and support of those in need? The agenda has always been ultimate control of the populace through an oppressive government regime while insulating the "enlightened" elite, like themselves, from the same requirements and restrictions.

And their mission is succeeding. The Centers for Disease Control and Prevention (CDC) reports that between the years 2005 and 2014, the percentage of abortions in the United States increased 110 percent. How is that government-sponsored contraception plan working, Sandra Fluke? Let us journey a little further. Sanger's 1939 "Negro Project" designed to "discourage the defective and diseased elements of humanity" from "reckless and irresponsible swarming and spawning,"⁴⁶ is succeeding. African American women comprise only six percent of the American population; however, an astounding thirty-five percent of abortions performed annually are African

---

44. Margaret Sanger, "My Way for Peace," MSM Margaret Sanger Papers, 1932.

45. Margaret Sanger and Paul Avrich Collection (Library of Congress), *Margaret Sanger: An Autobiography* (New York: Dover Publications, 1971).

46. M. Hodges, "CDC: 35% of aborted babies are black," LifeSiteNews.com, December 5, 2016, https://www.lifesitenews.com/news/cdc-statistics-indicate-abortion-rate-continues-to-be-higher-among-minoriti.

American.[47] This statistic only included twenty-nine of the fifty states in the nation, therefore, the actual statistic could be much greater.

Modern feminism has contributed to the death of untold millions of babies, much of whom, are African American. Imagine how many cures to cancer and HIV have been aborted. Imagine how many potential Billy Grahams, Beethovens, Mark Twains, Einsteins, presidents, senators, congressmen and congresswomen, artists, scientists, philosophers, professors, and leaders have been sacrificed to Moloch for the sake of covering a transgression. Again, I ask, where is the church? Where are the nation's religious leaders? Frankly, they are too busy propagating a false gospel of health, wealth, and motivation. When cornered, many of them will refuse to take a stand for Christ on any topics of consequence. They are spineless, greedy, inconsistent, inconsequential ear-ticklers, spewing damnable doctrines that will result in lives lost to sin.

Unfortunately, it gets much worse. There has been a movement afoot among liberal ideologies that an unborn baby is not a "person." Mary Anne Warren argued an unborn fetus is not actually a person and, therefore, cannot be considered human until it has achieved at least two of her five qualifications for such.[48] Allow me to reiterate her five qualifications for "personhood."

1. Consciousness (of objects and events external and/or internal to the being), and in particular, the capacity to feel pain;
2. Reasoning (the developed capacity to solve new and relatively complex problems);
3. Self-motivated activity (activity which is relatively independent of either genetic or direct external control);
4. The capacity to communicate, by whatever means, messages of an indefinite variety of types, that is, not just with an indefinite number of possible contents but on indefinitely many possible topics;
5. The presence of self-concepts, and self-awareness, either individual or racial, or both.

Warren admitted there were problems with enumerating such an exhaustive list of criteria for personhood; however, she asserted that if

---

47. Ibid.
48. Mary Ann Warren, "The Personhood Argument in Favor of Abortion Rights," 1973, *The Monist*, 57, no. 1.

numbers one and two (and possibly three) were achieved, then personhood could be assumed. Ladies and gentlemen, I submit to you, the reader, the dangerously destructive psychology of a maddening theoretical position of an abortionist's love of death. This list of criteria is quite disturbing and, frankly, sickening. If individuals in charge of whether we all should live or die adhere to this list, which is probably a little more stringent than most modern abortionists' perspective of criteria for personhood, then I submit to you that we must all pray that God not allow any of us to slip into a coma at any point in our lives.

Science will support that little is known about the brain functionality of an individual in a coma. Essentially, any one of us in a coma would not be able to attain any of these criteria. Let us go one step further: I am sure many of the readers know at least one individual who is severely and profoundly mentally disabled. If we were to apply this list to their lives, they, too, would not be able to attain to these criteria. In fact, Warren *supported* such a notion in her statement,

> A man or woman whose consciousness has been permanently obliterated but who remains alive is a human being which is no longer a person; defective human beings, with no appreciable mental capacity, are not and presumably never will be people; and a fetus is a human being which is not yet a person, and which therefore cannot coherently be said to have full moral rights.[49]

Are there any readers highly offended by this insanity yet? The insanity has not yet, however, reached full capacity. Let us consider artificial intelligence for a moment. With the vast functional capacity of computers in our modern world, there is little a computer cannot do. In fact, a computer by the name of "Watson" even defeated the greatest *Jeopardy!* champion of all time, Ken Jennings. By Warren's definition, Watson is a person. We do not even have to go as far as Watson to find a person. The computer in the reader's living room would qualify just as well. Warren even acknowledged and approved of the potential for artificial intelligence to one day be considered people.[50]

Ladies and gentlemen, I personally question the mental capacities of people like this who would rather deny the humanity of an unborn baby, an individual with developmental disabilities, or one of us who may lose the ability to function cognitively but would readily accept the assignment of

49. Ibid.
50. Ibid.

personhood to an inanimate object such as a computer, while concurrently advocating for the destruction of those deemed "less than people." Not to mention, Ms. Warren was an associate professor at a major American university. It is nice to know there are such special people training our future leaders in this nation, is it not?

Can it possibly get any worse? Unfortunately, it can. Long-term senator from California, Barbara Boxer, was confronted by then-Senator Rick Santorum in 1999 to explicitly define the precise moment a baby actually becomes a baby and thus protected by the Constitution. Senator Boxer's response should have left every listener aghast and should have resulted in her immediate dismissal from the Senate. Her response to the question was, "I think when you bring your baby home, when the baby is born . . . the baby belongs to your family and has all the rights."[51] Santorum, likely astonished by the response, attempted to allow Boxer to correct her response. He asked her, "Obviously, you don't mean they have to take the baby out of the hospital for it to be protected by the Constitution?" Senator Boxer refused to acknowledge in the affirmative and ended the debate with, "I don't want to engage in this."

But her colleagues are now more than willing to engage in this. As of January 24, 2019, the abortion religion nearly completed its decades-old mission. The state of New York passed abortion legislation allowing mothers to abort babies up to the moment of birth "when a woman's health is in danger."[52] It is critical to understand the full ramifications of this legislation that other states are now adopting. Ninety-four percent of abortions in the United States are elective. Less than one percent are performed to save the life of the mother. In fact, doctors resoundingly testify that there is never a reason to perform an abortion after 20 weeks.[53] In the instance of late-term abortions, it is a diversion tactic of the Left to cite the life of the mother as a reason to perform late-term abortions.

As heinous and disgusting as is the legislation from New York, it sadly worsened. Governor Ralph Northam of Virginia, a pediatrician by trade,

---

51. George Will, "George Will: Barbara Boxer's Position on Abortion," *Newsweek*, July 31, 2010.

52. C. O'Kane, "New York Passes Law Allowing Abortions at Any Time if the Mother's Health is at Risk," CBSNews.com, https://www.cbsnews.com/news/new-york-passes-abortionbill-lateterm-if-mothers-health-is-at-risk-today-2019-01-23/ (accessed March 1, 2019).

53. Tony Perkins, "Late-term Abortions: A Tough Fact to Follow," FRC.org, https://www.frc.org/updatearticle/20190207/tough-fact (accessed February 7, 2019).

publicly advocated for infanticide.[54] In fact, he advocated for this sickening act after the baby is born should he or she have severe health problems. To be clear: an elected official in the United States of America who previously worked as a pediatrician and took an oath to preserve life wherever possible, advocated for murdering a baby after it had been born due to "severe deformities" if that was the wish of the mother. As is the case in the New York legislation, who makes the judgment call? What should be the circumstances that determine a mother's life "is in danger" and an abortion is necessary? Who decides deformities are sufficiently severe to warrant murdering the baby after it is born?

In truth, the Left wishes these decision points to remain undefined. One could argue that simply being pregnant places a mother in a circumstance in which her life is changed. Could one possibly argue that her life is "in danger" because her life, as she knows it, will be radically changed by the responsibilities inherent to parenthood? Are children with Down syndrome, physically deformed, or presenting with other developmental disabilities before and after birth now, more than ever, in danger of failing to meet the threshold of normalcy that would save them from Governor Northam's infanticide? Does it also surprise anyone knowing the history behind Planned Parenthood that Governor Northam had to make public apology after public apology for appearing in a racially charged blackface and Ku Klux Klan photograph in college? Are the racist foundations of progressivism sufficiently clear?

The culture of death embraced by leftists in this nation is nothing short of demonically induced. The demon spirit of Moloch is running rampant through individuals like Boxer, Northam, and those who support them and who openly support actions that are no less than infanticide. Let me be clear: anyone who votes for candidates who support abortion is also responsible for perpetrating and continuing state-sponsored and approved abortions on demand. God will not accept the argument of a voter who suggests they are "not voting for a pastor." Clearly, that is the case; however, a voter who supports the agenda of a candidate by his or her vote is implicated in the subsequent actions that are made possible by the election of that candidate. The voter may as well perform the abortion him- or herself.

So, then, what is the correct, biblical form of feminism? First, it is important to address the proverbial elephant in the room: the biblical role of

---

54. S. Jennings, "Ralph Northam Should Be Remembered for Advocating the Slaughtering of Deformed Babies," *USA Today*, February 5, 2019.

women. The apostle Paul had much to say about the roles men and women should perform in relationships and in the church. According to the divine order, men are called of God to be the spiritual leader of the house.[55] Where there is no man or the man relinquishes his responsibility as such, the woman is responsible to provide that leadership. Let me be clear on this: *both* the woman who aspires to lead the household where a man is present and in a right relationship with God *as well as* the man who shirks his biblical responsibility are operating in rebellion, which is a sin.[56]

The reason it is vitally important for the man to perform his responsibility according to Ephesians 5:22-33 is that when done correctly and in order, the woman will be placed in a wonderfully dynamic position. She will be loved as the man loves himself and as Christ loves the church (His bride). Remember, Christ died so we could become His bride. When in its proper balance, the man will give everything he has to ensure his wife is loved, honored, and esteemed. In its proper balance, the man will treat his wife as his partner and the relationship will operate as God intended from the beginning. It is essentially a symbiotic relationship designed to be actively supported and performed by both parties. Two people become one flesh.[57]

God never intended for this relationship to be a power play between the sexes. He never intended for women to overrule the husbands nor for men to subjugate their wives. The correct perspective of feminism includes the belief that God views the value of men and women equally with equal opportunity to serve the Lord.[58] Marriage is often difficult enough. Partners should be struggling together rather than struggling for control against one another.

I have been married to Shannon for eleven years. People rarely believe me when I say this but it is true: we have never fought. Sure, we have disagreed with one another but I can honestly affirm that we have never argued. Are we perfect? No. Do we have the perfect marriage? Hardly. We have troubles just like everyone else. There are circumstances beyond our control that we wish, hope, and pray the Lord will intervene and correct. At the end of the day, however, we love, honor, and respect one another. I often go to Shannon with major decisions that will affect us. I attempt to get her opinion and perspective. It often ends with "whatever you think."

---

55. Ephesians 5:22-33.

56. Samuel 15:23.

57. Mark 10:8.

58. G.G. Hull, "Biblical Feminism: A Christian Response to Sexism," *Priscilla Papers: The Academic Journal of CBE International*, 1990.

3. THE DIRTY BOMB: SECULARISM

As a man who is trying to operate in the biblically supported office of priest of the home, that statement can be frustrating. I *want* to know what she thinks and how she feels. In the biblical relational balance, this should be the case. It is really frustrating when we go out to eat. Sitting the car, I will say, "Where would you like to go?" This is *always* met with either, "I don't know," "It doesn't matter," or "Wherever." I am almost to the point in which I will use the phrase my pastor emeritus, Troy Wilhelm, would use when asked his preference on dining establishments: "A place that serves food."

I was twenty-seven years of age while Shannon was twenty-five when we married. I dated many young ladies, some godly and some not, who I knew were not the spouse God had for me. While I have not always lived in perfect accordance with the will of God, in this specific instance, I have no doubt I acted in total accordance with God's will in marrying Shannon. Let this be a lesson to young men and women: I believe in arranged marriages. When God arranges the marriage, there will be peace, harmony, and joy in the married life. I am not naïve. It will not be without its problems but with God at the center, the problems will not overcome.

Shannon and I have a great relationship. I would never attempt to silence, subjugate, or restrain her in any fashion. We both have a responsibility to each other that has been divinely established. We know our role in the play and do our best to perform it. Radical, progressive feminists would likely perceive Shannon's role in our relationship as subjective and toxic. Shannon would vehemently disagree. However, there are many Christian women in this same situation whom progressive feminists work tirelessly to castigate, relegate, and silence. The same feminists who supposedly struggle against "the system" to ensure women have equal voices are the same feminists who, sometimes, violently, often virulently quell the voices of women who do not fit their narrative.

Hillary Clinton, the recent champion of feminism, in speaking at a press conference in Des Moines, Iowa, in 2015 stated, "Today, I want to send a message to every survivor of sexual assault. Don't let anyone silence your voice. You have the right to be heard. You have the right to be believed and we're with you."[59] To this, progressive feminists all over the world cheered. Of course, when President Clinton's accusers came forward once again weeks later, these women were liars, concocting such stories that are

---

59. Real Clear Politics, "Hillary to Sexual Assault Victims: 'You Have the Right to Be Heard, You Have the Right to Be Believed,'" RealClearPolitics.com, https://www.realclearpolitics.com/video/2015/09/14/hillary_clinton_women_should_be_believed_when_they_claim_rape_have_to_increase_prevention.html, (accessed August 6, 2019).

politically motivated. But, I thought Hillary Clinton said these women have a right to be believed. Again, it is the height of hypocrisy on full display where some women's voices that do not fit the narrative are shunned in order to advance the progressive agenda.

There is another point to be made regarding Mrs. Clinton's statement. Why do accusers have "the right to be believed?" Certainly, they have the right to be heard and they have the right to an investigation. Do these accusers, even President Clinton's accusers, have a right to be believed simply because they are women? The truth of this statement is perhaps more simplistic rather than nefarious but it sets a dangerous precedent. Mrs. Clinton was most likely pandering to women for a vote; however, this simple statement should be a clarion call to anyone who believes everyone is innocent until proven guilty. Simply because one is accused of sexual misconduct does not automatically mean he or she is guilty.

The #MeToo Movement

As I write this, the #MeToo movement is in full operation. Women are coming forward by the dozens making accusations against men who allegedly forced them into a sexual situation of which they were not agreeable. If these men are indeed guilty, they should be punished to the fullest extent of the law; however, they should be provided the decency of presumption of innocence until an investigation has concluded. Unfortunately, the converse is actually happening. A simple accusation results in most men picking up the pieces of their destroyed lives.

Justice Brett Kavanaugh was accused of sexual misconduct, even up to and including rape, by three women during events that occurred thirty-six years ago. None of the three women, to date, have produced any evidence for their accusations. In stunning precedent, Democrats have called for the withdrawal of Kavanaugh as the Supreme Court nominee, even going as far as to indicate he was clearly guilty. In an absolute shocking statement, Hawaii Senator Mazie Hirono even refused to indicate Kavanaugh deserved the right to be presumed innocent until proven guilty. Simply because his accusers are women is the ultimate reason they should be believed.

Of course, this was a political ploy to keep the president from seating a presumed conservative justice on the Supreme Court. Many Democrats refused to support anyone the president would nominate. It should send chills down the spine of the reader that the rule of law and the Constitution was completely discounted in the proceedings. In essence, anytime a man is accused of sexual misconduct by a woman, even without evidence, he is automatically guilty. This is the message the leaders of this nation were conveying. These are indeed perilous times. Again, this is radical linguistic constructionism in which one's beliefs are contingent on nothing more than words and those words constitute truth, no matter the evidence to the contrary.

However, there is and always will be a double standard. Former Vice President Joe Biden, a Democrat, was accused by Lucy Flores, also a Democrat and Nevada legislator, of unwanted physical behavior.[60] The same members of the media and politicians who resoundingly declared Justice Kavanaugh's accuser, Dr. Ford, must be believed, began to openly question these accusations by Lucy Flores and others. When it is someone of the same ideology they wish to protect, the media and fellow politicians have short memories. Should not Joe Biden's accusers be provided the same unequivocal benefit of the doubt that Dr. Ford was supplied?

Lucy Flores supported Bernie Sanders for president in 2016. Most likely, the attack on Vice President Biden was politically motivated, as was the attack on Justice Kavanaugh. However, Kavanaugh's life, credibility, and family were ripped apart because of the Left's politically-motivated witch hunt, whereas the Left has, for the most part, rallied around one of their own—for now. See, Joe Biden is considered too moderate for the insanely socialist and leftist agenda Democrats wish to perpetrate on the United States. If politicians such as Bernie Sanders, Alexandria Ocasio-Cortez, and Rashida Tlaib have their way, the Democrats will sacrifice Joe Biden on the altar of #MeToo.

The #MeToo Movement has placed a cultish, god-like status on femininity. To be a woman is to be sacred and unable to lie. Simply being born a woman entitles one to preferential treatment, regardless of legality, fairness, or qualification. As I watched the Kavanaugh hearing, the Lord brought to my mind the scriptural parallel for what this nation saw unfold.

The writer of Mark chapter six details the grisly account of the imprisonment and death of John the Baptist. Herod Antipas, having been recently divorced, married Herodias, his half-brother Philip's wife. In fact, Herodias was not only the wife of both Herod and Philip, but she was also their niece. While not specifically named in Scripture, Josephus, the Jewish historian, provided the name of Herodias's daughter/grandniece and

---

60. B. McGinnis, "Who is Lucy Flores? Nevada Politician has Accused Joe Biden of Unwanted Kiss on Back of Her Head," *USA Today*, March 30, 2019.

Herod's step-daughter/grandniece as Salome. Having been pleased by a dance performed by Salome, Herod decreed that she should receive whatever she wished. Herodias, the devious mother, encouraged Salome to ask for John the Baptist's head in a charger. Having obeyed, she requested this grotesque act. Herod ultimately fulfilled his promise and Herodias was presented with John the Baptist's head in a charger. Likewise, the radical Left sought the head of Justice Kavanaugh and will seek the heads of others who dare oppose their radical agenda.

In essence, the modern #MeToo Movement is a progressive attempt not at discovering actual acts of violence against women but to seize control through accusation, intimidation, and slander. While there are, indeed, women who have been unjustly and horrifically sexually abused with little or no earthly recompense to the perpetrator, this movement will, in reality, do nothing for them. That is not the mission. One must realize the narrative is that men control every seat of power and it is critical for men to be upended by women by any means necessary.

John the Baptist and his message was dangerous to the incestuous, vile lifestyle of the Herod household. Herodias, under conviction for her evil deeds, determined John had to be silenced by any means necessary. Seizing the opportunity, Herodias encouraged Salome to request something so sinister that it even grieved Herod. Without legitimate provocation and evidence, John the Baptist was unjustly imprisoned and sentenced to death based on the whims of one woman. Through the trial of Brett Kavanaugh, the nation has witnessed the spirit of Herodias call for the destruction of a man based simply on the words of one woman. Could Justice Kavanaugh be guilty? Certainly. However, with no evidence whatsoever, only God can make that judgment.

Other women in Scripture like Jezebel and Delilah made mockeries of men and acted brazenly to destroy the lives of others. Jezebel was the motivation behind Ahab's unjust, illegal, and wicked murder of Naboth in order to take his vineyard.[61] Jezebel's efforts to destroy the prophet Elijah resulted in self-exile[62] for fear of his life, considering Jezebel had a record of murdering prophets.[63] She simply needed no evidence for these and other heinous acts she inflicted mostly upon men. Her whims were satisfied by willing parties with no ethics or morals. Delilah's mission was to destroy

---

61. Kings 21.
62. Kings 19.
63. Kings 18:13.

3. THE DIRTY BOMB: SECULARISM

the champion of Israel. Samson, having achieved great public notoriety, was dangerous to the enemy. Like the circus perpetrated by the Democrat Party in the Kavanaugh hearing, the puppet masters recruited Delilah to destroy Samson, which she accomplished.

Sex is a powerful tool Satan is utilizing in his efforts to destroy a generation. It is a great motivator for a history filled with heinous acts against humankind. Certainly, any man who sexually harasses, sexually abuses, or rapes a woman should be prosecuted to the fullest extent of the law. Furthermore, anyone who falsely accuses another person of an insidious crime such as rape should be prosecuted and, if found guilty, carry the same sentence as one who has perpetrated the crime of rape. The nation is witnessing the blatant use of unequal balances in the judiciary. Proverbs 11:1 and 20:23 clearly establish the use of unfair balances as an abomination to the Lord. This idea was best encapsulated by the comments of South Carolina Senator Lindsey Graham during the Kavanaugh hearing when he stated that if Kavanaugh wanted a fair hearing, he had come to the "wrong town" (Washington D.C.) at the "wrong time" for that.

Perhaps an even more concerning result of this movement is the fact that after sexual consent is granted for sexual intercourse, either participant can withdraw consent at any point during the activity.[64] In fact, North Carolina is currently the only state where this is not the case. The issue here is not whether sexual intercourse should continue or whether or not it should be considered rape. The issue is that if consent is withdrawn after sexual intercourse has commenced, how would anyone restrained by the law prove it? Essentially, it is one's word against another. Radical, progressive feminism would refer to it as toxic masculinity. It is, however, another perfect example of why young men and women should wait for sexual intercourse when in the bonds of a marriage God has instituted and ordained.

The feminism of the modern age; progressive, secular, and radical, is primarily designed to advance a humanist agenda that God has not ordained. The goal is not the advancement of equality for women. On the contrary, the goal is subjugation of all under the authority of the progressive elite who desire to eradicate God from the equation and control the populace. Feminism is not the bra-burning episodes of decades past nor the schizophrenic babblings of the misguided and anti-christian Betty Friedan. It is certainly not

---

64. S.F. Colb, "Withdrawing Consent During Intercourse: California's Highest Court Clarifies the Definition of Rape, Supreme.FindLaw.com, https://supreme.findlaw.com/legal-commentary/withdrawing-consent-during-intercourse.html, (accessed March 1, 2019).

promoted and encapsulated by the operations of the National Organization for Women (NOW) that only supports women who are politically and ideologically aligned with progressivism and liberalism. Feminism ordained by God, outlined by Scriptures, and authentically practiced promotes women, respects their contributions, amplifies their voices, generates equality of opportunity, and rewards the proper relationships.

Universalism

Many definitions of "universalism" exist. One definition essentially mirrors that of pluralism in which any path to God is universally accepted as legitimate. Because I deal specifically with pluralism in a separate chapter, I will address a secondary meaning that is prevalent in modern Christianity that was highlighted, in part, by Michael LeMay.[65] Christian Universalism, in a secondary sense, relates to heavenly rewards. It is a prevailing belief that all people, regardless of religious belief, will be in heaven.

On the face of this assertion, a fairly orthodox Christian would balk at such a belief; however, think about it for a moment. When was the last time you attended any funeral where the minister did not publicly state the deceased had entered into the heavenly portals? My pastor emeritus, Troy Wilhelm of Randleman Church of God, often states that no one in the past twenty years who died in Randolph County (the county where my church is established) has gone to hell. Please do not misunderstand me: I hope that everyone who has passed away has indeed made it into heaven but simple logic and statistical reasoning would betray such a hope. So, what is happening?

Could it be that pastors and ministers are making an admirable effort to comfort the grieving families? Perhaps. While it is indeed admirable, it is ultimately detrimental to those who, hearing the message, know the deceased and who, themselves, are living in a similar sinful condition. Truthfully, this is the best assumption one could make. A more unfortunate scenario may be that the minister truly believes that regardless of the circumstances of death or the life led by that individual, he or she has made it into heaven.

The simple fact is that people are dying in a sinful condition. Revelation 21:27, among many other Scriptures, records the fact that sin will not

---

65. Michael D. LeMay, *The Suicide of American Christianity: Drinking the "Cool"-Aid of Secular Humanism* (Bloomington, IN: WestBow Press, 2012).

enter into heaven. Frankly, any other philosophy on this matter is false and unfounded scripturally. Let me clear: while I am a minister, I am not a pastor. I have never had to fulfill the unfortunate responsibility of conducting a funeral for one who has passed away in a sinful condition. I cannot imagine the difficulty with which a pastor struggles in delivering a message that is comforting to family members while adhering to such troubling but truthful concepts as the damnation of souls not in accordance with the salvation of Jesus Christ. One can only hope that the Lord will intervene and direct the minister tasked with such an unenviable job. In my lifetime of church experience, I have often heard from pastors who performed such tasks recount how the Lord has indeed granted wisdom in such positions.

One may ask how cruel it would be to preach to grieving families about how their deceased loved one has been damned to hell by his or her life choices. Once again, it is critical the minister in such a position be led by the Holy Spirit and careful to employ wisdom. However, this particular question underscores the unfortunate perspective of many in our modern society. This perspective often includes the notion that truth must be tempered in order to refrain from offending people. Furthermore, this notion assumes that the act of conveying the truth of the Word of God cannot be synonymous with love, care, and respect. On the contrary, one who refuses to share the whole truth as expressed by the infallible Word of God is, in fact, exhibiting a lack of love for one another. In fact, the writer of Hebrews 12:6 reminds us that the Lord loves those He chastens.

Frankly, the truth is offensive at times. Hebrews 4:12 records how the Word of God is sharper than a double-edged sword piercing to the dividing asunder of soul, spirit, and body. A double-edged sword, of course, lacerates both entering and exiting—cutting those hearing *and* those delivering the message. This Scripture reminds us that the effects of the truth of the Word of God will most often not be a pleasurable experience. It was never intended to make one feel good. It was always designed to change, mold, and shape a flawed flesh that wishes to do nothing but evil. Sacrificing the truth on the altar of political correctness is the order of the day among some of the highest-profile Christian leaders.[66]

I want to briefly explore universalism in the context of Calvinism. Many Christian brothers and sisters believe that once one has been saved from sin, he or she has been forgiven of sins past, present, and future. Indeed, once Christ's blood has been provided to cover one's sins, his or

66. Ibid.

her sins past and present have been forgiven and forgotten. However, it is deleterious to the conditions of men and women to assume Jesus has already forgiven future sins.

Let me be clear: I am a fundamental Pentecostal and a minister in the Church of God, Cleveland, Tennessee. I do not adhere to the teaching of eternal security. I attest that the teaching of eternal security (rooted in Calvinist doctrine) is a form of Christian Universalism in that one is taught his or her sins are *universally* forgiven from birth to death. The Church of God teaches that one can "backslide;" knowingly and intentionally committing a sin in which condition the individual is without Christ, considering God cannot be a party to sin.

Our brothers and sisters who do adhere to eternal security have, in the past, argued that one in such a condition did not truly accept Christ and relinquish sins. While this argument is convenient, it is dubious. The Scriptures make it clear how one can be saved from sin and, simply stated, it is not rocket science. If an individual has declared he or she is a sinner needing the salvation of Christ and has confessed those sins to the Lord, believing in Him, the Lord said He is "faithful and just to forgive."[67] Are we to believe this is inaccurate? Are we to believe Christ is unable to fulfill this promise?

I challenge our brothers and sisters who adhere to the eternal security universalism doctrine on a couple of points. If an individual asks the Lord for forgiveness of sins but later succumbs to the sin of homosexuality, lives out the entirety of his or her life in that condition, and, subsequently, dies in that condition, will he or she be forgiven and enter heaven? Would our brothers and sisters allow that individual to assume leadership in their churches while living in the homosexual lifestyle? In essence, this belief of eternal security is a belief in a universal "get out of jail free" card. Such a belief ignores the human free will. We have the choice of whether or not we want to continue living in a saved condition.

So, what is the answer? Thankfully, the Lord is not willing that any should perish but that all would come to repentance.[68] He stands ready to forgive of sins we have committed if we simply ask. The Lord will not force us to live for Him at any point. He is faithful to convict us of our sins; however, His Spirit will not always strive with man.[69] But, did not Romans 8:38-

---

67. John 1:9.
68. Peter 3:9.
69. Genesis 6:3.

39 assure us that nothing can separate us from the love of God? Is this not proof that even sin cannot separate us from salvation? Too often, churches conflate Christ's love with His saving grace. While it is the ultimate act of love for Jesus to have ascended to Calvary to give His life for us, His love and the miracle of salvation are not synonymous in this sense. Romans 5:8 reminds us that even when we were in our sinful conditions, Christ loved us and died for us. Jesus loves the sinner. In fact, Jeremiah 3:14 reveals to us that God is married to the backslider. He exhorts the backslider to turn from the sin in which he or she has engaged.

Christ's love for us will never fade. He died for all so that we might have life more abundantly[70] but, ultimately, it is still our choice whether we will live for Him or not. One cannot live a life of sin and still be saved, as evidenced by 2 Corinthians 6:14-17. Light and darkness cannot coexist. It is, therefore, impossible for one in a backslidden or sinful condition to still remain saved. As God removed the Spirit of the Lord from Saul in 1 Samuel 16:14, He will, likewise, remove His Spirit from those who were once saved but revert to a sinful lifestyle.

Universalism is a tactic of the enemy that has infiltrated modern society as well as the church on a grand scale. It is a tactic by which Satan has deceived many people, saved and sinner alike. The doctrine of universalism is a means to excuse haphazard living and soothe the conscience when one wants to commit sins. It is the Diet Pepsi of Christianity: no benefits and less filling. Satan wishes to deceive an entire generation with this tactic in order to continually keep them defeated by enslaving them to sin. Universalism is a method by which he has enslaved the sinner while convincing them they are in a right relationship with Christ. Sadly, the enslaved no longer hears the voice of the Savior and either does not realize it or does not care.

I have had many discussions of this nature with fellow Christians. Of late, I admittedly attempt to stay out of the weeds of this discussion and have reverted to providing two responses. First, I have told people that if they feel so moved to sin, they have the right to sin but they should not try to justify their actions by God because He has made it clear how He feels about it. Second, I concede to people that if eternal security is indeed correct, then my asking for forgiveness for sins is simply icing on the cake; however, if I am correct and eternal security is incorrect, then they will lose everything when we stand before a holy God. Why gamble with one's eternal soul? I choose not to.

70. John 10:10.

Antinomianism

In some ways, antinomianism is the converse of universalism, but in other ways, the first cousin. Allow me to first define antinomianism and then provide a more modern and perhaps well-known term in its place. Antinomianism, in its purest form, simply means "against the law." An antinomian is one who defines him- or herself as a Christian but believes that God has no definite law by which he or she should conduct him- or herself. While this seems to mirror relativism rather closely, it is not quite that overt. Many antinomians reject the law of God as presented in the Old Testament. In fact, many will even go as far as to indicate the Old Testament has no relevance for the modern Christian, believing it is even anti-Christian. The argument is often that we are "living in the dispensation of grace" and, therefore, we no longer need the old covenant or law. The slippery slope of antinomianism is the belief that there is nothing that one cannot do that will not be covered by grace. Enter the doctrine that is quickly gaining adherents in modern Christianity: hyper-grace.

Essentially, antinomianism is the polar opposite of neo-Judaic doctrine. Each, in his or her own way, is not pleasing to the Lord. Neo-Judaism is a popular hybridization of Christian doctrine and Judaism. Many followers of this doctrine will present themselves with prayer shawls, yarmulkes, and many other Jewish symbols. Let me be clear: if one believes he or she needs these items in order to reach God, then he or she should have no issue with the Catholic needing rosary beads and a priest. In fact, one needs none of those items in order to reach God. I contend the inordinate need to possess those items when praying is tantamount to idolatry and witchcraft. The Lord is not more likely to hear and answer one's prayer over the other simply because he or she is wearing a prayer shawl, lights a menorah, or wears a yarmulke. Adopting those items into one's Christian life is tantamount to expressing one's rejection of the ultimate sacrifice Christ made on Calvary and replacing it with the Judaic rituals and laws that are pre-Christ or even anti-Christ.

Neo-Judaism is not synonymous with Hebraic study. Many study the Hebraic roots of Christianity in order to gain further insight into the origins of our faith. Indeed, Jesus was a Jew and was reared to be an adherent to Jewish law and customs. There is no doubt that a more in-depth analysis of Jewish law, customs, traditions, and feasts will provide unique insight into many of the messages Jesus preached to His congregations. In fact, understanding the ancient Jewish perspective will, in many instances, provide meaning to parables and statements of Jesus that will allow one to delve deeper into his or her relationship with the Lord. One should have a desire to know more about the Scriptures; not simply more about how the message applies to our modern lives but also more about how the message related to the ancient perspective. This understanding can provide a multidimensionality to Christ's message that would help believers today.

Unfortunately, the hyper-grace movement is often found among those who eschew the eternal security route but, unbeknownst to them, they are essentially the same. If one believes that he or she can do anything and still make it to heaven, whether it is grace or eternal security that serves as the catalyst, there essentially is no difference whatsoever in those beliefs.

Many tenets of the hyper-grace movement are not biblical. The dissolution of the law was rejected by Christ when He declared that He did not come to abolish the law and the prophets but to fulfill them.[71] Jesus is not a proponent of tearing out the first two-thirds of the Bible. He is the very embodiment of the law and prophets that antinomians or hyper-grace followers wish to eliminate. Imagine trying to understand the prophetic nature of Jesus's birth, life, and death without the prophets. In fact, the Old Testament is perhaps more prophetic about Christ's birth, death, resurrection, transfiguration, and second coming than the New Testament books. Talk about relevance!

For example, when we read, "But as the days of Noah were, so shall also the coming of the Son of Man be,"[72] how would we know anything about the days of Noah had it not been for the law and prophets? How would we know how Jesus resisted Satan in the wilderness[73] if we did not know the passages of Scripture from Deuteronomy He quoted? Jeffrey Kranz is correct in that Jesus was the most learned Old Testament scholar the world has ever witnessed.[74] Kranz goes on to count down Jesus's most referenced Old Testament Scriptures with the top four being Psalms, Deuteronomy, Isaiah, and Exodus. If Jesus found relevance in the Old Testament, how much more should we continue to read, study, and apply it?

---

71. Matthew 5:17-20.
72. Matthew 24:37-39.
73. Matthew 4:1-11.

74. Jeffrey Kranz, "Which Old Testament Book Did Jesus Quote Most? *Biblia blog*, April 2014, http://blog.biblia.com/2014/04/which-old-testament-book-did-jesus-quote-most/.

Paul warned against antinomianism and hyper-grace in Romans 6:1-2: "Shall we continue in sin, that grace may abound? God forbid. How shall we, that are dead to sin, live any longer therein?" Jude writes about how certain men have crept in "unawares" turning "the grace of our God into lasciviousness"[75] and how we should "earnestly contend for the faith that was once delivered unto the saints."[76] The faith for which we should contend is that faith of our fathers, in its original context and meaning, and unaltered or unadulterated. Paul, in Romans 7:12, writes how the law is holy and righteous. He further explains the purpose of being filled with the Spirit is so that the law would be fulfilled in us.[77] The antinomians are correct in that it is impossible to live according to the law.[78] No one has been able to accomplish this feat hence the scores of sacrifices made at the temple in ancient Hebrew times. The Lord, however, expects His followers to adhere to His moral law, which is the basis for sanctification clarified through the office of the Holy Spirit.[79]

Joseph Mattera enumerates the signs of a church that is operating in the hyper-grace movement.[80] These signs are worth repeating:

- The preachers never preach against sin in the context of standing against sin other than those of "legalists" and "Pharisees."

- The lead pastor never takes a cultural stand for righteousness but shies away from opportunities to stand against the ills of modern society like abortion, homosexuality, and other overt abominations.

- The Old Testament is almost totally ignored with the exception of remarks toward types and shadows of Christ.

- No accountability: leaders are allowed to hold office while leading immoral, ungodly lives.

- The pastor will often reference and denounce the "old school" or "conservative" church.

---

75. Jude 1:4.
76. Jude 1:3.
77. Romans 8:4.
78. Romans 3:19.
79. Romans 3:20.
80. Joseph Mattera, "8 Signs of 'Hypergrace' Churches," CharismaNews.com, https://www.charismanews.com/opinion/40060-eight-signs-of-hyper-grace-churches, (accessed March 2, 2019).

- The lead pastor will denounce tithing as a godly practice.
- Health, wealth, and prosperity: Sermons have transformed into motivational messages.
- Key church members lead openly sinful lives.

Galatians 3:24 reads, "Wherefore the law was our schoolmaster to bring us unto Christ, that we might be justified by faith." It is clear the Scriptures of the New Testament relate back to the Old Testament while the Scriptures of the Old Testament portend the activities and lessons of the New Testament. The Bible, rightly divided,[81] holistically portends the first and second coming of Christ. Every book, Scripture, jot, and tittle of the Bible points to an omnipotent, omniscient, omnipresent, soon-returning Christ.

Antinomianism is a tactic of the enemy to confuse a generation and promote a secular agenda. Hyper-grace is a secular doctrine that has invaded the church destined to promote haphazard lifestyles among those who proclaim to be Christian. I have grown up in the Church of God and listened to many pastors refer to "riding the fence." This phrase essentially defines those who want all the benefits of Christianity, none of the trials, and all the while continue to engage in activities the Bible clearly denounces as sinful. Followers of the hyper-grace movement want to continue to ride the fence but they fail to realize that God requires 100 percent. Anything less is unacceptable and will result in disaster for one's eternal soul. Too many in the modern church have become professionals at fence riding.

While there are instances of church attendees who can ride the fence without anyone knowing the condition of their lives, most who are fence riders will often betray their seemingly private conditions. When people begin to neglect to assemble together[82] and resist the fellowship, there is an issue in their lives. When Christians begin to relax their standards and accept sinful practices such as alcohol consumption, drug use, sexual immorality, and the like, it is clear there is a backsliding occurring in their personal conditions.

Humanity has a proclivity for taking the path of least resistance. If there is an easier path, why should anyone choose to work hard? The problem is that in a Christian journey, there is no easy path. In fact, Matthew 7:13-14 assures us that an easy path leads to destruction in which many will access but it is a challenging path that leads to life in which few will access. There

---

81. Timothy 2:15.
82. Hebrews 10:25.

is a variety of televangelists who preach health, wealth, and prosperity and make the earthly Christian existence seem like tulips, daisies, and puppy-dog tails. Many proscribe to such a program only to be greatly frustrated, discouraged, and dismayed when the enemy offers the slightest bit of resistance. Sadly, many of those new converts fail to continue on the narrow path because they had been sold a bill of goods by a charlatan.

The Christian journey is a difficult, challenging, and often troublesome one. Be assured Satan will fight with everything he possesses in his arsenal. Sometimes, God allows trials and tribulations to occur in order to strengthen the Christian. Much like the athlete prepares the body for competition by lifting weights, it takes resistance to make one stronger and prepared for the event. Pushing through the trials and tribulations, whether initiated by God or Satan, will only serve to make one stronger and prepared for the next hurdle.

Paul compares the Christian journey to a race in 1 Corinthians 9:24-27. My wife is an avid runner. She has competed in variations of races including an entire marathon. When preparing for the marathon, she trained by running various distances in an effort to prepare for the ultimate 26.2 miles that she would complete. This training consisted of consuming certain foods and beverages, building leg strength, and preparing her mind for such an enormous task. It would have been impossible for her to run the marathon had she not first conquered other shorter races as well as besting her own times while training. Her mission was to slowly improve herself until the moment she had to compete in the ultimate event.

In this Christian journey, the goal is not the place in which one finishes—it is to finish strong. I do not want to barely crawl across the finish line on that day, but I want to run through those gates, shouting and praising God for His mercy. Too many new converts are placed in this race under the impression that they can simply crawl their way through the entirety of the event. They are never challenged by anointed preaching to live a life of holiness before God. They are often encouraged to seek their best life now when, in actuality, their best life is waiting for them on the other side of the finish line. If this life is our best life now, we are in trouble.

New converts who are listening to these motivational speeches rather than sermons are never encouraged to build the strength necessary for competing with the enemy. Building the necessary strength will be difficult and painful at times but is invaluable for being able to contend with the enemy and win. Sadly, too many Christians remain in an emaciated state of spiritual existence, unable to contend with the weakest devil. They flee in the face of the simplest resistance.

We can certainly rely on the powerful grace of Christ when we falter and fail. Be assured, we will falter and fail the Lord. As long as we live in this corruptible flesh, there will be moments when we do not perform according to Christ's standards. We can rest assured that He will be there to extend His grace and mercy to forgive us of our sins, restore our lives, and restart us on the path of righteousness. But, we must not take His grace for granted. He will not dispense His grace to those who have no remorse for sin and no intention of ending the behavior.

Evolution

Allow me to first offer full disclosure: I am not a biological scientist. I am a scientist in as far as I understand and implement the scientific method when conducting statistical analyses and experimental research related to my profession. While I understand scientific experimentation, statistical data analyses, and procedural implementations, I am not a scientist, per se. However, I am of the opinion that it does not require a vast scientific comprehension to fully grasp the basic concepts of evolution; particularly, the socio-political underpinnings of its modern iteration and projection.

Evolution is a concept that is clearly a tactic of the enemy to destroy a generation. It is peddled mostly to children by some of the best salespeople in the world. Some, perhaps even most, scientists the world over believe and promulgate this concept as the absolute truth of how the world came into existence and how humankind appeared on the earth. Most schools in America teach evolution as a scientific fact when, in truth, it is a theory. Those same schools mostly refuse to teach creationism. Those who teach creationism devote a paltry amount of time to it and ultimately dismiss it out of hand as myth and legend.

Where did such a concept originate? "Originate" is an interesting choice of wording because the origins of evolution began with Charles Darwin in his 1859 seminal work, *On the Origin of Species*. While the term "evolution" is not utilized by Darwin in this work, he does introduce the overall concept by theorizing that all current species on earth may have descended from a single primordial form. He introduced the term "natural selection" as nature's way of ensuring only the strongest and most abled survive. The phrase "survival of the fittest" was not coined by Darwin but rather Herbert Spencer, a social Darwinist, in 1864.

To be clear: evolution can be a concept utilized to assist in defining many progressions. The simple evolving from one form to another in, say, liquid to solid to gas is a legitimate evolutionary concept. Trees evolve from saplings to full-grown oaks, maples, or birches. Frogs evolve from eggs to tadpoles to fully developed adults. When discussing evolution, it is critical to delineate between microevolution and macroevolution. Microevolution is biblical and accurate. This is the frog developing from an egg to a fully formed adult frog. Macroevolution, the concept most often utilized in areligious settings, is the development from one species to an entirely different species. This would be the conventional apes developing into a human concept. For our purposes, when I refer to evolution, I will be referring to macroevolution.

The scientific method is the framework by which any legitimate scientist will operate. Essentially, scientists observe, question, hypothesize, develop testable predictions, gather data, test predictions, revisit hypotheses, and develop theories. Notice that the end state of that process is to develop theories. A theory is an action that is not universally observable, may explain an observation, may become obsolete, and may be replaced by a better theory. A scientific law is one that is universally observable, obviously factual, had no observable alternate, and has no exceptions. For example, unless we are standing on the moon, submerged in water, or in a hyperbaric chamber, when one tosses a ball in the air, it will eventually fall to the ground every time. This is a law. It happens without fail when conditions are normalized.

Newton's *third law of motion* states, "For every action, there is an equal and opposite reaction."[83] I will crudely provide an example for this. If a ball is rolled toward a child and the child kicks the ball, there is force exerted on the ball as well as on the child's foot. The ball will move in an opposite direction as a result of the greater force exertion from the child's foot. If the ball happens to (strangely) be greater in mass or moving at such an accelerated rate of motion greater than that of the foot, the ball will exert a greater force than the foot, causing the foot to move in the opposite direction. In normal circumstances, it happens that way every time, thus it is a law.

---

83. Isaac Newton, *Newton's Principia: The Mathematical Principles of Natural Philosophy* (New York: Daniel Adee, 1846).

3. THE DIRTY BOMB: SECULARISM

For evolution to be considered a law, it must be observable and occur the same way every time. In other words, our living in the present world should produce examples of observable evolution occurring naturally. We should be bearing witness to species changing into other species. In fact, this is not occurring nor has it occurred in recorded history. Some of the most ancient texts in history record evidence of animals in forms with which we most equate them even today. Ancient Egyptian texts record evidence of cats, dogs, monkeys, fish, crocodiles, and hippopotamuses. Perhaps the oldest book of the Bible, Job, records the leviathan, behemoth, ox, and ostrich. There is debate on whether behemoth and leviathan were dinosaurs but this is unlikely. It is more likely they were either crocodiles, hippopotamuses, rhinoceroses, or elephants; however, I do not doubt what God can do. Other animals appear in other books of the Bible like cattle, snakes, donkeys, horses, chickens, sheep, lions, bears, and others. Even within the millennia that has transpired, none of these animals have changed into another species.

The very concept of evolution as described by Darwin requires a more advanced, complex form ultimately exterminating the less advanced and improved parent. This has simply not occurred within recorded history. Darwin also hypothesizes the need for what he calls "transitional species," otherwise known as "the missing link." However, to date, there have been no fossil records for such species. In Darwin's day, he even questioned himself why this was the case.

Evidence is paramount when operating as a legitimate scientist within the confines of the scientific method. Nicolas Wade wrote that the evidence supporting man's ancestors are so limited, it would fit on a billiard table.[84] Dr. Lyall Watson also conjectured that there were more scientists than specimens supporting claims of evolution and that all those specimens would fit inside a normal-sized coffin with room to spare.[85] For scientists to treat evolution as an irrefutable law is dishonest at best and nefarious at worst. It is clearly malpractice. If science requires results to be proven to a near absolute, is it not clearly bias in operation for something with such scant evidence to be treated as irrefutable, obvious, factual law? Let me be clear: I have no issues with evolution taught as a theory. In fact, I support evolution being taught *as a theory*. There is nothing wrong with

---

84. Nicholas Wade, "The Editorial Notebook: How Old is Man?" *The New York Times*, October 4, 1982.
85. Lyall Watson, "The Water People," *Science Digest*, 90, 44.

people theorizing about whatever they wish. This, however, has not been how dishonest, biased scientists have operated.

Darwin, himself, stated, "Life was originally breathed by the Creator into a few forms or into one . . . and from so simple a beginning endless forms most beautiful and most wonderful have been and are being evolved."[86] Clearly, Darwin believed in a "Creator" who breathed life into man. If he truly believed in a God so powerful as to create man, it is senseless to believe He was not powerful enough to create everything else. It is also senseless to believe He relied on evolution to take over from there. This idea is, incidentally, the basis for a prevailing thought called *process theology* espoused by some modern churches.

Essentially, process theology attempts to marry Christian ideals, morals, virtues, and beliefs with radical postmodern secularism. For instance, process theologians use Scripture in an attempt to validate man-caused climate change.[87] In fact, they validate man-caused climate change while referring to its deniers as demonic. Among their rather ridiculous beliefs is that God created life in the beginning and then stepped back to allow evolution to progress. This begs a couple of questions. Given that God is omnipotent (all-powerful) and omniscient (all-knowing), would He not have discerned that evolution would produce mankind, plants, and animals? And, given that He would have recognized where evolution would lead (if evolution was true), then why, in His infinite power, would He not have just made humans, plants, and animals as they are from the beginning?

Evolutionists teach that 99.999 percent of the universe is not necessary for human life; therefore, they determine that it is illogical for an intelligent designer to create more than necessary. Thus, there is no Intelligent Designer. Furthermore, evolutionists have determined there is no reason for stars to exist, so an intelligent designer could not be very intelligent in creating something so useless. Perhaps, they are correct in that ninety-nine percent of the universe is not necessary to sustain human life; however, last time I checked, humans only occupied one planet.

I do not purport to know exactly why God created the vastness of the universe. Perhaps, it is because He can. Perhaps, it is for us to use as a playground when He comes to take us home to be with Him for eternity.

---

86. Charles Darwin, *On the Origin of Species by Means of Natural Selection, or, the Preservation of Favoured Races in the Struggle for Life* (London: J. Murray, 1859).

87. David Ray Griffin, *Process Theology: On Postmodernism, Morality, Pluralism, Eschatology, and Demonic Evil* (Process Century Press: Anoka, MN, 2017).

Perhaps, it is simply not currently usable but will be in the near future. Who knows? I do know, however, that planets, stars, and the universe worship God. How is that? Job 38:7 refers to when the morning stars sang together. Richard Gray reported how scientists have discovered that stars and planets produce harmonic sounds.[88] So, the stars, quite literally, sing together just as the Bible records.

Closely related to evolution, scientists constantly struggle with the origins of the universe and often ignorantly endorse asinine theories like the big bang. Again, I have no problems with theorizing about the beginnings of the universe but, ultimately, I do have a problem with scientists reaching disingenuous conclusions unsupported by science. There are, however, good questions that have arisen from such research. One such question is that if science teaches us that something cannot come from nothing, how did God create the universe *ex nihilo*, or "from nothing?"

Genesis chapters one and two teach us about the formation of the earth and everything on the earth. Genesis 1:2 teaches that "the earth was without form, and void." So, science will teach that it is impossible to create something from nothing and, therefore, Genesis 1:2 is inaccurate. While I know Genesis 1:2 is completely accurate, I am of the opinion that it is indeed impossible for something to come from nothing. We have to realize that if we are to defend our faith, we must be truthful with ourselves, earnestly studying the Word of God, and allowing the Holy Spirit to teach us. We cannot honestly defend that something came from nothing when God created the heavens and the earth while simultaneously debating scientists who proclaim the universe exploded from nothing into the form we now know. If we defend that something came from nothing, we have no claim to reject that molecules or gases came from nothing to create the big bang.

So, what happened? This is another question with which I struggled for many years. Please understand, I fancy myself a logical, rational, scientifically minded individual. To me, the Bible is fully logical and rational. Faith, while completely nonsensical to the world, makes perfect sense to me. So, I can easily believe science and Scripture. They are not contrary to one another. God is the Author of all knowledge and nothing under the sun is new.[89]

---

88. Richard Gray, "Star's song captured by scientists," Telegraph.co.uk, https://www.telegraph.co.uk/news/science/space/8114694/Stars-song-captured-by-scientists.html (accessed February 16, 2019).

89. Ecclesiastes 1:9.

I fully realize the response to "how did God create the universe out of nothing," which is the go-to response for many Christians, is "Because He's God and He can do anything." Of course, He is God and yes, He can do anything but this is, in my honest opinion, a cop-out answer the world will reject when we attempt to defend our faith. It is an answer born out of ignorance of the Scripture and a lack of understanding as granted by the Holy Spirit. I am not the ultimate, super-Christian who has learned everything I have ever needed to know from the Holy Spirit. I am far from it. In fact, I still count myself very much a learner of God's Word. Furthermore, the ready-made response still did not answer the question. I wanted to know *how* God created the universe out of nothing. While studying Genesis chapter two, the Holy Spirit let me see what I believe is the answer.

Allow me to present a theory of my own for your enjoyment that personally makes me rejoice when I contemplate it. Genesis chapter one indicates God spoke the world into existence. If one reads Genesis, one will find the words, "And God said" throughout the chapter with one significant exception: Genesis 1:27, which reads, "So God *created* man in his own image." Genesis chapter two, often cited by atheists and evolutionists as a contradiction to Genesis chapter one but, in reality, is a more detailed account of the marvelous work of God, indicates God decided to get His hands dirty when He made humankind.

Carving man from the very dust of the earth He spoke into existence, He inspired or breathed *His own breath* into humankind's body. The very breath of God is the substance of our souls. He breathed our souls into existence. My theory entails that God did not create the universe and life from nothing but the very sound of His spoken words were, are, and always will be tangible; even producing physical matter. In other words, God created the universe and life from the very essence of His being, even placing this same essence into humankind, so His creation may, in turn, return praise and adoration while utilizing His very substance He embodied in His creatures.

In my opinion, we, as Christians, need to reverse course on the idea that the earth is 6,000 years old. I fully realize that this opinion may not be popular among my fellow brothers and sisters but consider it. Dinosaur fossils prove the earth was in existence long before 6,000 years ago. It is comical but I have even heard a conspiracy theory that dinosaur bones were planted in order to falsely prove the age of the earth was older than

3. THE DIRTY BOMB: SECULARISM

6,000 years. Admittedly, I cannot substantiate or disprove that claim but I highly doubt the validity of the theory.

Where does the number 6,000 originate? Simply stated, God spent six days creating the earth and when combined with 2 Peter 3:8, believers have historically equated an exact thousand years with each day of Creation. This is, in my opinion, a misapplication of Scripture. Even if God spent one thousand years creating each day, there is no record of the progress of a day. We consider a day from the rising to the setting of the sun. There may have been millennia between each day of Creation. God may have spent minutes creating the five days and millennia creating man. It simply is not measurable.

In my opinion, each day of Creation (and the time between days) lasted as long as God desired it to last. Second Peter 3:8 essentially assures the reader that God does not measure time in the same way humans do. He is transcendent to space-time as we know it. To assert the age of the earth is a mere 6,000 years limits the vastness and omnipotence of God. Science suggests the earth is 14.5 billion years old. Certainly, there is no way to validate this claim either, however, if it is true, we can rejoice in that God is amazingly ancient! How awesome is our Lord to be an unfathomable number of years in age! Amazingly, He is simultaneously younger, too. God simply does not exist with the confines of conventional time and space. To continue to argue for a 6,000-year-old earth is a battle not worth the effort. If it is 6,000 years old, wonderful. If not, so be it.

Evolution and random universal design are favorite beliefs among atheists because they offer explanations for life devoid of God. Because atheism, and its cousin agnosticism, is a major tactic of the enemy, we will investigate it later. I will also share the cosmological first cause argument for the existence of God that generally ends debate with atheists and agnostics.

Evolution is, quite frankly, an irrational, unscientific, unfounded, illogical attempt at explaining the natural order. Simply stated, if evolution is taught to children as fact, it is educational and scientific malpractice. There simply exists no significantly sound evidence for the theory of evolution to be considered fact. I challenge parents to confront teachers in school who do teach evolution as scientific law. Do not allow such satanic influences to go unchecked and unanswered. Evolution is generally utilized by the enemy as a gateway to atheism, secularism, and postmodernism. Because it is generally taught early in school and revisited more in-depth in high school biology class, parents should be vigilant to examine school textbooks, homework assignments, class materials, and children's teachers' personal opinion on how evolution should be taught. Remember, it should be taught but only as a theory.

Atheism and Agnosticism

I had originally planned to treat this topic as a separate chapter but, to be honest, atheism and agnosticism are simply too easy to refute. Most atheists argue that there is no God. Agnostics argue that either God is unknowable or that they are unsure as to whether there is a God. To support these claims, atheists and agnostics will often refer to the impossibility of absolute truth. When an atheist claims there is no God or God does not exist, that is a definitive "truth" statement spoken from a position of knowledge. In other words, the individual making such a statement is certain of a supposed fact.

When one makes a factual statement, he or she must be ready to prove such a statement. Therefore, atheists should be called on to prove such a statement. Both atheists and agnostics make a truth claim that there are no truth claims90. If there are no truth claims, then the same truth claim made by atheists and agnostics cannot be true, thus truth exists. Much like when Satan continually attacks God's people, telling them they are sinners and on their way to hell, the opposite must be true because Satan is a liar. Do not allow him to gain the upper hand.

The *law of noncontradiction* states that something cannot simultaneously be true and false.[90] If something is true, it cannot also be false and vice versa. Philosopher David Hume stated that meaningful ideas can only be true if by definition or by sense experience. His ideas were encapsulated by Ayer's "principle of empirical verifiability." This principle essentially states that something can only be meaningful if it is true by definition or if it is empirically verifiable (testable). To be empirically verifiable something has to be observed with the senses and replicable to achieve the same outcomes each time. Hold up a pen and let go. It will drop to the floor every time. That is empirically verifiable because it is observable.

The principle is self-defeating. It is neither true by definition nor empirically verifiable therefore it is meaningless. Immanuel Kant, an agnostic philosopher, thought he would be able to get beyond the meaningless of the principle of empirical verifiability by stating there was no way to know the

---

90. Norman Geisler and Frank Turek, *I Don't Have Enough Faith to Be an Atheist* (Wheaton, IL: Crossway Books, 2004).

real world, even empirically verifiable information. Again, Kant is an example of a philosopher trying to prove the inability to know God exists and refuting his own statement. Because Kant stated he knew there was no way to know anything about the real world, he provided a truth claim. If Kant's view was correct, there is no way he could know reality is unknowable.

Either something is or it is not. Either God exists or He does not. Either I am a human or I am not. This is the *law of excluded middle*. There can be no equivocation, thus there is always true and false. We empirically observe our world and make conclusions about it that makes sense to our innate sensibilities. This is induction. We analyze those conclusions to make meaningful statements. This is deduction. Humans do not possess omniscience; therefore, our inductions, and consequently, our deductions can be wrong.

We can, however, be reasonably sure about basic empirical evidence. For example, all human beings are from the planet Earth. While we can be reasonably sure this is a true statement, no human has omniscient knowledge about the universe. While we can be ninety-nine percent sure this statement is true based on everything we know, we cannot be perfectly sure. Geisler and Turek suggested that even though God Himself is unobservable, we can induce knowledge about God by studying the effects of God.[91] This is nothing short of what we, as humans, do on a daily basis. While we cannot observe gravity, we can observe its effects. While we cannot see the entirety of the universe, we can fairly assume all human beings are from Earth. This is all based on rational conclusions made by rational observations.

The *law of causality* states that everything that had a beginning also had a cause. The universe had a beginning; therefore, the existence of the universe is dependent on a cause. So, what caused the universe? Atheists will argue the universe has always existed and has been expanding and contracting forever. The *second law of thermodynamics* disputes this. According to this law (again, something tested thousands of times with the same results), the universe contains only a finite amount of energy. Once the energy is dissolved, the universe will cease to exist. Because we can observe that we are still alive and the universe is still functioning, this "cosmic rebound theory" holds no validity. In fact, nothing possesses perpetual energy. We rest in order to refresh our strength. Machines that operate constantly will eventually

---

91. Ibid.

break. A pendulum will eventually stop swinging. Everything that God has created will eventually run out of energy.

There is, essentially, no other explanation for the cause of the universe other than a Cause outside of space and time. God has to be the cause. But what caused God? Simple: because God is outside time and space, He is not dependent nor contingent on the natural laws that govern humanity. God has forever been and will forever be. If atheists wish to ascribe this nature to the universe, then the universe itself would be God. However, the universe cannot be God. Why? Because the universe is losing energy and will dissolve, thus the universe demonstrates it had a beginning and a cause to that beginning.

The *anthropic principle* refers to the evidence that the universe is specifically tuned to sustain human life. To recap a dilemma I presented earlier: if God created the universe and everything in it and considering that humans occupy less than 0.1 percent of the universe, then what is the purpose of the planets, galaxies, stars, moons, and suns? Why would God create Jupiter when it really has no purpose that I can see? I partially answered my own question. There are many purposes that I cannot observe so I must induce those purposes. However, I recently heard a startling astronomical fact that made me rejoice. Jupiter serves as a "cosmic vacuum cleaner." Essentially, Jupiter, because of its gigantic size and gravitational pull, redirects cosmic trash, asteroids, meteors, and comets that would otherwise threaten Earth.[92] Additionally, there appears to be no other galaxy with a planet like Jupiter that performs this function.

But if this was not the case, the Bible declares the function of the universe. Psalms 19:1 reads, "The heavens declare the glory of God; the skies proclaim the work of his hands." Even before there were telescopes or Albert Einstein, the Bible revealed the expanding of the universe. Science is not an anathema to Scripture. It does not disprove the existence of God. In fact, J. P. Moreland argued science supports Scripture. It is *scientism* (the philosophical belief that only hard science can contribute to knowledge) that conflicts with Scripture.[93]

There is a *moral law* whereby every human being innately knows to do good and shun evil. It is a law that "keeps one in check." It is this same

---

92. M. Davis, "Why humanity owes a lot to Jupiter." BigThink.com, https://bigthink.com/surprising-science/how-jupiter-protects-earth?rebelltitem=1#rebelltitem1 (accessed November 9, 2018).

93. J. P. Moreland, *Scientism and Secularism* (Wheaton, Illinois: Crossway, 2018).

3. THE DIRTY BOMB: SECULARISM

law whereby one inherently knows that murder, theft, rape, and other sinful, heinous practices are wrong. Relativists would argue that there is no absolute truth or absolute moral law. Of course, by their making such a statement, they have highlighted what they believe to be an absolute truth and moral law, which means their argument is self-defeating. Applying the *law of noncontradiction* to this, that means there must be an absolute truth and absolute moral law. If there is an absolute moral law innate to all human beings, how did it get there? There must be an absolute Moral Law Giver. In fact, Jeremiah 31:33 tells us Who that is: "I will put my law in their inward parts, and write it in their hearts; and will be their God, and shall be my people."

This does not mean that one does not have the choice to violate this moral law and commit sin. If there is a moral law and God put it in every human mind as well as wrote it on every human heart, how does one fall so far from this standard that he or she commits atrocities like murder, child molestation, elder abuse, and more? Jeremiah also has an answer to this: "Were they ashamed when they had committed abomination? nay, they were not at all ashamed, neither could they blush: therefore shall they fall among them that fall: in the time of their visitation they shall be cast down, saith the LORD."[94] In other words, the sinners to whom God was referring had willingly violated their own conscience and rejected the moral law so often they were cast down or, as the writer of Romans 1:28 stated, "[given] over to a reprobate mind." Ravi Zacharias encapsulated this point when he wrote about atheists: "I strongly suggest that the real issue is not an absence of moral order but an insistence on determining for oneself what is good and what is evil, in spite of what we intuitively know to be true . . . to believe that there is no moral order, one must assume knowledge of what a moral order should look like if there were one."[95]

In fact, atheists even agree with moral law, albeit unwittingly. Without moral law, atheists would not even be permitted to believe as they wish to believe. Without moral law, there is no objective right or wrong. Atheists who believe murder is wrong are applying moral law to make such a statement. They are admitting to a truth. Tolerance is a principle of moral law. Those preaching tolerance are advocating for the application of a moral law truth. These are often the self-same people who declare there is no absolute

---

94. Jeremiah 8:12.
95. Ravi Zacharias, *The End of Reason: A Response to the New Atheists* (Grand Rapids, MI.: Zondervan, 2008).

truth. Again, the atheistic, relativistic argument is self-defeating. As Geisler and Turek stated, a plea for tolerance is an automatic and inherent acknowledgment that the activity for which tolerance is requested is wrong.[96] There is no need to tolerate an activity that is moral and good.

In short, atheism and agnosticism are simply cop-outs. Atheists and agnostics simply wish to be able to do as they wish. Ravi Zacharias suggested atheists possess a covert desire to have a world without God.[97] He further explained that Aldous Huxley, famous author, atheist, and hedonist, wrote that he wanted the world not to have meaning so he would be free from all of religion's moral demands. Transcending value must come from someone of transcending worth.[98] If one is completely resting value in a world of matter alone, then there can be no intrinsic worth. Foucault, a twentieth-century philosopher, was a sadomasochistic sex deviant atheist who taught his students that it is forbidden to forbid. Foucault followed his deviancy to his early death in 1984 due to AIDS. He is the product of a self-aggrandized atheist who dismissed the moral law because he wanted to live as he pleased with no boundaries.

This is, in effect, the root of atheism and agnosticism. It is a denial of God's moral law and a desire to live unconstrained in a hedonistic and masochistic lifestyle. It is a total, conscientious rejection of moral law in favor of sin done so with some measure of guilt. Guilt is the natural reaction that God has instilled in humankind. In order to sufficiently dismiss this guilt rather than succumb to God's moral conviction and their own consciences, atheists and agnostics choose to pretend God does not exist in a cowardly attempt to appease their own conscience so they may continue in the sinful lifestyle they have chosen. Ultimately, they believe their own lie, and true to the nature of God, He has already underscored as the natural outcome.[99]

The moral law of God applied to our minds and written on our hearts, as Jeremiah 31:33 reads, is that special inner voice God has granted us that we call conscience. Atheists have seared their consciences with a hot iron[100] in order to live according to their own self-indulgent laws. But what is the conscience exactly? How can it save from a life of devastation and destruction?

96. Geisler and Turek, 2004.
97. Zacharias, 2008.
98. Ibid.
99. Thessalonians 2:7-12.
100. Timothy 4:2.

3. THE DIRTY BOMB: SECULARISM

Summary

Secularism, in all its iterations, cannot be injurious without activism. Without activism, it is nothing more than a meaningless philosophy. The evil root of secularism is the weaponization of its tenets to hold accountable those who do not agree with or adhere to the philosophy. There is zero tolerance for those who do not walk in lockstep with the ideology. In fact, it is the source of much violence spreading across the world. Failure to agree with the ideology can result in physical harm. Speaking out against the ideology can result in death. What, then, should we as Christians do? The untold story of the Scriptures is not the gaps in the life of Christ, His disciplines, and the forefathers of the faith.

The untold story is the activism of those who believed in Christ but were not among those who are chronicled in the historicity of the Scriptures. Thousands were saved during Christ's life on earth and during the ministry of the disciples and apostles. However, we only read of a select few. Where were the thousands of believers? Throughout Scripture, believing in Christ and eschewing the lies of the enemy resulted in harsh persecution and even death. History repeats itself; we are now living in those times again. Will we be among the thousands who believe but refused to speak for fear of retribution? Or will we be among the few who will be chronicled in history as those who spoke out against the lies of Satan? More importantly, will we be among the few who stand before our Creator and hear, "Well done, thou good and faithful servant"?[101]

---

101. Matthew 25:21.

4. THE SHIELD: OUR CONSCIENCE

IN EARLIER GENERATIONS OF American society, and other societies for that matter, the church was generally the centerpiece of life in the community. It was the place where families came together to meet in fellowship with other families. It was the place where families publicly participated in worship with other like-minded families. Church was the place where morals, that were ideally taught at home, were reinforced and elevated to provide families with the opportunity for a closer walk with Christ. The church was the purveyor and guardian of the community's conscience.

What Is Conscience?

Conscience is a divine element gifted to humanity. What does this mean exactly? The human conscience extends back to the very dawn of humanity. In Genesis, the Bible records that God would actually come down in the garden of Eden "in the cool of the day" to walk with Adam. While Genesis does not explicitly indicate that God and Adam engaged in direct conversation during these walks, one may definitely, and probably accurately, assume they engaged in interesting dialogue. Imagine the possible content of the conversations between God and Adam! We must understand: God Himself descended from His throne in heaven to walk on the face of the earth He created in the garden He created to hang out with the man He created.

Adam and Eve's conscience intervened when presented with the forbidden fruit. Genesis 3:3 records how Eve, while talking with the serpent, recited God's warning not to eat of the tree, underscoring the consequence of death should she disobey. Following their disobedience, Adam and Eve hid from God during one of His walks.[1] Eve's acknowledgment of God's command and the subsequent attempt at hiding, demonstrated the first recorded act of conscience intervention and display of guilt. Eve's conscience reminded her of God's command, dissuaded her from disobeying, and then

---

1. Genesis 3:8.

when disobedience did follow, shamed her and Adam for their sin. When allowed, the conscience God has given every human being will bring remembrance of what is good and what is evil.

Is Conscience the Actual Voice of God?

The conscience is a divine gift. Some may argue that human conscience is the actual "still, small voice" of God reminding humankind of basic moral truths.[2][3] Others believe the conscience is a divine gift that bears witness to universal truths of Christ.[4] Still yet, there are those who believe the conscience is nothing more than a paradigm, designed by the mind's developmentally appropriate reaction to societal norms and expectations.[5][6]

An Analysis of Conscience in Genesis Chapter Three

An analysis of Genesis chapter three would lead one to conclude Moore's and Hutcheson's premise is correct, given Adam and Eve's seemingly innate concern with God's command. Conversely, it is expedient that we consider this analysis in light of God's initial command to not eat of the tree. Simply stated, without that command, there would have been no need to consider disobedience, therefore, no sin and no need for shame.

Perhaps an understanding of the word "conscience" is important. The word is a compound of "con," meaning "with," and "science," meaning "to know" or "knowledge." Essentially, the word means "with knowledge." The reader would do well to remember this specific definition as biblical Scripture will illuminate that specific rendering of the word later. In Greek (the language of the New Testament), the word for "conscience" is *synderesis*, meaning "pain suffered as a result of betraying one's personal moral

---

2. Francis Hutcheson, "Reflections on the Common Systems of Morality," In *Francis Hutcheson: On Human Nature*, ed. Thomas Mautner (Cambridge: Cambridge University Press, 1993), 96-106.

3. G. E. Moore, *Principia Ethica* (Cambridge: University Press, 1903).

4. Thomas, *The Summa Theologica of St. Thomas Aquinas* (London: Burns Oates & Washbourne, 1912).

5. Jean Piaget, *The Moral Judgment of the Child* (Glencoe, Ill: Free Press, 1960).

6. Sigmund Freud, "The Ego and the Id," In J. Strachey (Ed. and Trans.), *The Standard Edition of the Complete Psychological Works of Sigmund Freud*, vol. 19, 3-66. (London: Hogarth Press, 1961), (original work published 1923).

principle." Considering the Greek definition of *synderesis*, it would be logical to conclude conscience is, in essence, the punitive action of betraying an innate sense, be it self-actualized or God-actualized. However, one may ask how it is possible to betray a personal moral principle without that principle being first personalized. Is it possible Moore and Hutcheson are correct and God has created all human beings with an innate sense of right and wrong? This question leads one to consider the nature versus nurture debate.

Thomas Aquinas considered *synderesis* as reason: the ability to do good and prevent evil.[7] Consequently, he considered *conscienta* as the ability to distinguish between right and wrong, apply this knowledge, and make a moral decision. *Synderesis* and *conscienta* are necessary for each to succeed. In order to do good and prevent evil, one must possess the ability to distinguish between right and wrong. Conversely, a moral decision is impossible without the ability to do good and prevent evil. Still yet, one may correctly question how humankind can arrive at the point of simply choosing good over evil without the knowledge of what is good and evil. Again, this leads us to the Moore and Hutcheson conclusion that knowledge of good and evil must be an innate human quality, divinely inspired.

However, our study of Genesis chapter three contradicts this perspective. If an innate knowledge of good and evil is divinely inspired in humankind, would not have Adam and Eve been created with this knowledge, thus no need to "eat of the tree of knowledge of good and evil?" Conversely, did not Eve, before she ate of the fruit, recall God's commandment not to eat of the tree while conversing with the serpent? Is not this evidence of an innate conscience prior to eating of the tree?

One must consider the circumstances of Adam and Eve. Eden was a paradise but perhaps Christians incorrectly consider the garden to be a place devoid of all sin. A rereading of Genesis chapter three indicates the beguiling serpent was already present in the garden. Of course, the serpent is a representation of satanic influence throughout Scripture. Clearly, disobedience, the first recorded sin, occurred in the garden of Eden; therefore, the garden was not entirely sinless. However, Adam and Eve, prior to consuming the forbidden fruit, had not known sin. Genesis chapter three alluded to the fact that Adam and Eve had no knowledge of their nakedness, given Adam's reasoning for hiding from God being "[they] were afraid because [they] were

7. Thomas, 1912.

naked"[8] and God's response being "who told thee that thou wast naked?"[9] Nakedness, in this sense and truly in the modern sense as well, is a reference to the sinful condition. Many who live in sin do not realize their own nakedness; however, many do indeed realize.

Prior to eating of the forbidden fruit, Adam and Eve essentially possessed no knowledge of good and evil. They could not, as Thomas Aquinas posited, reason between good and evil and apply to an innate moral principle. Genesis records God's instruction to not eat of the tree. It is reasonable to theorize that God also instructed Adam and Eve in other endeavors, as well, given His clear instruction in this instance. Simply put, Adam and Eve did not need knowledge of good and evil because they relied fully on God's instructions. Their innate moral principle did not exist as God's audible word was their sole guide.

Following Adam and Eve's actions, sin was realized and propitiation was necessary for restoring humankind's relationship with God. At this point, humankind began to develop a moral center. Also, due to this sin, humankind today is born into sin.[10] Yes, those precious babies, indeed gifts from God, are sinful creatures. Yes, those little two- and three-year-old darlings are sinful and have a propensity to sin. In fact, there are none good, no not one.[11] If you do not believe your little darling is sinful, put him or her to the test. Leave a giant cookie out with instructions that he or she is not to eat it. Research indicates as much as eighty percent of children five years of age or younger will not only eat the cookie, they will, when confronted, either lie about it or create a diversion to avoid trouble.[12]

Genesis chapter three indicates God made Adam and Eve clothes of skins to cover their nakedness.[13] One can conclude God sacrificed an animal to obtain those skins for Adam and Eve, thus the beginning of the practice of sacrifice for propitiation for sin. Ultimately, Jesus became the final sacrifice for sin and Christians are clothed in His righteousness. Indeed, the apostle Paul was correct in Romans 3:10-12—there is none good; however, it is only through Christ Jesus that we are made righteous. It is His precious

---

8. Genesis 3:10.
9. Genesis 3:11.
10. Psalm 51:5.
11. Romans 3:10-12.
12. Tali Sharot, *The Influential Mind: What the Brain Reveals About Our Power to Change Others* (New York: Henry Holt and Company, 2017).
13. Genesis 3:21.

blood that flowed from Calvary through the ages to touch sinful man and restore his relationship with an Almighty, Holy God.

Because humankind is born into sin, this lends partial credence to the theories of Piaget[14] and Freud.[15] Children, born into sin, are not able to reason between right and wrong as Thomas Aquinas suggested. This inability to reason between right and wrong lends itself to an oft-cited concept of the "age of accountability." To be clear, there is no scriptural reference to the concept of an age whereby one becomes self-accountable for his or her sins. So, does this mean that since children are born into sin, should they die in that condition, they will suffer eternal damnation? No. We must remember God is a just God.[16] Children of an early age have not sufficiently developed cognitively to the point whereby they fully understand the difference between good and evil. They are, in essence, subjected to a sinful, Adamic nature that was thrust upon them from a single act in a garden millennia ago.

The Age of Accountability?

What, then, is the age of accountability? When considering the vast research on cognitive psychology in concert with the Scriptures, the answer to this question is not clear and truly depends on the individual. In some instances, like those with cognitive and mental disabilities, an individual may never reach a specific age of accountability. Most consider the age of twelve or thirteen to be the primary age of accountability because that is the age at which Jesus ministered in the temple and is when the account of Jesus's life in Scripture resumed subsequent to His birth account. This being the age at which all individuals become accountable for him- or herself is arbitrary at best. Some may arrive earlier or later at the cognitive ability to reason the difference between right and wrong.

Ultimately, then, how does one arrive at the point of reasoning between what is good and evil, applying that knowledge, and choosing good rather than evil? As we discussed, Moore's and Hutcheson's theory of an innate conscience is not altogether tenable, given the assertions made by Scripture and cognitive psychology. Conversely, it is not altogether untenable either. While humankind is not born with the ability to distinguish between good and evil, there is an inactive, innate conscience, divinely

14. Piaget, 1960.
15. Freud, 1961.
16. Job 34:12.

inspired, within each human being. While Piaget and Freud incorrectly dismissed God as the source of any such conscience development, they were correct in that cognitive development is necessary for concurrent conscience development. This is the core of the nature versus nurture debate: is every human being naturally imbued with moral principles upon birth or are they developed over time? The answer is "both" to a degree.

Nature vs. Nurture

To be more specific, every human being is imbued with the *natural mechanisms* to develop moral principles. One may think of it as such: humans have a latent conscience that, with careful conditioning, will progressively awaken with time. Conversely, if humans are allowed to grow without any moral conditioning, the conscience will not develop appropriately, resulting in an essentially and *theoretically* amoral individual. This is why Proverbs 22:6 is critical for parents to understand and practice: "Train up a child in the way he should go: and when he is old, he will not depart from it." The emphasis in this Scripture is the word "train." Think of that child running wild in the grocery store. We have all seen and experienced the scene. Furthermore, we have all commented either aloud or mentally, "This child has had no training." Clearly, the parent neglected to apply appropriate correction to the rearing of the child. Sadly, in my professional experiences, these are the children who grow to be incorrigible in school, underperform academically, and progress to be a strain on society, rather than a contributing member.

The Case of the Transgendered Child

In my secular capacity as a school district administrator, I recently encountered a very troubling situation. A Christian teacher approached me, very concerned about a potentially controversial situation in which state expectations were conflicting with her religious beliefs. A first-grade female student (to be crystal clear: a six-year-old) was dressing, acting, and portraying herself as a boy. In fact, her parents were supportive of her action by using a male name and male pronouns. The expectation of the school was to follow suit. The teacher indicated to the principal that while she would comply with calling the student by her chosen name (because it is not unusual for all children to prefer middle names or nicknames), she could not refer to the female child with male pronouns. To do so would violate her natural sensibilities, given she is female and that cannot change and would, in effect, require her to lie to herself and her students while projecting an acceptance of this action to all her students.

Tearfully, she explained the principal would not support her. He exclaimed, "This is not about what you want and need; this is about the student." Finally, she asked how she should conduct herself with this student. My first point of explanation to her was that the parents should lose custody of the child for child abuse. A first-grade student! Second, I explained to her that it is her right not to refer to her as "he, him, or his." She then replied, "How am I supposed to refer to the student in class then?" I responded, "Rather than use pronouns, call the student by name every time. Yes, it will sound silly but if the situation were not so unfortunate, it would be silly itself."

It is evident in this situation that the parents were contributing to the future mental instability of the child. In fact, the results could be potentially even more devastating. Research indicates that forty-eight percent of transgendered youths attempt suicide, compared with 2.4 percent of adolescents in general.[17] Proverbs 22:6 should not only be affirming to the parents who work to instill biblical morals and values but should be a warning to parents who either neglect or refuse to do so. Parents who elect to "train up children" in a way not founded in biblical moral principles but in politically correct ideologies are essentially condemning their children to a life of ruination.

Train Up a Child

But what about those children who were trained according to Scripture but then choose to live in sin at some point in their adult lives? It would seem Proverbs 22:6 is untrue, would it not? Clearly, Proverbs 22:6 assures parents that when the child is old, he or she will not depart from that training. While it may seem that the promise proposed in this Scripture sometimes fails to deliver, that could not be further from the truth. Scripture provides us with another promise I like to refer to as the antecedent, or backup, to Proverbs 22:6. We should take comfort in the words of Isaiah, "So shall my word be that goeth forth out of my mouth: it shall not return unto me void,

---

17. R. Carmody, "Trans young people at alarmingly high risk of suicide and depression, report reveals," *ABC News*, September 1, 2017, http://www.abc.net.au/news/2017-09-01/young-trans-people-at-higher-risk-of-suicide-report-finds/8861156.

4. THE SHIELD: OUR CONSCIENCE

but it shall accomplish that which I please, and it shall prosper in the thing whereunto I sent it."[18] God's Word is living and powerful.[19] Be encouraged that when a child strays from that which has been taught; if it is built on the immutable Word of God, those words will continually "haunt" him or her while he or she is living in sin.

While I was growing up, my mother always made sure God was first and foremost in my life. I will never forget my mother reading the words of life to me. There were times she would also pause in the midst of a Scripture and expect me to fill in the blanks. That exercise ensured that not only was I listening but that I was able to memorize. She ensured that I "hide [God's Word] in my heart, that I might not sin against [Him]."[20] Did this ensure that I would not sin? No. However, it did ensure that, in sin, I would know how to come back to Christ. It ensured that, in sin, I would not languish in the putrid stench of this world but that I would return to the path that while it is straight and narrow, it ultimately leads to everlasting life.[21]

I am reminded of the parable of the prodigal son.[22] The son who spent his inheritance partaking in the pleasures of the world ended up, as a Jew mind you, in the pigpen. Anyone who was raised in the country is well aware of the smell (and contents) of a pigpen. It certainly is not a pleasant place to find oneself. There is a small and sometimes overlooked section of this parable that indicates the process by which one who is trained according to Scripture finds him- or herself living in sin. The first words of Luke 15:17 indicate the prodigal son, while in the pigpen of life, "came to himself." In other words, he came to his senses. Often, those who were reared in church and trained according to the Word of God but chose a life of sin, however short or long, makes one question what is wrong with him or her.

We must remember the words of the writer of Hebrews 11:25, in that sin is pleasurable for a season. Proverbs 14:12 supports this assertion and assists in explaining why the prodigal son, who had everything while in the house with his father, would choose to give it all away for a short season of sin: "There is a way that seemeth right unto a man, but the end thereof are the ways of death." As with the prodigal son, there is an attraction, perhaps related to the Adamic nature of humankind, to sin. The allure of sin is

18. Isaiah 55:11.
19. Hebrews 4:12.
20. Psalms 119:11.
21. Matthew 7:13-14.
22. Luke 15:11-32.

sometimes too enticing to ignore. Satan lures individuals to his spider web of sin and actually provides a modicum of pleasure for a season. Ultimately, his goal is destruction. When he is finished, sin bringeth forth death.[23] It is the goal of the enemy to destroy God's creation.

However, we can be thankful that the powerful Word of God, when instilled from the beginning of life, comes back to remembrance in those desperate moments when sin has run its course, leading one to his or her senses. I have often been amazed at how the soundtrack of my conscience sounds so much like my mother! I grew up hearing my mother pray for me and my family until the Holy Spirit began to speak. It is a wonderful feeling to know the Holy Spirit is praying to the Father for you. It is also a profound moment in a young person's life to hear parents calling his or her name in prayer. Regardless of the life condition of a scripturally trained adult, he or she will never depart from the knowledge of how to be saved and forgiven.

Why Not Ask "Why?"

One must be careful with the modern inculcation of doctrine. Indoctrination is literally the practice of teaching a set of religious tenets to be accepted uncritically. This may not be a popular perspective but follow me through this explanation. I do not believe Christ expects followers to blindly accept this doctrine. As Thomas Aquinas posited, humans have the innate ability to reason. God provided humans with a brain and a will. He expects His followers to *choose* Him. How can one make a choice without weighing the options? Please understand, God is not afraid of our questions. The Almighty, Who is the Architect of the universe, is plenty capable of fielding the insignificant queries of His creation. In fact, I believe God enjoys the communication! Do we not believe the gospel is sufficiently strong enough to withstand questioning? If we discourage our children from "questioning God" or questioning our faith, how else will they be able to "earnestly contend for the faith"[24] when the world will relentlessly work to discredit God's Word? This is the essence of apologetics.

Paul, in Philippians 2:12, wrote, "... work out your own salvation with fear and trembling." Many misinterpret this Scripture in order to satisfy their own desires to live haphazardly, all the while soothing their own consciences by justifying a favorite sin as not being "a personal conviction."

23. James 1:15.
24. Jude 1:3.

On the contrary, working out one's own salvation is a personal mission to fully understanding why one follows Christ—to learn everything possible about the nature of our faith. Our faith is most logical and reasoned. It has endured millennia of criticism, attempts at destruction, aspersions, and blatant hatred. Surely, it can endure and thrive in light of questioning.

Shame

Conscience, divinely inspired, albeit latent in humankind from birth, must be nurtured in order for it to appropriately govern one's future actions. However, conscience is subject to another divinely appointed characteristic of humanity: the free will. While the conscience will alert one of an action that is contrary to his or her cultivated moral center, imploring that individual to turn from the wicked way,[25] ultimately, he or she can choose to obey or ignore. The apostle Paul discussed the consistent disregard of conscience in 1 Timothy chapter four by comparing it to the action of searing with a hot iron. The act of searing one's conscience is the continual and blatant disregard of his or her own moral center as informed by his or her conscience. When the conscience is seared, all sense is lost. One can no longer feel ashamed of the sin in which he or she is engaging. The prophet Jeremiah best summarized this condition in chapter 8, verse 12 when he wrote, "Were they ashamed when they had committed abomination? nay, they were not at all ashamed, neither could they blush: therefore shall they fall among them that fall: in the time of their visitation they shall be cast down, saith the LORD."

The inability to feel shame for ungodly, immoral conduct is a dangerous condition in which one may find him- or herself. In fact, it is near to the condition Paul described as "reprobate mind."[26] Interestingly, one arrives at such a condition when, as Paul wrote, "they [do] not like to retain God in their knowledge." Recall the word "conscience" is a compound word meaning "with knowledge."

---

25. Chronicles 7:14.
26. Romans 1:28.

Sanctification

As Thomas Aquinas theorized, humans have the ability to reason what is good and evil (*synderesis*) and then apply that reasoning to make a moral judgment (*conscienta*). When confronted at the proverbial crossroads of good and evil; ultimately, one must *choose*. Earlier, I indicated the reader should mentally mark the definition of "conscience" as being "with knowledge" because Scripture is clear on the choice one makes when standing at that proverbial crossroads of good and evil. The writer of James unequivocally indicated, "Therefore to him that knoweth to do good, and doeth it not, to him it is sin."[27] In other words, those who know to *choose* good but *choose* evil are living in a sinful condition. Those who continually make this choice are in danger of searing their conscience, leading to the inability to feel shame. Those unable to feel shame for their perpetual sinful condition are in danger of God turning them over to a reprobate mind.

The method for eschewing this progressive descent from making a wrong choice to outright sin, a seared conscience, and a reprobate mind is a scriptural term that is not a popular concept in modern society: sanctification. My church, the Church of God (Cleveland, TN), teaches that sanctification is the second definite work of grace subsequent to salvation and prior to baptism in the Holy Spirit. The church also teaches that sanctification is also a progressive work to which Paul alluded in Colossians 3:10 when he wrote about a process of daily spiritual renewal. Sanctification is perhaps best defined in 2 Timothy 2:21, "If a man therefore purge himself from these [works of iniquity], he shall be a vessel unto honour, sanctified, and meet for the master's use, and prepared unto every good work." Essentially, the Christian must separate him- or herself from the sinful practices of the world—made holy in order to be used by God. The Christian must strive to live holy. It is a commandment from God in 1 Peter 1:16 to, "Be ye holy; for I am holy." Furthermore, God warns us in Hebrews 12:14 that without holiness, "no man shall see the Lord."

This treatise on the development of the conscience is critical for fully understanding the condition in which our society now exists. In modern society, conscience is trivial, evil is good, good is evil, hypocrisy reigns, deception is commonplace, absolute truth is rejected, and tolerance of sin is demanded. It seems as though Satan is winning in every situation and controlling the world. The church has abdicated its rightful position

27. James 4:17.

4. THE SHIELD: OUR CONSCIENCE

as the guardian and purveyor of biblically centered moral truth in favor of the prosperity gospel; hyper-grace; seeker-sensitive, politically correct ear-tickling; and a hell-less, everyone goes to heaven existence. The church, as a whole, has exchanged its effectiveness for a more tolerant and accepting image. As a result, sin has run amok, even in the church, generations are lost, fear of the Lord has waned, and society is in danger of losing a moral center entirely. The focus of this book is how these elements are combining to perpetuate a most dangerous scenario for our children. Satan is determined to destroy this generation but we must be reminded, however, to, "Be strong and of good courage, fear not, nor be afraid of them: for the LORD thy God, he it is that doth go with thee; he will not fail thee, nor forsake thee."[28]

---

28. Deuteronomy 31:6.

5. THE WOLF IN SHEEP'S CLOTHING: SOCIAL JUSTICE

> Take a moment to investigate the cartoon located at http://culturalorganizing.org/the-problem-with-that-equity-vs-equality-graphic/

THE IDEA BEHIND THIS illustration is to convey that when a teacher, principal, or educational administrator enacts equality, often cited as noble, he or she does not actually serve the child. The crates in each picture represent the pedagogical actions in which an educational professional might engage in a learning environment. To clarify a little further: the crates could represent a teacher's work in the classroom through lesson delivery or the amount of money a district provides to a specific school. In the equality illustration, all three children, regardless of height, are provided the exact same crate. Educationally, all three children are provided the same treatment in the classroom or all three schools are provided the same amount of capital. The more vertically challenged child is unable to see over the fence when he is provided equal services. The message to the viewer is that if services are provided to all children or schools equally without regard to his or her specific needs, then the student in most need with the least preparation will still be unable to succeed.

This message is, in fact, true! When a teacher or educational services entity fails to consider the inherent needs of the child, the student will not succeed. Unfortunately, this message is resoundingly negated by the illustration. Social justice warriors determined that a more nefarious, child-endangering goal was more appropriate. Let us consider the "equity" illustration. At first glance, one may notice all three children can now see over the fence and surmise the mission has been accomplished. Such is the conclusion social justice warriors would wish.

In fact, one must consider the illustration in terms of a graph. Consider the fence line as a passing score. It matters not what subject area the reader considers. In the equity illustration, the teacher or school district has successfully implemented interventions to assist the more vertically challenged child to finally rise above the passing score. But what happened to the vertically enhanced child? He regressed from well above the passing score to just above the score. In fact, notice how his crate no longer exists. Does the social justice warrior suggest teachers and school districts should *remove* services from this child in order to provide services to the vertically challenged child? Consider the middle child. Are social justice warriors suggesting teachers and school districts should *ignore* the educational needs of the middle student?

Regrettably, these images have circulated extensively in teacher professional development sessions with social justice professionals expounding on the virtues of implementing equity versus equality in the classroom. In fact, I challenge every reader to take this image to his or her child's teacher and principal and ask him or her to provide an explanation of the illustration. If he or she responds with the social justice mantra of providing extra services to the vertically challenged student without acknowledging the endangerment and injustice perpetrated on the other two students, then the reader should remove his or her child from that school.

Consider the illustration as a graph once more. If the viewer drew a line across the heads of the students, one would see a straight line. This is indicative of zero growth. With educators teaching "to the middle," the excelling students will regress to the mean, moderately performing students will remain at the mean, and underachieving students will never rise higher than the mean. Essentially, the vertically enhanced student, representative of students who are academically gifted in one form or another, not only lose teaching interventions but are purposefully regressed in order to make the academically underperforming students *appear* as though they have progressed. This is called *teaching to the mean* or *teaching to the median*. Do not be mistaken, the social justice advocate is only interested in equalizing everyone to the median.

Without discussing too much detail, this is the result of the hyper-testing culture in which our nation's schools have been inculcated. Notice the fence line again. The reader must understand that is referred to in standardized testing and statistical methodologies as a "norm." It is the middle point or median. It is where the majority of test participants will likely score based on preparation. In most educational instances, that norm is sixty percent. Consider a doctor who only understood sixty percent of medical treatments. How about a pilot who only understood sixty percent of the controls and data required for flying? Why, then, is it acceptable for *any* child to only understand sixty percent of the material the state government has deemed necessary for a holistic education?

How, then, should the illustration appear? In short, there should be no limits to the number of boxes any child receives. Why should the fence line be the point at which learning stops? Perhaps the view from a higher perspective would be an even better one. Students, regardless of prior preparation, should be given the tools necessary to excel. This is the very definition of an educational term often quoted but rarely understood: differentiation. *Differentiation* is a term that is not synonymous with the social justice agenda. Social justice advocates are concerned only with the *perceived* disenfranchised. If in order to provide the necessary methods and materials for the disenfranchised to succeed requires inflicting punitive measures on the *perceived* empowered, then so be it. Differentiation would require an educator or educational entity to provide whatever methods and materials is necessary for each individual student to succeed, regardless of prior preparation or current perceived power status.

Furthermore, education should not serve to simply get students past the goal line. Education should serve to provide access to the training by which doors will be opened that would otherwise be closed without said training. Learning should be personal; therefore, mastery learning is the method by which students must demonstrate, unequivocally, not only their grasp of the material but also the ability to fully iterate it to another person.[1]

Let me be clear: the social justice advocate, concerned only with median performance, is, in essence, openly admitting their personal beliefs that the perceived disenfranchised can never excel beyond the norm. Essentially, sixty percent is the ceiling for those who perhaps did not have access to prior preparation that others may have possessed. Let me state this categorically: this is a bigoted position designed to leverage personal power for the avowed social justice agenda by exploiting classism and pitting the perceived powerless against the perceived powerful. It is an attempt to vilify and enslave contingencies of people because of some observable trait such as skin color, gender, wealth, class, ethnicity, or any other qualifier.

Let me pause for a moment. I have utilized the term "perceived" often when referring to the disenfranchised and empowered. Allow me to explain: there are, indeed, power structures working within the modern society.

---

1. Alan D. Wimberley, *Reshaping the Paradigms of Teaching and Learning* (Lanham, MD: Rowman & Littlefield, 2017).

5. THE WOLF IN SHEEP'S CLOTHING: SOCIAL JUSTICE

These power structures are real and not perceived; however, there are prevailing perspectives among the so-called social elitists and progressives who are applying disenfranchised (powerless) and empowered (powerful) statuses to classes of individuals who are not designed to empower others but are designed to continue to divide and conquer. Remember, the goal is not to improve another's condition, it is to depress the conditions of others to the median level in order to make the disenfranchised positions *appear* to be improved like the equality/equity illustration. If all are on the median level, then all are easier to control—hence, the socialistic inclination of the vast majority of social justice advocates. Primarily, the progressive social justice advocates base perceived power structures on obvious characteristics like race, class, socioeconomic status, gender, age, and sexual orientation. These are hot-button issues, easily exploited, easily observable, and offer the most accessible schemes to a payday. In reality, disenfranchisement knows no characteristics. Poverty is not exclusive to a racial or ethnic group. To suggest such is inherently racist. Inability to access services is not exclusive to gender. To suggest such is inherently sexist.

Make no mistake, progressive social justice aims and goals are Marxist in nature. They are not designed to improve the conditions of their fellow man; they are designed to disintegrate the advances of others they perceive are not worthy of such advances so as to equalize all at the same level. They are not designed to provide access to services the perceived marginalized could not previously access. They are designed to shunt and block access for those they have deemed who possess too much access already. Ultimately, it is all designed to segregate and compartmentalize groups of people based on observable characteristics and nurture hostility and enmity between those groups in order to continue their mission of equalizing conditions, controlling actions, and reserving financial posterity for themselves.

Karl Marx and Friedrich Engels asserted in the seminal work, *The Communist Manifesto,* that the bourgeois (wealthy landowners) will oppress and exploit the labor of the proletariats (working class) resulting in continual class struggles and revolutions.[2] According to them, the only answer is communism whereby all classes are erased. The Communists would focus solely on the so-called proletariats, essentially ignoring the needs of the so-called bourgeois, while confiscating and controlling all commerce, property, and labor. Sound familiar? One can clearly distinguish

---

2. Karl Marx and Friedrich Engels, *The Communist Manifesto* (New York: Penguin Books, 1847).

how Marxist philosophy is at work in the agenda of the progressive social justice advocate. The Marxist wishes to focus only on the perceived disenfranchised, while confiscating from the perceived empowered to redistribute as the state sees fit, thus equalizing the conditions of everyone. This is synonymous with the equality/equity philosophy captured in the aforementioned illustration. What the progressive fails to reveal in this false utopia is 100 percent of history bears out that the equalized condition is often one of poverty except for those in control of the state. They also fail to mention that when there is no reward for hard work, the laborers will refuse to work. The results are untold thousands who are enslaved by the government in forced labor camps.

Many Americans do not realize the Pilgrims once attempted to live by communist principles when they arrived. The Pilgrims, upon arriving in the New World, found themselves in less than ideal conditions. In order to survive, Governor William Bradford in 1620 implemented the colony's "common stock and goods."[3] Essentially, Bradford implemented the then-future Marxist philosophy, "From each according to his ability, to each according to his need."[4] The results of the socialist commune experiment were that able men and women resented the work, began to refuse to work for others' benefits, and starvation began to set in. Patton recounted how Bradford, seeing the experiment was failing, abolished socialism, enacted free-market principles, and asked God for forgiveness.[5] Once the free market principles were enacted and socialism reversed, the colony began to prosper.

For the progressive postmodernist, social justice is a punitive measure designed to exact a measure of retribution for past sins. The dogma entails that an immoral and unjust majority has illegitimately repressed certain segments of society characterized by an observable characteristic or quality not observed in the conceptualized majority. Terms such as "equality" and "equity" are routinely and often inappropriately utilized to justify behavior that is designed to not only ensure "marginalized" voices are amplified but other voices deemed "in the majority" are repressed. While this, in and of itself, is contrary to the Word of God, the progressive postmodernist

---

3. Judd Patton, "The Pilgrim Story: Vital Insights and Lessons for Today," *Bellevue University Economics Department*, 2000, http://jpatton.bellevue.edu/biblical_economics/pilgrimstory.html.

4. Marx and Engels, 1847.

5. Patton, 2000.

5. THE WOLF IN SHEEP'S CLOTHING: SOCIAL JUSTICE

takes it to another level by validating and legitimizing all philosophy and perspective deemed not "of the majority." This is no more evident than in how modern society has legitimized all religious and irreligious philosophy contradictory to Christianity. The homosexual agenda, transgenderism, and socialism are universally legitimized in the progressive postmodern society with no supplementary qualifications, while scripturally based counterpoints and dissents are relegated, and often ostracized, as biased, intolerant, antiquated, and dubious.

Hence the inclination toward socialism and communism as evidenced by the writings of Marx and Engels. The so-called majority philosophy is no longer valid and useful; therefore, it must be silenced. Furthermore, the Christian dogma is antithetical to the agenda of the communist, therefore, it must not only be silenced but delegitimized. No doubt, generations, past and present, have committed abhorrent sins against humanity not just in the United States, but also all over the world. The simple fact is this world is sinful. As long as Satan is active, there will be atrocities committed every day.

Past, present, and future atrocities are, by no means, justified by attributing them to Satan. On the contrary, it is a clarion call to reject Satan's attempts at diverting attention away from his devious work by causing people to continually dwell on issues insoluble by man, while simultaneously castigating one another, rather than taking it to the Lord in prayer. Where progressive, postmodern social justice initiatives seek to punish and deliver retribution, Christ seeks to forgive and forget,[6] bind up the brokenhearted, set the captive free,[7] and bind believers together.[8]

While the church must minister and exhibit love to all sinners, regardless of sin, it is imperative the church not accept, justify, legitimize, and promote the sin. By refusing to preach the unadulterated Word of God in a derisory effort to be "seeker-sensitive" and "politically correct" for the sake of bolstering church statistics, while positioning practitioners of sinful lifestyles in leadership, the church promotes sin. It is crucial the church tolerates the sinner but rejects the sin by preaching truth, regardless of offense. To do otherwise would be tantamount to canceling the effectiveness and anointing of the church. This is a progressive, postmodern approach to church fraught with political correctness and an ungodly social justice.

6. Corinthians 5:17.
7. Isaiah 61:1.
8. Ecclesiastes 4:12.

I am reminded of the saying, "The ground is level at the foot of the cross." Equity and equality can only be achieved through the liberating power of what Christ did for all on Calvary. If we, as Christians, lift up Jesus so He can draw all men,[9] while honoring one another above ourselves,[10] proclaiming the gospel to every creature,[11] and loving one another,[12] we will not have cause to worry about social justice. To be clear: exhibiting true love is to provide the truth, regardless of how offensive or politically incorrect it may be and irrespective of who it may upset.

The Robin Hood Principle in Social Justice

Let us return to the equality/equity cartoon and apply it to modern societal efforts. In the recent past, we were treated to the spectacle of a then-presidential candidate Barack Obama engaging a potential voter (Joe "the Plumber") in a conversation in which, among other conversational topics, he indicated that for the country to be successful, the answer would be to "spread the wealth around." Four years later, then-President Obama, in a rally, took to the pulpit to inform Americans that if they owned a business, they did not "build that" but someone else did. To be fair, perhaps many Americans took his comments at face value and did not consider the implications. Of course, anyone who owns a business, sacrificed, worked hard, and endured hardship in order to be successful. No one should deprive any successful person of his or her hard-earned success. However, what I believe then-President Obama meant was there were people who contributed some service along the way to help make that success a reality. This, however, is where the goodwill ends.

A central tenet to the social justice agenda of the modern era is, to state it most simply, the Robin Hood principle—steal from the rich and give to the poor. Progressive social justice advocates entreat the government to act as Robin Hood, but rather than simply stealing from the rich, they want the rich to be castigated and punished in the process. Punished for what? Punished for being rich? Well, yes, to a degree because they did not get rich on their own.

---

9. John 12:32.
10. Ibid.
11. Mark 16:15-16.
12. John 13:34.

5. THE WOLF IN SHEEP'S CLOTHING: SOCIAL JUSTICE

There is a dangerous sentiment being espoused in the modern era in which success and wealth is automatically considered ill-gotten gains and must be confiscated by the government. Bernie Sanders, 2016 and 2020 presidential candidate, proposed a tax plan that would have resulted in a tax increase on every American, regardless of income level[13] while simultaneously leveling a nearly seventy percent tax on top earners.[14] Sanders, an avowed socialist, believes the wealthiest one percent in the nation are a detriment to the working class,[15] of course, completely ignoring that according to his own tax documents, he earned roughly one million dollars in 2015, putting him squarely in the top one percent of American earners.

While some earnings are undoubtedly ill-gotten gains with some working-class laborers treated unfairly, the vast majority of business owners achieved their success through hard work and fair play. Too many Americans are willing to perpetrate punitive measures on someone who has been painted as the "evil rich" by so-called social justice advocates seeking to continue class warfare. The sentiment is becoming "shoot first and ask questions later." The answer is to strip top earners of their livelihoods because "they did not build that" business that was earned on the backs of low-wage earners and redistribute it to those who either do not work or make very little.

Fair warning: I am about to climb on my soapbox and the next discussion may be quite offensive. Nearly half of Americans paid no federal income tax in 2016.[16] There are too many lazy Americans who are not willing to work but would rather exist on government benefits, demanding those who will work to pay their share. While there are those who legitimately need financial assistance, there are far too many who have learned how to game the system in order to accrue maximum benefit for minimum input.

---

13. A. Smith, "Bernie Sanders' income tax brackets: How much would you owe?" *The Motley Fool*, May 12, 2016, https://www.usatoday.com/story/sponsor-story/motley-fool/2016/05/12/motley-fool-bernie-sanders-income-tax-brackets/32607881/.

14. P. J. Reilly, "Bernie Sanders and the 90% Income Tax Rate That He Does Not Call For," *Forbes*, https://www.forbes.com/sites/peterjreilly/2015/12/18/bernie-sanders-and-the-90-income-tax-rate-that-he-does-not-call-for/#7e3a44bc69dc.

15. J. Glum, "Bernie Sanders, Who is Rich, Complains that Wealthy People Always Want 'More, More and More,'" *Newsweek*, November 13, 2017, http://www.newsweek.com/bernie-sanders-net-worth-assets-cnn-column-oligarchy-709692.

16. C. Hill, "Almost half of Americans won't pay federal income tax," *New York Post*, April 8, 2017, https://nypost.com/2017/04/18/almost-half-of-americans-wont-pay-federal-income-tax/.

Essentially, we are quickly returning to the failed Pilgrim socialist commune. If, in order to equalize all earners to the median, Senator Sanders and other social justice warriors want to stifle business by taxing it into oblivion for the sake of dishing punishment to the evil rich, then the evil rich will relocate or simply stop working, like the Pilgrims did in 1620.

Paul wrote in 2 Thessalonians 3:10 that if a man does not work then he should not eat. God expects people to work for what they own. The writer of Proverbs records many verses on the subject of work.[17] Perhaps one of the most famous Scriptures in Proverbs dealing with work ethic is Proverbs 6:6-11:

> Go to the ant, thou sluggard; consider her ways, and be wise:
>
> Which having no guide, overseer, or ruler,
>
> Provideth her meat in the summer, and gathereth her food in the harvest.
>
> How long wilt thou sleep, O sluggard? when wilt thou arise out of thy sleep?
>
> Yet a little sleep, a little slumber, a little folding of the hands to sleep:
>
> So shall thy poverty come as one that travelleth, and thy want as an armed man.

This Scripture specifically references ingenuity and initiative. The ant has no guide, overseer, or ruler but works constantly to have plenty for the times when she cannot work.

"Dr. Street, you are being too harsh! Not everyone has the same opportunities." I will concede this as partially true; however, I will not concede that everyone cannot make opportunities for themselves. I did not grow up in a wealthy home. My father worked a very hard job building chicken houses. I will never forget the brutal winters and sultry summers when my dad would still go to the job, rain or shine, sick or well, and work daylight to dark. My mother worked as a teacher assistant and bus driver. That is certainly a thankless and meagerly paying job. My parents raised four children, of which, I am the fourth. I did not have every new invention, every new craze or fad, and I did not wear the most expensive clothes. By modern standards, my parents should have had a very difficult time making ends meet.

---

17. Proverbs 10:4; 12:11; 13:4; 14:23; 16:3; 20:4; 20:13; 21:25; 22:29; 28:19.

But what happened? While I did not have everything at my fingertips, I did have what I needed. The reason is my parents saved, spent sparingly, and lived frugally. We existed within our means. "But, Dr. Street, look at you now. You own your home, two cars, have multiple degrees, and have a good job." I attended public school through to graduation. Throughout school, I worked diligently to earn top grades so when it came time for college, I was able to attend with practically a full scholarship. While in college, I worked for the university so I could pay for other incidentals like gas, food, and clothing. Knowing I did not want to cease my education after undergraduate school, I worked diligently to graduate with a decent grade point average and university honors. I earned my master's degree and doctorate by funding my own education. I paid off two cars, am still paying on the house, and fulfilling my obligations. How can this be possible? Shannon, my wife, and I work every day from daylight to dark, live within our means, and often forego luxuries in order to fund the necessities. I have maintained my job through countless hours of hard work, often outside of normal work hours.

This is the divergence—there is a cadre of Americans who live as though they are millionaires but do not want to put forth the effort to possess the financial standing to be such. There are also many Americans who would rather exist from the generosity of those who do work and pay taxes so the government can fund their lifestyles. Many of these Americans are of a younger generation who are part of the "trophy for everyone generation." In an effort to bring everyone to the median, it became in vogue a couple of decades ago to reward children for participation. Even if they did not win or succeed, all children were rewarded with a trophy. Essentially, we began rewarding the future generation for failure and for doing nothing. We did not want any child to have hurt feelings or low self-esteem because he or she did not succeed on the level of another.

We now see this in action with students going to college to major in a subject that has no job prospects, spend hundreds of thousands of dollars, go in deep debt, and then demand the government cancel the student loan to which they agreed to pay. While I am discussing this topic, I would like to stress that college is not for everyone and that is perfectly acceptable. Some students may not need or want a college education. Some may need or want to learn a trade instead. God only knows the level of earnings that future mechanics, plumbers, electricians, and tradespeople will attain because we no longer teach these skills in public schools. Furthermore, there is no need for students to "over college" themselves. One does not need to attend Harvard to be a teacher. By doing so, students accumulate serious debt to earn a degree for a job whose pay will never support the debt. There is no need to go to college for "gender studies," "queer theory," "basket-weaving" and other asinine majors that will never result in a lucrative job.

Victimology 101

The practice of rewarding for failure has created a generation of adults who believe they are entitled to a reward, even when they do nothing to earn it, and they will support candidates for public office who promise to continue that reward system. The progressive social justice advocates continue to coddle them by assuaging their feelings of inadequacy and ensuring them it is not their fault they do not have what the Joneses have. Besides, the Joneses achieved their success at the detriment of others, so they do not deserve it.

Sometimes failure is the best thing that can happen to a person. What would have happened if Thomas Edison had been patted on the head, told his failures (approximately 1,000) were not his fault but those of others trying to keep him from succeeding, and given a reward each time? Perhaps, he would not have succeeded in inventing the light bulb. What would have happened if Ludwig van Beethoven had been coddled upon going completely and profoundly deaf and told it was not his fault that he had to take extreme measures to feel the vibrations of his keyboard in order to compose perhaps the greatest symphonic work known to mankind: Symphony No. 9? In fact, I have studied the actual manuscripts of Beethoven's pre-deafness works in Vienna, Austria. He often made mistakes, scratched them out, and scribbled notes to himself on the page—often using profanities in German. Had he not worked through the failures himself, he would not have had the initiative to work through the impossible situation of being a composer and profoundly deaf.

We have robbed our children of their opportunities to fail. That statement may sound harsh but it is the truth. The natural human tendency is to overcome but when that tendency is replaced by a well-meaning adult who is attempting to keep fragile feelings intact, the fragility never has the opportunity to transform into persistence and the child will never learn how to overcome failures. Those children then grow into adults with an entitlement mentality whereby everyone owes them a reward for no work

5. THE WOLF IN SHEEP'S CLOTHING: SOCIAL JUSTICE

or success. Social justice advocates then harness that mentality, foster it, and exploit it to advance their nefarious agenda of socialism in which everyone is brought to the median except those in control of the onerous government.

As discussed before, the social justice warriors, armed to the teeth with their postmodern philosophies, then begin the slow process of "victimizing," literally and figuratively, people by assuaging their feelings of inadequacy by preaching that their situations are not of their own making—it is the evil "other" who is exercising oppression. Social justice warriors have a strong foothold in our nation's schools. Many teachers have converted to this ideology and espouse it often in school classrooms. Allow me to provide an example.

Such teachers say the United States of America is not great and never has been great because it was founded upon the backs of other people. The land was stolen from Native Americans. Mexicans were robbed of their lands. The wealth of the nation was made through the oppression of slaves. Women were never allowed a voice but were kept barefoot and pregnant with barely any status as a human being. Nothing about the founding of the United States was great and to suggest otherwise is an affront to the posterity of assaulted women generations ago. This nation is racist, homophobic, xenophobic, sexist, bigoted, etc.

While I am sure that many readers have heard this garbage from adult liberals, many fail to realize this garbage was first generated in schools. Everyone gets rewarded exactly the same and in the same manner, irrespective of the work or lack thereof that someone has performed. Like the Pilgrim's socialist experiment, the question must be posed, "What good is actually working hard and excelling?" As evidenced by the cartoon at the beginning of the chapter, there is no reward for working hard because it will be snatched away and given to another student to ensure everyone is equalized. Then, when the children become adults who were rewarded for nothing, the social justice mantra continues but with more nefarious and burdensome results. They generally become adults who do not want to work, expect top compensation for poor work, seek "management" jobs with no experience, expect banks to loan money with no credit, often live on government assistance, and, all the while, accuse the evil other or the biased system for their plight. They are the victims of racism, sexism, homophobia, etc.

The insanity does not stop there. Social justice warriors have ensured the madness will continue, regardless of how well their victims are treated. When no one can be directly blamed for the victim's situation, there is a phantom source that is quite convenient. The phantom source of the victim's troubles is such because no one can fully define it in any situation—and that is the purpose. That phantom source is encapsulated in *institutional racism* and *microaggressions*. Our children are taught that political and social institutions are inherently racist, biased, and bigoted. The power and resources are inequitably distributed within that system to favor white, heterosexual men. Often cited examples of institutional racism include the wealth gap, food deserts (areas with no access to grocery stores) and food insecurity, incarceration rates, and lack of health services.

Social justice warriors assert that the gap between the rich and the poor continues to widen. This, in and of itself, is not the point. The social justice warrior's point is that this gap is not the fault of the poor. The system is "rigged" so that the white, rich men maintain their power and control with little to no effort. Hence the statement by President Obama, "You did not build that." In essence, poor people, especially those of color, can never attain wealth because the "system" will not allow it.

Food deserts and lack of health services are interrelated. The social justice warriors contend that in communities of color, there are severe shortages of grocery stores, access to healthy foods, and health services. They assert that this shortage is due to the inherent intricacies of a system designed to ensure people of color are repressed, live in poor conditions, and hopefully die an early death. To ensure further lack of resources, men of color are incarcerated at higher rates than any other identity subgroup. To the social justice warrior, this reflects the innate racism that exists among the criminal justice system.

In all the institutional racism examples, the common thread is victimhood. It is not remotely possible that those who experience success and failure is by their own hand. The victim cannot be at fault. Rather than explaining to people how to lift themselves out of poverty, the social justice warrior tells them it is not their fault but the fault of evil, rich, white men who intentionally hold them down. Rather than explaining that perhaps businesses refrain from building in communities of color is because of high crime rates or a simple marketing strategy, the social justice warrior reminds them that these businesses are run by evil rich people who want to see the victim die. Rather than explaining that men of color disproportionately commit crimes, hence the disproportionate incarceration rates, they further ensconce them in their misperception of victimhood by blaming the police. The results are violent acts against police, increasing criminal activity in communities of color, destitution, and hatred.

Microaggressions are subtle prejudicial slights, often unrealized, against a group of people based on some perceived common characteristic of that group. For example, it would be considered a microaggression to assume a person of Hispanic descent speaks Spanish. It is considered a microaggression for a teacher to say, "I do not see skin color in my class. I see children." It is considered a microaggression to assume an African American person listens to hip hop. In fact, I am likely committing a microaggression by this statement—microaggressions are, to those who live in reality, most often nothing more than an assumption based on common anecdotal evidence.

Most Mexicans speak Spanish so it is not beyond the realm of possibility to assume a specific Mexican that one encounters to speak Spanish. Hip hop is a cultural phenomenon developed, most often performed, and distributed by African Americans. When one encounters hip hop blasting through the car stereo (yes, the ones that actually rattle the car), it is most often an African American person in the seat. Most people of Asian descent have a different eye shape than other ethnicities. Is it true of *every* Mexican, African American, or Asian? Certainly not. It is, however, an anecdotally evidenced characteristic.

Simply stated: People are different. Cultures are different. People of Asian descent will look different from people of African descent. People of Mexican descent sometimes prefer experiences that differ from people of European descent. Simply pointing out differences does not equate to bigotry. The social justice warriors, in their breathless attempts at equalizing every factor of humanity, often perpetrate the very overtly racist actions they purport to abhor.

Teachers who state that they do not see race are simply stating they are not treating anyone differently based on external characteristics. We are now told that teachers must teach differently, based on race. Fifty years ago, segregationists expressed the exact same sentiments. Social justice is nothing more than racism dressed up in victimology in order to ensure Leftists continue to control segments of the population for political and social gain. It is the Leftist who demonstrates racism by implying an African American cannot be successful in this culture because of his or her ethnicity. It is the Leftist who demonstrates prejudice by automatically categorizing people based on external characteristics in order to ensure victimization.

There are those among us who are in need and we should help them. I am of the opinion that if I ever fall on hard times, I will not expect another to offer to assist me until I have done everything within my power to make it on my own. This means that I will turn off the cell phone, disconnect the cable, sell a car, forego eating out, purchase basic food staples on which to survive, work multiple jobs, even if they are considered beneath my education level, and trim the fat where possible. If, after I exert those measures, still need assistance to survive, that is when I will seek it. The Scriptures entreat us to serve the "fatherless and widows;"[18] "deliver the poor;"[19] "uphold the cause of the oppressed;"[20] and lift up the downtrodden.[21]

Boaz commanded his men to intentionally leave the corners of his fields for Ruth to glean while concurrently leaving "handfuls of purpose" for her; however, notice Ruth and the other widows did not expect to obtain this without working for it.[22] There are those who are unable to work. There are those who have served this nation honorably, some giving their limbs and mental stability in service, who should be served by this nation. There are those who may not possess the mental capacity to work. This is not the focus of this discussion and, sadly, these individuals are not the focus of the progressive social justice advocates either. See, they actually need help. The progressive social justice advocate is not interested in those who actually need help because they are not politically expedient for the advancement of a socialist agenda.

The mentally and physically competent should work. Not everyone will be a millionaire but Christ never promised millions. Paul wrote, "But my God shall supply all your need according to his riches in glory by Christ Jesus."[23] What are our needs? Food, shelter, clothes, and love are the basic staples. If one has those, his or her needs are being met, but the Lord, in His infinite love and grace, supplies us with so much more. We are a generation most blessed with more modern comforts and amenities than any previous generation. I do not wish to see the wealthy person punished because, one

18. James 1:27.
19. Job 29:12.
20. Psalm 82:3.
21. Psalm 147:6.
22. Ruth 2:16.
23. Philippians 4:19.

day, I would like to be one! I am content with what God has provided. He knows the effect wealth may have on me or my family. I trust in Him and His judgment. It blesses me to see others richly blessed by God. I pray everyone in my church becomes a millionaire. See, if they pay tithes, then the church will be blessed, too!

Oh my, I mentioned the T-word: tithes. Since I have dug quite an offensive hole, I might as well end this chapter by going all in. If the reader proclaims to be a Christian and does not pay tithes, he or she is a thief.[24] In fact, I believe the church economic system of tithes and offerings instituted by God is so rational that the nation should implement it as the tax system. If everyone paid ten percent of his or her earnings to the government and the government existed within its means, then all would be well. There are a lot of major "ifs" there, I know. Let me state this as simply as possible: the money and property I have is earned by the good grace of God Almighty; therefore, all of it is His. He asks that I return at least ten percent of it to him to be maintained in the place where I offer my worship so there will be sustenance in His house: the church.[25] He allows me to live on the ninety percent. It is the least any of us can do and I truly mean it is the *least*.

Well, if the reader *is not* thoroughly offended at this point and has not thrown this book in the garbage or across the room, then I encourage the reader to keep reading. I am sure there will be some offense at some point. If the reader *is offended*, perhaps he or she should inventory his or her life practices and search the Scriptures. I am careful to provide several Scriptures throughout this treatise for further exploration. I am certainly not inclined to coddle the reader, flash a telegenic smile, tickle his or her feelings, pat him or her on the head, and send him or her home in the same condition. I will leave that up to America's favorite televangelists. Change is often unpleasant. Deal with it.

---

24. Malachi 3:8-9.
25. Malachi 3:10.

6. THE ENEMY WITHIN: SECULAR HUMANISM

Humanism is a tricky and often difficult concept to understand. It is also a concept that has been resoundingly accepted by mainstream, so-called Christian leaders in a way one might not completely understand. Secular humanism is a teaching that often pervades a lifestyle and belief system while going unnoticed. This is why secular humanism is an enemy within. It is within the individual and within the church as an organism. It is often ignored at best and cultivated at worst. While main tenets of secular humanism may not be readily measurable in the church, there are elemental aspects of those tenets that are steadily increasing.

Secular humanism is related to secularism and atheism but appeals to the most basic and often most destructive aspect of humanity: narcissism and pride. The Council for Secular Humanism loosely defines this concept as a belief that humans were not designed or created.[1] Furthermore, there is no transcendent being. God, essentially, is a creation of human beings in a meaningless search for "something more than self" and the known natural world.

The Council for Secular Humanism describes its philosophy as naturalistic and scientific with a consequentialist ethical system. The human being's earthly life is all that exists. There is no higher power, but yet, there is almost a mystical power inherent in the human being itself. Proponents of secular humanism follow individualism whereby the human is "emancipated" from the controls of family, church, and state. He or she is free to live his or her life according to his or her wishes. The scientific method is the natural order of things whereby humankind may firmly establish answers to questions. Any other answers obtained by any other methods are unreliable. Evolution is key to understanding how humankind has achieved its current state. Ethics are consequential in that the results of any action judge

---

1. Council for Secular Humanism, "What is Secular Humanism? *Free Inquiry,* 2018, https://www.secularhumanism.org/.

6. THE ENEMY WITHIN: SECULAR HUMANISM

the action. In essence, the ends justify the means. This, of course, is in contrast to command ethics whereby right and wrong are defined in advance of actions, in which subversion of such command is punishable.

Further examination of secular humanism allows one to discover a categorical rejection of "transcendentalism." While one may hearken back to high school English class and relate to the transcendentalism of Emerson or Thoreau, this is not the same. In fact, secular humanists would most closely align with the philosophies of Emerson and Thoreau. Transcendentalism, in the humanist sense, involves anything spiritual or religious. God, Satan, Allah, Buddha, Mohammed, demons, ghosts, and all other real and folkloric conceptions are not scientifically provable and are, therefore, rejected by the secular humanist.

Secular humanists admit they are atheists but stress their journey does not end there. While most atheists would argue, secular humanists consider their worldview as ethical, whereas atheism does not necessarily include an ethical stance. Humanist ethics essentially originate and exist within the human. Atheism is strictly a position that says there is no God. Humanism is a way of life and thought.

The statement I will make in this section is, admittedly, very strong and will likely be met with great opposition from those who are either overt practitioners of secular humanism or covert practitioners, like many high-profile Christian television preachers. I understand the statement I make is provocative and potentially upsetting. I also understand that some, even within the church, may think this statement is over the top, considering secular humanism does not seem to be as critical an issue in our society as is progressivism, secularism, or relativism. That could not be further from the truth. I make this statement following extensive research, prayer, and thoughtful consideration. The thesis statement of this chapter is simply: Secular humanism is demonic and its belief structures are rooted in the ritualism and dogma of satanism.

With that bold statement, I realize it is incumbent upon me to explain. I encourage the reader to remain engaged in this explanation as it can become confusing and heavy at times. Throughout this explanation, I will refer primarily to the humanist ideas of consequentialism, individualism, and how this dogma is encroaching on the church in profound but often silent means. Furthermore, within this treatment of secular humanism, the reader should begin to see many of the topics of this book (i.e., relativism, progressivism, feminism, atheism, etc.) begin to converge.

Consequentialism

Consequentialism demands that the results of an action determine whether the action is morally and ethically just. While a secular humanist would likely argue with the encapsulating phrase, there can be no doubt he or she subscribes to the philosophy that the ends justify the means. This means that the result, if deemed just, ethical, and moral, justifies whatever course of action on which one progressed to obtain those results. Major news media outlets have been salivating for two years about the possibility that President Trump colluded with Russians to "hack" the election of 2016. While my purpose is not to debate the possibility, I will state that any media that relishes in the possibility of a major crime perpetrated that would inevitably cause panic and destruction to a nation resulting in devastation is sick. If President Trump is guilty of high crimes, one should be in mourning for the destruction that such a revelation would cause. Of course, in the United States of America, one is supposed to be innocent until proven guilty. In the modern era, one is often guilty until proven innocent at best and "innocent but let us find a way to make him or her guilty" at worst.

Recently, CNN and *The Washington Post* unveiled a story whereby reporters breathlessly iterated an anonymous source was privy to a secret meeting between Donald Trump, Jr. and Russian agents whereby President Trump, who has previously denied knowledge of such meeting, did, in fact, know about the meeting in advance. Subsequent to the story, the attorney, Lanny Davis, who represents Michael Cohen, the scandalized former attorney for President Trump, was the anonymous source who began to change his story and "walk back" his allegations.[2] CNN and *The Washington Post*, to date, have refused to recant the report but is doubling down by reiterating they "stand by the story." Since the release of the Mueller Report, so-called news agencies still refuse to acknowledge the findings.

What reporters of this sad situation involving the declination of American media as trustworthy outlets for news fail to underscore is that CNN, *The Washington Post*, and other such media outlets are not really concerned about the veracity of their claims. In progressive ideology, truth is not necessarily important. Appearance is far more important. If one can be made to *appear* as though he or she is ethically corrupt, that is far more effective than if he or she is *actually* ethically corrupt. Because

---

2. Post Editorial Board, "Why is CNN avoiding the truth about Lanny Davis' lies?" *New York Post*, August 29, 2018, https://nypost.com/2018/08/29/why-is-cnn-avoiding-the-truth-about-lanny-davis-lies/.

6. THE ENEMY WITHIN: SECULAR HUMANISM

the progressive Left in America, who, by and large, control most major media outlets, concur and conclude that an individual or entity is evil, then that individual or entity is irrevocably and undeniably evil. Should one disagree with such a conclusion, then he or she is also evil or, at best, ignorant. Sadly, this underscores the declination of mainstream media as guardians of truth in America.

The major American media outlets have definitively concluded President Trump is evil, morally bankrupt, and ethically corrupt. Again, whether or not this is true is not the subject of this treatise but the media have already served as judge, jury, and executioner on someone who is just as human and American as me. This is not the American way intended by the framers of the Constitution. Indeed, the modern American way, motivated by major media outlets who are fully progressive, is to slander and smear anyone who disagrees or dares to resist their progressive agenda. Because it appears as though President Trump is resisting and intends to resist the progressive agenda, the progressives in control of major American media outlets view him as an enemy and must, at all cost, destroy and discredit him.

This is not just because President Trump is the American president or because he is Donald Trump. To the progressive Left, it does not matter who it is. Their attack on him is because he happens to control one of the most idealized bully pulpits in the world and he dares to resist their agenda. It could literally be anyone else in that same situation and the result would be the same. In their minds, he opposes their agenda, therefore, he must be eradicated, and it doesn't matter how it is accomplished. This means that if a story is proven false, it does not matter because the damage has already been accomplished, and that is more important than truth. Much like how Christians fail to study the Word of God enough to know the promises and warnings God has declared, Americans routinely fail to research a story to determine its veracity but rather take the first statement provided at face value. Essentially, a progressive media can easily promote its nefarious agenda without much repercussion because most will believe the lies hook, line, and sinker.

There is no better example of this than what happened to then-candidate Mitt Romney in 2012. Senate Majority Leader, Harry Reid, took to the United States Senate floor and declared Mitt Romney had failed to pay his taxes. At the time, the major news media outlets chose to take Senator Reid's word for it, even though Mr. Romney had released his tax returns, proving he had indeed paid taxes. CNN didn't confront Senator Reid about his false accusation until 2015, to which he responded, "Romney didn't win, did he?" Clearly, in Senator Reid's ultra-progressive mind, the ends justified the means. He even expanded his statement later to indicate this action was "one of the best things [he's] ever done."³ To further underscore the point, Reid, when questioned whether there were any lines he would not cross when it came to political warfare, he responded, "I don't know what that line would be." One would think someone as untrustworthy as this would easily lose reelection bids. Sadly, Nevadans continued to elect Senator Reid until he chose to retire, far wealthier than when he was first elected.

Senator Reid, like the major American news media, desired to promote an agenda of progressivism in which the government controls every aspect of American life for the benefit of the elite. It is a nefarious agenda rooted in Marxism. To that end, there are no ethical or moral lines that cannot be crossed in order to fulfill the mission of furthering that agenda. Clearly, Senator Reid understood he unabashedly lied on the floor of the United States Senate but that was deemed appropriate in order to achieve the grander goal of advancing progressivism. Clearly, the news media in 2012 chose to ignore the falsity of Senator Reid's statement because it would have impeded the grander goal of advancing progressivism. When reviewing the results (President Obama's reelection), the means implemented to achieve that goal were worthy, just, moral, and ethical.

Secular humanism paves the way for such destructive behaviors to pervade everyday life because the fulfillment of the agenda they deem right and just is more important, even if it means the methods to achieve that goal are destructive, distasteful, and disgusting. To further substantiate the clear connection between progressivism and communism, Leon Trotsky, a communist revolutionary, wrestled with how the ends may justify the means; ultimately concluding that as long as the ends include securing humanity's power over nature and abolishing one's power over another, then ends are justified.⁴ Again, the agenda must drive the action, regardless of the nature of said agenda.

Clearly, the belief that the ends justify the means stands in direct opposition to Scripture. Throughout Leviticus, Numbers, and Deuteronomy, God provided laws to Moses in order to govern the actions of the people.

---

3. Chris Cillizza, "Harry Reid lied about Mitt Romney's taxes. He's still not sorry," *The Washington Post*, September 15, 2016, https://www.washingtonpost.com/news/the-fix/wp/2016/09/15/harry-reid-lied-about-mitt-romneys-taxes-hes-still-not-sorry/.

4. Leon Trotsky, *Their Morals and Ours* (New York: Pioneer Publishers, 1939).

6. THE ENEMY WITHIN: SECULAR HUMANISM

Subversion of God's laws resulted in sometimes strict punishments. In the New Testament, the Pharisees sought to trap Jesus and accuse Him of subverting the governmental authority. In Matthew 22:21, Jesus confronted one such instance. Jesus persuaded the people to pay their taxes and submit to the authority of those in whom God had arranged in such positions. Jesus could have easily, and perhaps been justified in doing so, encouraged the people to revolt against Roman and temple taxation. Clearly, taxation in these days was onerous and unfair. However, Jesus was careful to encourage the people to not just be hearers of the Word, but doers, as well.[5] Regardless of the outcome, we must walk in the light[6] and according to the Spirit.[7]

Christianity, in stark contrast to secular humanism, teaches that the means lead to a desired end. How we lead our lives on earth will determine how we will spend eternity. When we stand before a holy and righteous Judge, He will weigh our lives. Like Belshazzar, will we be found wanting?[8] Will He look at you and say, "Well done, thou good and faithful servant: thou hast been faithful over a few things, I will make thee ruler over many things; enter thou into the joy of thy lord?"[9] Will he look at you say, "I never knew you: depart from me, ye that work iniquity?"[10]

Do not be deceived: how we live our lives on this earth is critical. The ends do not justify the means, except when those means involve the trials and tribulations of this life. The trials and tribulations will all fade away one day. When surrounded by the glory of the Lord in heaven, we will look back at those trials and tribulations and declare they were worth it. We must live holy lives because without holiness, no one shall see the Lord.[11]

Although this treatment of consequentialism should be, in itself, significantly substantial to eschew the ills of such a destructive doctrine, there are more nefarious aspects. Another adherent to the doctrine of "the ends justify the means" brings in a more sinister, satanic influence. One of the most prolific progressive champions of the modern era, often referenced by conservative pundits in attempts to appropriately castigate his doctrine,

---

5. James 1:22.
6. John 1:7.
7. Romans 8:5.
8. Daniel 5:27.
9. Matthew 25:21.
10. Matthew 7:23.
11. Hebrews 12:14.

is Saul Alinsky. Alinsky significantly influenced many of the most prolific progressive liberals of the twenty-first century, like President Barack Obama, First Lady Michelle Obama, and Secretary of State Hillary Clinton.

In fact, Michelle Obama cited a previous statement of President Obama's in the Democratic National Convention of 2008 that was a direct reference to Alinsky's seminal work, *Rules for Radicals*.[12] Referring to neighborhoods in Chicago, Obama referred to "the world as it is" and the "world as it should be." This is a direct reference to Alinsky's doctrine of "the ends justify the means." In essence, Alinsky argued for the rejection of ethics and morals as impediments to political success.[13] Clearly aligned to the doctrine of consequentialism, the Obamas portrayed their vision of America requiring "fundamental transformation."[14] Those who rejected such a vision resulted in their being labeled a racist and bigot. In fact, President Obama had previously worked for Alinsky organizations as a community organizer, often employing Alinsky tactics. Secretary Clinton was a student of Alinsky; even dedicating the subject of her college thesis to him.

What is so disturbing about progressives like the Obamas and Secretary Clinton manifesting a fascination with the tenets espoused by Saul Alinsky? Aligned to the doctrine of "the ends justify the means," Alinsky desired for the system to be utterly destroyed and encouraged the incitement of violence, struggle, and constant agitation to make that happen. It did not matter if the violence, struggle, and agitation were founded in reality. The goal was deconstruction of the current system by any means necessary via the "agent of change." Adams correctly surmised the goal of Alinsky was change while the agent was also change.[15] Alinsky and his followers seem to wish for shared power among the masses but offer no solution for how to wield that power once it has been transferred. The ultimate ideal is a utopian society with social justice for those deemed worthy.

To achieve such a society, one must be pragmatic. Pragmatism, in this sense, essentially means "by any means necessary." Sound familiar?

---

12. Saul D. Alinsky, *Rules for Radicals: A Pragmatic Primer for Realistic Radicals* (New York: Random House, 1971).

13. D. L. Adams, "Saul Alinsky and the Rise of Amorality in American Politics," *New English Review,* January 2010, https://www.newenglishreview.org/DL_Adams/Saul_Alinsky_and_the_Rise_of_Amorality_in_American_Politics/.

14. Victor Davis Hanson, "Obama: Transforming America," *National Review,* October 1, 2013, https://www.nationalreview.com/2013/10/obama-transforming-america-victor-davis-hanson/.

15. D. L. Adams, "Saul Alinsky and the Rise of Amorality in American Politics."

6. THE ENEMY WITHIN: SECULAR HUMANISM

Incidentally, John Dewey, one of the world's most infamous progressives and influential educators proudly labeled himself a pragmatist. Many of our systems of schooling in America are based on the teachings of John Dewey.

When reading Alinsky's *Rules for Radicals*, one will see an interesting dedication. Alinsky dedicated his work to Lucifer.[16] Indeed, he dedicated his work to the devil, while exalting him as the first revolutionary. This is the same individual who is revered by people like President and Mrs. Obama as well as Secretary Clinton. But, it makes sense for someone like Alinsky, who is a true secular humanist, to be a Luciferian. Isaiah 14:12-15 describes the mission of Lucifer. He stated he would exalt himself above God and essentially take His throne. In other words, Lucifer, in an act of ultimate narcissism and pride, desired to overthrow God Himself. He sought to act in a manner opposite of God's order, essentially emancipating himself from God's authority, acting in direct rebellion against Him. We, of course, know where that track took Lucifer.

Sadly, Alinsky, in an interview just before his death, stated, "Let's say that if there is an afterlife, and I have anything to say about it, I will unreservedly choose to go to hell . . . hell would be heaven for me."[17] If Mr. Alinsky failed to repent of his sins, he has been experiencing the utter torment and torture that is hell since his death until now and will experience it for all eternity. Surely, if Alinsky could return to earth with the knowledge he now possesses and proceed with his life, he would change his tune.

Alinsky, the perfect Luciferian, and his followers sought to ultimately deconstruct the foundational, or *fundamental*, moral and ethical fabric of the nation. Unfettered from the confines of morals, ethics, and law, one can choose to do what he or she wills, without repercussions. This is the central theme of the secular humanist doctrine of individualism.

Individualism

Interestingly, this is also related to another topic we have already discussed: relativism. When foundational truth is no longer accepted, and when truth differs from one person to the other, there are no limitations on how one can or should lead his or her life. Furthermore, modern feminism with its almost god-like status assignment to women embraces the individualist doctrine. Because one is a woman, she should not have to conform to

16. Alinsky, 1971.
17. D. L. Adams, "Saul Alinsky and the Rise of Amorality in American Politics."

traditional standards. Women have become *emancipated* from the traditional chains that men once utilized to enslave her.

We must understand; however, this evil doctrine of individualism was not founded by the Council for Secular Humanism. While this doctrine of individualism was perfected by Lucifer in his attempt to overthrow God, it would be later codified by an individual about whom many modern people know very little but has dramatically influenced generations of popular culture: Aleister Crowley. More on Crowley later.

Where can individualism lead? One must understand the secular humanist's approach to individualism is rather extreme. Simply stated, the desire to emancipate oneself from the controls of family, church, and state in order to live one's life as he or she wishes is the height of rebellion against all that is ethical, moral, and just. While I am certain many secular humanists are not willing to take the most extreme position such a doctrine potentially entails, the very adherence to such a doctrine lends itself to limitless actions conducted with impunity.

Like Lucifer, the mental corruption that it must take to believe one is not subjected to controls, especially from family, church, or state, can potentially be highly intoxicating to a species that, in its natural state without Christ, possesses proclivities to sin. It is amazing to think that a being like Lucifer who habited the halls of heaven and knew the unassailable might and power of God, his own Creator, decided, in his narcissism and pride, to attempt an overthrow of the Creator of the universe. It is the same nature present within humankind that will attract him or her to the most basic source of evil. It is the Adamic nature of man that Christ came to destroy.

Lucifer attempted to assume god-like status. It is this same kind of intoxication that Satan now attempts to sell to humankind. Satan, in the form of the serpent in the garden of Eden, said to Eve that eating of the forbidden tree would not cause her to die as God had warned but that it would open her eyes and she would be like God.[18] Satan continued his intoxicating temptation to humankind in order to provoke similar action he, himself, attempted. He sprinkled the temptation with a bit of narcissism and pride by implying God was hoarding all the god-like powers for Himself, not wanting to share with humankind through his statement, "For God doth know . . ."

One would think Satan would have learned his lesson. Luke 4:5 and Matthew 4:8 illustrate how Satan endeavored to tempt Jesus with world

---

18. Genesis 3:5.

domination during His wilderness fast. How narcissistic (and subsequently foolish) must Satan be to tempt Jesus with something over which he has no authority but that is something over which Jesus already had all authority. It is the same as if someone tried to sell my own house to me!

It is this same course of temptation Satan continues to project upon humankind today—one can sin and God will look the other way. One can sin and God will ignore it. God is not going to punish for a simple foray on the other side of the fence where the grass is always greener. These are among the favorite lines Satan utilizes to ensnare God's greatest creation into performing acts that are a direct affront to the law of God.

Our pastor emeritus, Troy Wilhelm, utilizes a quote from Ravi Zacharias that best summarizes the course that a small sin will pave for the sinner. He often states, "Sin will take you farther than you want to go, keep you longer than you want to stay, and cost you more than you're willing to pay." It is a spiderweb that when ensnared, the more one struggles, the more one seems to become more deeply enslaved.

This continued deeper foray into a life of sin encourages one to think he or she can act with impunity. Jeremiah stated that sinners, so deep in their sins, are no longer embarrassed by what they do.[19] The goal of secular humanist individualism is the complete eradication of conscience whereby one can behave any way he or she wishes.

This Luciferian doctrine has evolved into complete satanic ideology. Perhaps the most prolific adherent to such a lifestyle who codified, perfected, and promulgated this doctrine that, to this very day, continues to inflict a profound influence on popular culture all over the world is the man once deemed "the wickedest man in the world," Aleister Crowley.

The Luciferian Doctrine and Its Influence on Popular Culture

Before I enter this section of the discussion, the reader must be forewarned that I discuss potentially troubling topics in a very graphic, unabridged manner. It is imperative the topics be completely exposed in order for the reader to fully comprehend the magnitude of the evil with which generations continue to struggle. Too many Christians are asleep in Zion. Too many fail to read and study for themselves. Therefore, before the reader progresses into this section, I strongly encourage him or her to read 1 Thessalonians 5. While the passage is too lengthy to reiterate

19. Jeremiah 8:12.

here, it is absolutely critical the reader understand the reason behind the explicitness of this section.

I will also forewarn the reader that I am not in a position to be concerned with the reader's feelings. I will address people and topics that may be the reader's sacred cow. The reader may be offended, upset, and in a state of disbelief. To be clear: I am writing what God has impressed upon me to write to a lost and dying generation. I am also writing to Christians who may be slumbering instead of readying for the battle or to Christians who are prepared for battle and need a little more encouragement and knowledge. I am only concerned with truth and souls; both of which are greatly endangered in this modern era by the vast topics covered in this book.

Most Christians likely do not know about Aleister Crowley; however, he is a man whose actions and lifestyle were putrid, satanic, vastly disturbing, and utterly disgusting. Even in light of his evil, there were and are many popular culture icons who revered him, practiced his self-created religion, and adhered to his satanic philosophy of life. He is a man about whom Christians should know so they can identify his teachings inherent in popular culture.

Crowley was born and reared in a rather fundamental Christian home in 1875; however, he completely rejected his Christian upbringing; choosing to act in total defiance. Katie Serena best described Crowley as a "mountaineer, poet, theologian, black magician, spy, drug fiend, and sex addict . . . branded as evil and egotistical, a raging genius, and a messiah of anti-Christianity."[20] Serena asserted there really were no words to describe how dark and evil Crowley truly was. He was so depraved that he was banned and deported from Italy by one of the most sinister men in history, Mussolini.

Crowley's father was a Christian preacher. Crowley strictly adhered to Christian teachings until his father's death when Crowley reached age eleven. Subsequent to this tragedy, Crowley began to completely reject all Christian teachings and embrace the polar opposite. He began his odyssey into evil by blatantly rejecting moral teaching, while embracing what was considered entirely evil in his day like smoking, masturbation, and sex with prostitutes. He was known as "the beast:" a moniker assigned to him by his own mother for the depravity he displayed.

---

20. Katie Serena, "How Aleister Crowley Inspired Led Zeppelin – and Terrified Most Everyone Else," *ATI*, October 24, 2018, https://www.allthatsinteresting.com/aleister-crowley.

6. THE ENEMY WITHIN: SECULAR HUMANISM

Crowley engaged in bisexual activities, practiced black magic, and began delving deeper into occultism. He joined the Hermetic Order of the Golden Dawn, which was an organization devoted to studying paranormality and occultism. His voracious sexual appetites led to more sadistic sexual activities with both men and women. At his home in Scotland, he attempted to summon the "twelve kings of hell." Of course, there are no kings in hell, so one can only surmise this was an attempt at conjuring demons. His attempt failed but resulted in many continued unexplained phenomena occurring at that home for generations. Crowley obsessed over conjuring and consulting with his "guardian angel" which was, in actuality, a demonic presence.

He eventually married the sister of artist Gerald Kelly and continued his world travels. Rose Kelly approved of his sinister lifestyle, including perverted sexual acts with other men and women. Rose served as the inspiration for Crowley to create his own demon-inspired religion. While staying in the great room in an Egyptian pyramid, Crowley and Rose meditated on conjuring his "guardian angel." Rose fell into a trance and spoke to Crowley, saying that "they were waiting for him." She proceeded to tell him to advance into the museum at the pyramid to where the display for the Egyptian god Horus stood. Incidentally, the display was numbered "666."

At this display, he consulted with "Aiwass" the "messenger" of the god Horus. Here, Crowley communicated with this demonic entity to pen his seminal work, *The Book of the Law*, which was the basis for his new religion: *Thelema*.[21] The thesis of his work and the basis for Thelema was simply summed up in the phrase "Do what thou wilt." Of course, this is the same mantra secular humanism espouses. It is a mantra rooted in satanism.

Not surprisingly, Rose eventually became consumed by alcoholism and descended into madness. Aleister continued preaching his brand of occultism, even opening an "abbey" in Sicily where he and his followers would engage in sadistic orgies mixed with black magic. Some of the orgies would even involve sexual acts with animals. Children would run naked and free around the compound, witnessing these perverse sexual escapades at any time.

During this time, Aleister consorted with a male assistant with whom he often performed sadistic sexual acts. During an attempted demonic conjuring with this assistant, Crowley placed the assistant inside of a so-called

---

21. Aleister *Crowley, The Book of the Law (Centennial ed.) (Newburyport, MA: Red Wheel/Weiser, 2004).*

"protective circle" so the demonic spirit would not inhabit the assistant. Crowley, on the other hand, remained outside the circle with the hopes the demonic spirit would inhabit him. During this conjuring, Crowley engaged in sodomy with his male assistant while simultaneously performing his black magic ritual and consuming high amounts of drugs. This scenario led Crowley to recount the methods for attaining the highest goals of black magic by mixing it with sadistic, perverse sex and drug use. Ritualistic sodomy and consumption of sexual fluids were recounted as the most effective means of achieving the highest levels of black magic when they were mixed with strong drugs. This had a profound impact on the music culture, even resulting in the famous phrase, "Sex, drugs, and rock and roll" that was terminology utilized for "free love," "peace," and "altered states of mind."

Crowley's writings would demonstrate the level of depravity in which he engaged. He often sacrificed animals in satanic worship. In his book, *Magick,* he included a chapter titled, "On Bloody Sacrifices" in which he wrote, "For the highest spiritual working one must choose that victim which contains the greatest and purest force. A male child of perfect innocence and high intelligence is the most satisfactory and suitable victim."[22] He revealed that he had, himself, performed this sacrifice "150 times per year between 1912 and 1928." Present-day followers of Crowley's religion attempt to sanitize such vile statements by asserting Crowley was being facetious in his statements on child sacrifice and that had he actually perpetrated that many sacrifices, he would have surely been caught.[23]

What Wilson likely realizes but hopes no one else does is that Satan likely protected Crowley since he was highly successful in influencing generations of people past, present, and future. Crowley often encouraged his followers to learn how to write and walk backward. He believed satanic messages were best revealed when one performed normal functions backward. This led to the infamous "backward masking" messages inherent in many rock songs of the 1960s, 1970s, and 1980s. Of course, in today's music, there is no need for backward masking. The satanic messages are front and center.

I must pause a moment to confess. Until I began this journey of research for this book, I was a fan of many rock songs from the 1960s through

22. Aleister Crowley, *Magick: Liber ABA, Book 4,* parts 1 to 4, 2nd rev. ed., edited by Hymenaeus Beta (Independently published, 1994).

23. R. A. Wilson, "The Enigma: Beyond the Legend of Infamy," Introduction to Israel Regardie, *The Eye in the Triangle* (2018), http://www.aleistercrowley666.co.uk/content/bookextracts_content_text.html.

6. THE ENEMY WITHIN: SECULAR HUMANISM

the 1980s. It was quite disturbing to learn of the vast influence Satan, through Crowley, had on many musicians of this time period. While I have absolutely no use for the vast majority of modern famous musicians, it still presented as a shock to learn the rather overt homages still paid to Crowley by some of music's most influential modern stars.

With that said, I am about to iterate popular culture icons who have been and are influenced by Crowley. I understand the reader may be disappointed to learn some of their most favorite songs may be satanic messages or that their favorite modern musicians are consumed in the occult. It is also critical to understand that while in heaven, Lucifer was among the highest, if not the highest, in hierarchy among the anointed cherubs. Described as being covered with precious stones, he was the star of the morning, visually stunning, and wise.[24] Ezekiel 28:13 also reveals that Lucifer was created with "pipes and "tabrets" within his being. In essence, he was a self-sufficient, purveyor of music. While some commentators have suggested the subject of the scripture was referring to the king of Tyre, it is most likely referring to Satan given the overall context of the scripture.

Perhaps the most astonishing musical group to have been influenced by Crowley were the Beatles. Their *Sgt. Pepper's Lonely Hearts Club Band* album features a picture of Crowley. While this may seem innocuous, it must be noted that those featured on the album cover were in a position of reverence by the Beatles. Other major music sensations with references to Crowley were Michael Jackson, David Bowie, Led Zeppelin, The Police, Pantera, The Jonas Brothers, Ozzy Osbourne, Iron Maiden, Nine Inch Nails, Eddie and the Hot Rods, Graham Bond, Daryl Hall, Lady Gaga, Jay-Z, Kanye West, Rhianna, and Ciara.[25] There are still persistent rumors that the Eagles were also influenced heavily by Crowley. The song, "Hotel California" is said to be referencing Anton LaVey's church of Satan or Crowley's mansion in Scotland. Other notable names that were heavily influenced by Crowley were Robert Anton Wilson, Rob Zombie, Jack Parsons, and L. Ron Hubbard (the father of Scientology).

As a musician, educator, and researcher, I have long been interested in the cognitive effects of music. Without going into much detail (simply because it would likely bore the reader to tears), music possesses an innate

---

24. Ezekiel 28:11-19.

25. R. Brett, "Turn and Face the Strange – Occultist Aleister Crowley's Influence on Popular Music," *Louder Than War*, November 17, 2017, https://louderthanwar.com/aleister-crowley-influence-on-popular-music/.

capacity to exert a monumental effect on the human brain. Recent fMRI studies have demonstrated that music, whether listened to or performed, engages more of the overall surface areas of the brain than any other activity in which humankind can participate. Make no mistake, Satan is fully aware of the power of music and has utilized it to his benefit rather successfully over the last sixty to eighty There is a reason Satan is the prince of the power of the air.[26] It is within his God-permitted ability to control the airwaves whereby radio, television, movies, and music are streamed. Is there any doubt as to why most of these media sources are profane? Furthermore, is there any doubt why, we as Christians, must have the power of the Holy Ghost in our lives to combat this evil?

The Paranormal Phenomenon

Because secular humanism essentially elevates humanity to an almost god-like status, another satanic-inspired phenomenon is becoming more pervasive and even affecting Christians. Television is rife with examples of programming whereby supposed "ghost hunters" are investigating local facilities in order to ascertain whether they are "haunted." Without fail, most of these shows employ specific devices that allow them to converse with spirits and spirits to subsequently converse with them. In technical terms, this is known as necromancy, or communing with the dead.

This type of occultism is secular humanism at work, in that individuals believe the human spirit is sufficiently strong to remain on the earth in one form or another. Unfortunately, many Christians believe that ghosts of the deceased continue to roam the earth. In fact, one in five Americans not only believe in ghosts but purport to have witnessed one.[27] Among those, thirty percent of Christians believe in ghosts.

The reason this belief is rooted in secular humanism is that when one believes the human spirit is innately and sufficiently powerful to *choose* to remain on earth or has been *trapped* on earth, he or she assigns a force to the human that is greater than God's Word and His power. This is because God, in His word, has expressly and unequivocally asserted the destination

---

26. Ephesians 2:2.

27. E. M. Miller, "What Does the Bible Say About Ghosts?" *Relevant Magazine,* October 21, 2017, https://relevantmagazine.com/god/worldview/what-does-bible-say-about-ghosts2.

6. THE ENEMY WITHIN: SECULAR HUMANISM

for a human soul and spirit following death is either heaven or hell.[28] Luke 16:23 recounts the scenario of when the rich man passed from this life to the next. According to the Scripture, he closed his eyes in death on earth and immediately lifted them in hell. There were no purgatories, intermediary states of being, or lights at the end of the tunnel.

So, are these people who claim to have seen a ghost lying? This is not necessarily the case. Some have mistakenly assigned something quite natural and normal as "paranormal." I am sure some have simply made up a tale. Some have likely convinced themselves they have seen something that is truly a figment of their overactive imaginations. There are also what I like to term, "pinto bean dreams." These are dreams that are often vivid and lucid but were the cause of something eaten before bed. Then, there are some who have truly seen something. Indeed, there are spirits roaming the earth, and while they may appear to be a long-deceased loved one, they are likely an evil, demonic spirit assuming the likeness of a human.

Spirits often take the form of a human because it is a *familiar* appearance. In fact, when grandma, who has been dead for years, appears in the home, this is most likely what the Scriptures refer to as a familiar spirit.[29] Interestingly, the same Latin word from which we derive *family* is the same from which we derive the word *familiar*. Demonic spirits appear in a familiar form in order to make one feel more comfortable with it. It will not likely come to someone in its true form unless its mission is to scare.

There is an instance of this occurring to one of my family members. A spirit appeared to a younger female member of my family several years ago in the form of an old, white man in a gray suit with a distinctively fetid smell. As she recounted the scene to us, she described seeing him walking down the driveway unnoticed by anyone else approaching the front door. When he knocked, she answered. He attempted to convince her to go with him. When she refused, he left the premises. He had lifeless, ice-blue eyes. Later, in a particularly tumultuous time in her life, he appeared to her again except, this time, he was in the house.

He walked into her room, undetected by anyone else, and approached her bedside. Once again, he encouraged her to leave the house with him. According to her, this man, clearly an evil spirit, visited her many times throughout her childhood. It was attempting to familiarize itself to her so she would feel more comfortable with it. Interestingly, I have heard strangely

---

28. 2 Corinthians 5:8; Hebrews 9:27.
29. Leviticus 19:31.

similar accounts from different children, all girls by the way, where they were visited by the same spirit, appearing the same way with acrid body odor, encouraging them to leave with it. These are the types of demonic spirits with whom so-called paranormal investigators are communicating and attempting to capture on recordings.

In essence, speaking to some random spirit in a purportedly haunted house or building is, in fact, an attempt to communicate with an evil spirit. Now, many of the so-called electronic voice phenomena (EVP) recordings, spirit box messages, and other electronic forms of spirit communication are simply natural phenomena or projections of our own minds. It is true that our mind, which is a powerful creation, will actually convince one that they have heard or seen something that was not actually there, simply because it is what one is attempting to see and hear. There are, however, times when these phenomena are real and are, in fact, communications from evil spirits.

The Scriptures even have an instance of this. Saul sought out the witch of Endor because he felt the need to commune with a deceased Samuel. The Lord had departed from him and was no longer answering his entreaties.[30] Interestingly, this same passage of Scripture indicated Saul sought out a woman with a familiar spirit. The Scriptures indicate that as Saul requested for her to summon Samuel, she looked and saw an old man in a mantle come up. As she saw him, she screamed.

The Christian world is unsure as to whether or not the witch summoned the actual Samuel or a familiar spirit who assumed the likeness of Samuel. I am of the opinion that she did not have a chance to summon anything. As Saul requested to speak with Samuel, he began to appear. His appearance frightened her. Had this been the spirit with which she was familiar, she would not have been frightened. Notice, also, how she screamed before she recognized Saul whom she feared would kill her. I do believe the Lord, in a remarkably rare act, allowed Samuel to appear. This could not have been an evil spirit because a prophecy was given that came to pass. Satan and demonic spirits do not possess the ability to know the future, otherwise, Satan would have done everything in his power to keep Christ from going to the cross.

This is why mediums, soothsayers, and fortunetellers are mostly inaccurate. I chose the word "mostly" for a reason. By and large, these charlatans are nothing more than pitiful individuals preying on the emotions

---

30. 1 Samuel 28.

6. THE ENEMY WITHIN: SECULAR HUMANISM

of others who are desperate to know circumstances beyond their control. Most of them are excellent readers of people and have an uncanny ability to tease out enough information to make educated guesses. There are, however, some who are in league with satanic spirits that provide insider information about their clients.

If a future is foretold and it comes to pass, most often it is self-actualized. This simply means the individual for whom the fortune was foretold knows the content of the fortune and subconsciously actualizes the contents of the fortune in his or her life. The individual then believes the medium is legitimate. Other times, when a fortune is actualized, it is simply a demonic spirit who happens to get it right. A blind squirrel can find a nut every now and then. But it might not be so difficult after all. The spirit knows the details of the person's life and is able to steer the course in the direction it wants him or her to go.

In short, the Scriptures are clear that witches, wizards, mediums, and the such should not be consulted. They are also clear that necromancy is detestable in the sight of the Lord; not because it is possible to commune with the dead, but because one is actually communing with a demonic spirit. There should be no mistake: if one wishes to capture some "evidence" that a spirit is among them, he or she will capture the evidence. I believe these television shows are attempts by Satan to normalize the practice of "paranormal investigation." He would like nothing more than to occupy more people with this practice in order to better familiarize himself with them. In short order, he will begin to assume control of areas of their lives and they will not understand how it happened. One should never open the door to communication with Satan because he will walk through it.

There are, however, instances in which, I believe, God allows certain visitations to occur. One such visitation occurred with my mother. My uncle Kelly passed away following a fatal brain aneurism. Kelly lived a rather ungodly life, even though he had been taught correctly. My mother and her family were concerned about Kelly's eternity. As the life support machine was powered down, my mother recounted a miraculous event. She saw Kelly's spirit come through the wall in the hospital room where she was sitting with his lifeless body. His spirit shown with a beautiful sheen that was simply otherworldly. He spoke to her in a way that was unique to Kelly indicating everything was alright. After this, he disappeared.

If God allows someone to appear, glory will be given to God. There will not be a sense of trepidation or fear. Additionally, there will be a clear purpose for this to occur. It will not be because a medium worked a magic spell to make it happen. God is infinitely powerful and mighty. He does not need magic spells to make His work a reality.

Secular humanist goals include attaching an almost god-like status to the nature of humanity. This seemingly pervasive perspective in modern society gives credence to paranormality when no such thing exists. Paranormality is not synonymous with supernaturality. There is a spiritual war ever-raging around us that we are not able to see. It is a supernatural war for our souls. The departed souls from this earth do not possess the power to remain here. They are either in heaven and they do not want to return or they are in hell where they wish they could return but cannot. While this obsession with all things paranormal seems to be infiltrating the church through casual experiences with Christians, there is an even more overt invasion of secular humanism into Christianity and it is most often welcomed with open arms and a million-dollar smile.

Humanism in the Church

Perhaps the most poignant Scripture for the quagmire in which we find the condition of the modern church is Isaiah 30:9-10. Isaiah wrote: "That this is a rebellious people, lying children, children that will not hear the law of the LORD: Which say to the seers, See not: and to the prophets, Prophesy not unto us right things, speak unto us smooth things, prophesy deceits." The world is rife with churches that no longer preach the unadulterated Word of God.

The seeker-sensitive movement has blossomed into politically correct, motivational speech, rather than an exposition of the Word of God. Church attendees have been conditioned to reject sound doctrine that challenges one's standard of living and promotes holiness. They have been conditioned to search for preachers that offer motivational words that will soothe their consciences and reassure them that their lifestyles are satisfactory before God when, in reality, they are not. These preachers offer no exposition on sin and the consequences thereof, while teaching them to pursue goals that are not godly.

Paul, in 2 Timothy 4:3, underscored Isaiah's assertion by writing, "For the time will come when they will not endure sound doctrine; *but after their own lusts* (emphasis added) shall they heap to themselves teachers, having itching ears." The Christian has forsaken the idea of subjecting him- or

6. THE ENEMY WITHIN: SECULAR HUMANISM

herself to comparison with the standards God has ordained in His Scriptures. Rather, they seek speakers who will match to their own ideals and they find a plethora of mainstream, so-called preachers who are more than willing to preach the Burger King doctrine of "have it your way."

One only needs to review some of the most popular bestsellers written by so-called church leaders. Most of the bestsellers focus on "you," "me," "my," "mine," and "ours." The focus is on the person and not on Jesus Christ. They are courses not in how to shun sin and cling to holiness; they are courses in how to continue in the same lifestyle of sin but do it just a little better in order to feel better about oneself. If Christ is the center of one's life, then he or she has all that he or she needs. Secular humanism in the church has supplanted God as the pinnacle focus of worship and replaced Him with the worshipper as the center of importance. We, as believers, do not attend church to make ourselves feel better; we attend to worship the Lord. He is the focus. Our programs, gimmicks, and desires should not be the focus. Church has become more about entertainment than true worship. Again, there is nothing wrong with the lights, smoke machines, audio/visual presentations, dance teams, skit teams, doughnuts, and coffee, as long as they are not the focus.

In the upper room on the day of Pentecost, the approximately 120 in attendance did not need any of those tools to launch the single greatest revival in history. The Holy Spirit will provide all the pyro and audio/visual any church needs if we will just allow Him to operate in the facility He desires to operate. A life lived victoriously is one led by the Holy Spirit—not a gimmick or a self-help book.

The major motivational speakers parading around like preachers of the gospel have relegated holiness as God's standard of living to the trash heap, while they work diligently to make parishioners feel good about themselves, regardless of the conditions of their souls. It is a vicious cycle: the devolving culture of the world created leaders like these and they are, in turn, continuing to produce sheep who sadly know nothing about the nature of God, His Word, and His expectations for living.

Their messages are consistently life-affirming for any and all hearers with absolutely no substance whereby one can hold a mirror in order to examine his or her life condition. As their conditions continue to remain sinfully stagnant or devolve into deeper despair, they are relentlessly bombarded with mantras on how to become better without relinquishing sinful practices. They are reminded each week that they are perfectly fine just the way they are. Subsequently, these parishioners will refuse sound doctrine that will confront their lifestyles, while fleeing back to the coddling embrace of the motivational speakers that confirm, whether overtly or covertly, their own lusts as perfectly acceptable. In essence, these motivational speakers who refuse to preach the whole gospel, rightly divided, are coddling millions of sinfully desperate people into hell.

As a parallel, 1 Kings 22 refers to the prophets ministering to King Ahab. These prophets routinely conveyed a message to Ahab that would make him feel good. When it was time to go to battle, these false prophets reassured Ahab and Jehoshaphat that God was on their side and that they would be successful in battle. The one prophet that prophesied negative news to Ahab, Micaiah, was imprisoned by Ahab for that very reason. Ultimately, at the behest of Jehoshaphat, Ahab called Micaiah out of the prison because Jehoshaphat apparently did not trust the all-affirming messages of his 400 pet prophets.

True to form, Micaiah prophesied a message of Ahab's doom that was contrary to those of the motivational speaker prophets. Under threat of potential death, Micaiah stood firm on the word of the Lord. Ahab, upset because he felt Micaiah always prophesied negatively of him, ordered he be returned to prison. In verse 23, Micaiah called out the 400 motivational speaker prophets by stating that the Lord has put deceiving spirits in the mouths of the prophets. Perhaps, this is exactly what is plaguing these modern motivational speaker prophets. They stand before large congregations and television audiences and speak deceptions ordered by evil spirits. Ultimately, they choose to prey on the most basic, animalistic aspect of humanity: emotions.

They preach that it is God's will for them to be wealthy. To accomplish this mission, they should "sow a seed" by sending thousands of dollars to fraudulent ministries. Sadly, tens of thousands in desperate situations heed this call and keep the coffers of the charlatans overflowing. They fail to preach that when one is saved, the road will not be easy, leaving many to, unfortunately, learn this on their own, resulting in great discouragement and apostasy. They make living a godly life seem like a cakewalk with no challenges and no reason to improve. They live glamorous lifestyles while presenting glitzy productions each Sunday that appeal to the sensationalist in all humans but they lack substance. They have traded the power of the Holy Ghost for the power of the smoke machine, strobe light, and lasers.

6. THE ENEMY WITHIN: SECULAR HUMANISM

People desperately seeking a change in their conditions are unable to find it amid all the sensation because, frankly, it is not there. In fact, the charlatans do not want it there. They would prefer to present a watered-down, spiritless, bastardized message in order to continue drawing large crowds with even fuller pocketbooks. In order to appeal more to the masses, it was necessary to edit messages by removing references to sin, holiness, standards, appropriate dress, the Holy Spirit, and, in some cases, even Jesus. When was the last time you listened to a message from mainstream preachers when they even mentioned the name above every name?

The doctrine is humanism. They wish to appeal to human nature by pacifying the flesh and deemphasizing the effects of sin. Many mainstream Christians even readily admit that they refrain from speaking about hell, sin, damnation, or anything that is not pleasing to the listening. Instead, they choose to use the pulpit to motivate people to "do better." How can someone do any better than when they eschew sin? Sadly, they simply choose to encourage them to "do better" in their sinful conditions. The result will be an eternity in hell. Ministers will be forced to account for the blood of millions on their hands for refusing to preach the gospel.

Michael LeMay, in asserting the effects of secular humanism on the church, stated, "Too many Christians attempt to mold God into our desired image of Him, instead of allowing the Holy Spirit to mold us into the image of Jesus."[31] Because the emphasis is on human emotion, the source for spirituality and truth comes from within rather than from God. The seeker-sensitive movement has led the church to the point of compromising on every fundamental belief central to the gospel. Popular culture rooted in secular humanism is not compatible with Christianity but the modern megachurch leaders have attempted to make it compatible, thus destroying the effectiveness of the gospel. The Holy Spirit will not bless and anoint something that is incompatible with the Word of God.

The future leaders of the church are taking notice. They see the compromising of principles and convictions in order to appeal to the masses. As a result, they are adopting a more liberal perspective on such tenets as morality, absolute truth, and the infallibility of the Word of God. Truth is subject to the whims and feelings of the beholder, more than on the steadfast foundation of the Word of God.

---

31. Michael D. LeMay, *The Suicide of American Christianity: Drinking the "Cool"-Aid of Secular Humanism* (Bloomington, IN: WestBow Press, 2012).

American Christianity judges the success of a church by the number of parishioners that attend, the size of the sanctuary, or the size of the bank account. LeMay correctly surmised that, in the view of modern Christianity, Jesus's ministry would have been considered an abject failure.[32] He primarily ministered to just twelve disciples, one of which betrayed Him, while another denied Him, and the others did not believe Him when He promised He would rise again on the third day. LeMay asserted many modern church leaders attempt to operate their churches like a corporation, attempting to relate to its customer base by providing what the customer wants. This is no more evident than when these motivational speakers are confronted with questions that, when answered scripturally, directly oppose the mantra of popular culture. In nearly every instance, the motivational speakers will give esoteric responses that ultimately avoid answering the question directly. Clearly, the results have been people heaping to themselves teachers having itching ears.

Desperate people are searching for something that is real. They desire something that is beyond themselves—something that lies in the realm of the supernatural. All the modern church has been able to offer them has been paltry amounts of platitudes for an hour on Sunday with a little bit of smoke and mirrors mixed in for effects. The songs of Zion in which one could literally perceive the electric anointing of the Holy Ghost has been given over to rock concerts where the name of Jesus is rarely mentioned. Children have been turned over to youth ministries with whom the highlight is playing silly games that have no realistic connection to eternity. The Word of God has been cherrypicked to just a few routine passages that are easily manipulated by the pastor to conform to his agenda of soothing the congregation in their sins. These are the churches that look like whited sepulchers, appearing outwardly beautiful but are, in reality, full of dead men's bones and uncleanness.[33] Across these churches, one can spiritually discern where the Holy Ghost has written "Ichabod:" the glory of the Lord has departed.[34]

The true church of the living God is one that may be small in number but mighty in power. This is not to suggest that a megachurch cannot be operating in the power and might of the gospel. On the contrary, I personally know of some. However, by and large, it is the churches that preach the

---

32. Ibid.
33. Matthew 23:27.
34. 1 Samuel 4:21.

6. THE ENEMY WITHIN: SECULAR HUMANISM

unadulterated gospel of Jesus Christ that often find themselves smaller in size. These churches should take heart: straight is the gate and narrow is the way that leads to life and few there be that find it.[35] These churches must never trade the power and presence of the Holy Ghost for the synthesizers, light boards, smoke machines, and other gadgetry. While there is nothing wrong with the technology utilized in the church, it should never supplant the Holy Ghost. He should be allowed to operate at will within each service. He can do more in seconds where it would take us a lifetime to achieve.

---

35. Matthew 7:14.

7. EQUIVOCATING COMMAND: PLURALISM

While I was in college, I had a friend who was recounting an experience he had in one of the religion courses in which he was enrolled. I attended a private, Christian college so one might expect a Christian worldview to persist in all courses. In this comparative religion course, my friend explained how the professor, a licensed minister, utilized presentation slides to demonstrate various religions from around the world. In each of the slides, the professor was praying to a particular god of that country's religion. Slide after slide, he prayed to Vishnu, Buddha, Mohammad, Confucius, and the multitude of other gods and prophets from around the world. At the end of the presentation, my friend, very confused, raised his hand and asked the professor, "Where is the picture of you praying to Jesus?" Ouch, that stung. Needless to say, the professor was unimpressed.

Of course, in a comparative religions course, one expects a focus to be on multiple religions but the professor certainly left himself open to such a criticism. On college campuses all over the world, liberal, progressive professors are teaching the ideology that has been exposed throughout this book. One such ideology is that other world religions and belief systems are just as valid as Christianity. An oft-quoted statement among such ideologues is that we are Christian because we were born in a nation sympathetic to Christianity but had we been born in Saudi Arabia, we would likely be Muslim. While this statement is relatively true, it makes no sense that this is the argument for the validity of other world religions.

Among the most overt tactics of the enemy to destroy a generation is the idea of pluralism. Simply defined, pluralism is the belief and doctrine that there is more than one legitimate path to God and, ultimately, heaven. Often, the acceptable mantra among pluralists is that as long as one consistently and wholeheartedly devotes oneself to whatever faith practice they choose, they will attain their ultimate goal of eternal life. In other words, as long as someone is the best Buddhist, Muslim, Wiccan, Hindu, or Christian

7. EQUIVOCATING COMMAND: PLURALISM

he or she can be, then that is sufficient. It does not matter the path. Only the sincerity of the traveler matters.

Popular culture relishes in the doctrine of pluralism because it is nonconfrontational, not offensive, and flexible with any lifestyle. For the Christian who proscribes to pluralism, it is an exercise in cowardice, biblical illiteracy, and compromise. Perhaps the most prevalent Scripture condemning the doctrine of pluralism is John 14:6 where Jesus commented, "I am the way, the truth, and the life: no man comes to the Father, but by me."

Throughout the Old Testament, Scripture indicates how kings of Israel led people astray in worship of other so-called gods and goddesses. Each time, Scripture condemned the practice and the king for promoting and enforcing it. Scripture regularly referenced the king's actions as performing "that which was evil in the Lord's sight." One must realize that our God is a self-described jealous God.[1] He has commanded that we put no other gods before Him.[2] We have also been commanded to put the Lord first in all that we do.[3] Ultimately, the Lord will be first in our lives or He will not be anything at all. He, the One true living God, will not share the stage with other false gods, thus subjecting Himself as being equal with lies.

There has, however, been a movement in progress for many years to deemphasize the singular authority and kingship of Jesus Christ. One very prominent pluralist, Oprah Winfrey, who was, incidentally raised in a strict Methodist home, stated in 2007 that "there are millions of ways to be a human being and many paths to what you call 'God' . . . there couldn't possibly be just one way."[4] In fact, she believes that it is a huge mistake to believe there is only one way to God. When she confronted both mainstream Christians with the question of whether or not all roads lead to God, they obfuscated the answer, literally saying nothing of substance. Let us try this together: Are there multiple roads to God? The answer is no. Jesus is the only way. See how easy that was? The problem is that this simple answer is not so simple for the charlatan motivational speakers parading around as preachers who are more concerned with attendance and offerings.

---

1. Exodus 20:5; 34:14; Deuteronomy 4:24; 6:15; 32:16; 32:21; Joshua 24:19; Nahum 1:2.

2. Exodus 20:3.

3. Proverbs 3:6.

4. C. M. Patton, "Oprah's Millions of Paths to God: Dealing with Religious Diversity," *Credo House*, May 20, 2008, https://credohouse.org/blog/oprahs-millions-of-paths-to-god-dealing-with-religious-diversity.

Pluralism is extremely easy to refute. One simply needs to provide a couple of examples. Aleister Crowley, discussed earlier, was clearly a Satanist. According to the dogma of religious pluralism, as long as one follows his or her faith with sincerity as best as he or she can, then that is a legitimate path to God. Pluralists, by their own statement of faith, would have to agree Crowley was saved and is presently in heaven. Osama bin Laden, the mastermind of the September 11, 2001 atrocities in New York City and Washington, D.C. was a devout, radical Muslim. Even though he viciously and wantonly slaughtered innocent people all over the world in the name of his religious beliefs, pluralists, when applying their own doctrine, would have to agree that bin Laden was saved and is in heaven.

However, it seems that no matter how idiotic this perspective seems to be, it is rather pervasive throughout the modern culture. One may ask how something so easily proven illegitimate can be considered so sensible. A component of the issue lies with human nature's innate aversion to confrontation. People simply would rather not be adversarial. They ultimately choose to get along. It is, indeed, easier to at least implicitly accept an argument for one's incorrect perspective than to confront it openly. In a sense, this is admirable. One should be able to disagree without being disagreeable. In the world of punditry that is pervasive in cable news, an accepted perspective is often the one that is shouted the loudest and longest. Civil discourse is, sadly, a thing of the past.

One must, however, never allow this lie of the enemy to progress without a challenge. For far too long, the Christian has stood idly by and allowed the enemy to promulgate lies with absolutely no protest. Because the church chose silence from the 1960s forward, the culture devolved into the absolute disarray in which we presently find it. Now, elements of the church that refuse to allow Satan to run amok throughout the culture are finding their voice but because the trajectory of the culture has progressed into amorality so far, it may, indeed, be too little too late.

Because Satan is targeting the younger generations in an effort to simply allow the fundamental Christian perspective to "die out" with the older generation, it is incumbent upon us to resist his efforts. We must remember that God will always have a remnant.[5] Will we choose to be a part of that remnant and bring as many along with us as possible or will we choose the path of least resistance and allow lies of the enemy like pluralism to be propagated throughout the culture?

5. Romans 11:5.

7. EQUIVOCATING COMMAND: PLURALISM

Let us explore this idea of pluralism a little further. David Ray Griffin, a theologian, asserted the opposite of religious pluralism is absolutism.[6] Absolutism, of course, is the belief that there is only one path to God. Inherent in the idea of absolutism are two forms. One form is exclusivism that posits that there can be no other way by which one can be saved than through Christianity. Inclusivism projects that practitioners of other religions can be saved but only by virtue of God's grace through the redemptive work of Christ. Certainly, the ideas of exclusivism and inclusivism appear to be separated only by semantics. One could argue that salvation by virtue of God's grace through the redemptive work of Christ is, in fact, Christianity.

John Hick, another rather progressive, liberal theologian argued that religious pluralism is the necessary reaction against centuries of Christian domination, resulting in what he terms as "Christian superiority."[7] In an absolutely astounding assertion, Hick argued anti-Semitic actions such as the Holocaust were results of Christian superiority. He theorizes that if Christians would eschew absoluteness and accept the notion that there are other ways in which people can respond to divinity, religion would be healing, rather than divisive. Of course, Hick's arguments are absurd.

While I am certain there existed and still exists self-professed Christians who are anti-Semitic, that perspective is wholly incompatible with Scripture. God's chosen people are the Jews.[8] We, the Gentiles, have been grafted into this divine order by the redemptive work of Christ.[9] To even remotely suggest Adolf Hitler and the Nazi regime were Christian and the Holocaust was perpetrated by Christian ideals is simply offensive. Hitler, while not likely an atheist, was, at least, agnostic and was the personification of social Darwinism in which the fittest of the social strata survive.[10] Ravi Zacharias contended Hitler was indeed an atheist or agnostic. If so, his atrocities were certainly not motivated by Christ.[11]

---

6. David Ray Griffin, *Process Theology: On Postmodernism, Morality, Pluralism, Eschatology, and Demonic Evil* (Process Century Press: Anoka, MN, 2017).

7. John Hick, *A Christian Theology of Religious: The Rainbow of Faiths* (Westminster: John Knox, 1995).

8. Deuteronomy 7:6-9.

9. Romans 11.

10. Samuel Koehne, "Hitler's faith: The debate over Nazism and religion, *ABC News*, April 18, 2012. http://www.abc.net.au/religion/hitlers-faith-the-debate-over-nazism-and-religion/10100614.

11. Ravi Zacharias, *The End of Reason: A Response to the New Atheists* (Grand Rapids, MI.: Zondervan, 2008).

Wilfred Cantwell Smith argued that Christianity was not the singular divine structure initiated by God. He suggested God inspired humans to construct the idea of Christianity just as "He/She/It inspired Muslims to construct what the world knows as Islam."[12] In such an argument, Smith essentially attempts to invalidate the divinity of Christ, deny His Sonship to God, place doubt about the essence of God by referring to Him as "He/She/It," and place Christianity on equal footing with Islam. Again, this approach is wholly incompatible with Jesus's own assertion that He is the only way to the Father.

While pluralism is inherently nonsensical and easily defeated, there is a relative ideology to the perspective that Satan has subtly generated for mass consumption. It is the favorite approach of many theologians, like David Ray Griffin, who proscribe to what is called *process theology*.[13] The ideology that is akin to pluralism but easy to accept is an attempt at a complete bastardization of Christianity. Sadly, many mainline Christian churches are treading into this territory with reckless abandon in an effort to demonstrate to the popular culture that we Christians are loving, kind, accepting, tolerant, and seek to coexist.

Religious syncretism is the blending of two or more religions into one singular religion or tradition. Griffin conveyed this idea by suggesting that what was considered contradictory ideas may actually be complementary.[14] The world's religions should communicate and cooperate to find common ground by which they may attain deeper religious understanding. Sadly, many of our churches, born out of what I consider sincere attempts at peace, are hosting meetings in the church where a local imam will sit with a local pastor on stage and discuss the commonalities between Christianity and Islam.

Without a doubt, there are some commonalities between Christianity, Islam, and Judaism. All three major religions are monotheistic, have common histories from Abraham back to Genesis, and share similar end-time prophetic teachings. However, to give credence to a religion that is falsely identified as peaceful in the house of God by equating it with Christianity is heretical.

---

12. Wilfred Cantwell Smith, "Idolatry in Comparative Perspective," In Hick and Knitter, eds., *Myth of Christian Uniqueness* (Eugene, OR: Wipf and Stock, 1987). 53-68.

13. Griffin, 2017.

14. Ibid.

7. EQUIVOCATING COMMAND: PLURALISM

But this is a trend. Fifty-seven percent of evangelical Christians believe that Jesus may not be the only way to salvation.[15] When parading imams in the church giving credence to their damnable doctrines, can there be any surprise that the evangelical Christians of the world are confused?

Many Christians believe that Yahweh God and Islam's Allah are one and the same—that Allah is simply another name for Yahweh God. The modern, progressive culture has perpetrated such a lie. In the Qur'an, Allah is an impersonal deity with no son, not represented in the Trinity, and with only one name. Furthermore, in pre-Islamic Arabic culture, Allah was a lunar god. Clearly, these descriptions of Allah are in total contrast to the God of Christianity.

So, why would high profile pastors give credence to such heresy? Indeed, one such pastor signed the abominable "Common Word Between Us and You" agreement. In 2007, several Islamic leaders published an open letter to Christian leaders asking for an interfaith dialogue, claiming both religions shared basic common tenets.[16] The goal was to have a dialogue whereby common ground could be established. LeMay accurately described "common ground" as the compromising of foundational doctrinal tenets in order to find common purpose.

The content of the letter was indeed beautifully written but one must not be deceived. The Qur'an teaches that in order to eradicate the earth of opposing religions, the Muslim is allowed to deceive and lie. Four scholars from Yale Divinity School, in response to the letter, published *Loving God and Neighbor Together: A Christian Response to a Common Word Between Us and You*.[17] In this response, the Christian leaders stated the foundational beliefs of both Islam and Christianity are virtually identical. This response was endorsed by one hundred Christian leaders, scholars, and pastors.

When attempting to bridge the gap between Christianity and Islam, some leaders will go so far as to pray in the name of "Isa." Many believe that Isa is the Islamic name for Jesus; however, one must remember that, in Islam, Allah had no son. Equating the name that is above every name, Jesus, with that of a character in a false book that claims Isa was a prophet

---

15. David van Biema, "Christians: No One Path to Salvation," *Time*, June 23, 2008, http://content.time.com/time/nation/article/0,8599,1817217,00.html.

16. Michael D. LeMay, *The Suicide of American Christianity: Drinking the "Cool"-Aid of Secular Humanism* (Bloomington, IN: WestBow Press, 2012).

17. A Common Word, "Loving God and Neighbor Together: A Christian Response to a Common Word Between Us and You," *Yale Faith*, https://www.acommonword.com/wp-content/uploads/2018/05/Response_300_leading_Christian_scholars.pdf.

is heretical. In 2009, a high-profile pastor spoke at the Islamic Society of North America—an organization with ties to radical Islamic terrorism. In fact, he shared the platform with Siraj Wahhaj, an unindicted co-conspirator in the 1993 World Trade Center bombing. In this meeting, he actually agreed to not evangelize Muslims. Additionally, Dr. Mehmet Oz has been invited to speak to his congregation. Dr. Oz is a follower of Sufi Muslim mysticism and New Ageism.[18]

This is not designed to single out any one individual by any stretch of the imagination but to underscore many of the religious syncretic activities in which Christians are engaging. Many such instances occur with those who would be considered evangelical leaders in America. Blending of the world's religions into one New Ageist doctrine is becoming rampant in our culture and even in the church.

LeMay and many others believe a bastardization of Christianity (namely Chrislam) will be the religion of the antichrist in the last days.[19] Many believe the Pope will lead such a merger of two main religions. Many believe this is the great whore as discussed in Revelation 17. I am not an eschatological expert in the slightest so I cannot thoughtfully comment on such assertions; however, I am certain that with the evidence we presently witness surrounding the overt merging of various religious teaching and practice, there must be some merit to such a claim that this adulterated religion will have a role to play in the last days.

Let us return, however, to one of the most dangerous and sinister human enemies American Christianity has ever witnessed: Oprah Winfrey. How in the world can someone who, by all accounts, has proven herself to be one of the most entrepreneurial and generous people alive be so dangerous? It is true that Oprah has, indeed, proven herself to be very generous with her time, efforts, and financial gain. Many people have benefitted from her graciousness. Her generosity should be admired and lauded. However, Oprah is perhaps the most powerful woman in modern American history. A media mogul with a near cult-like following among people from every walk of life from women to men; LGBT to heterosexual; areligious to super-religious; African American to every known race or ethnicity; and destitute to ultra-wealthy and powerful. Her influence has proven to know no bounds.

18. LeMay, 2012.
19. Ibid.

7. EQUIVOCATING COMMAND: PLURALISM

The First Church of Oprah, The "Me" Generation, "Little Gods," and Word of Faith

Having such unmitigated influence could be a tremendous blessing if utilized appropriately. Unfortunately, Oprah has chosen not to entirely use her influence for the spiritual benefit of others. In addition to her assertions that multiple paths to salvation through God exists, she has essentially created a cult of her very own.[20] This cult is a syncretic blend of many religions that has morphed into a New Age psycho-spiritual monstrosity that resembles no legitimate religious credo but uncannily resembles the message preached weekly by those she calls "friend."[21]

Through her media outreach, Oprah has introduced the world to individuals such as self-professed self-help guru Louise Hay who teaches the tenets of reincarnation as truth. Oprah has introduced her audience to Caroline Myss, a self-professed "medical intuitive" who is nothing more than an introspective medium. She has also introduced Rhonda Byrne, author of *The Secret*, which trains individuals that by simply thinking about wealth, it will lead one to be rich. A routine guest on Oprah's media platforms has also been renowned "psychic" John Edward who purports to commune with dead relatives of those in Oprah's audiences.

Oprah also introduced the world to another very dangerous character—Marianne Williamson—now a 2020 Democratic candidate for president. In 2008, Oprah, along with Williamson, introduced a worldwide audience to "A Course in Miracles." The origins of this heresy began in 1975 with Helen Schucman, a Columbia University professor, who claimed she had a "new revelation" designed to "correct" misinterpretations about Scripture. If Ms. Schucman actually knew her Scripture, she would know Galatians 1:8-9 clearly pronounced her as accursed for preaching any other gospel but the one presented in Scripture. As an aside, this is why Mormonism is also a damnable, anti-Christian religion. Mormons believe an angel came down to Joseph Smith and presented the Book of Mormon to him on golden plates. It is interesting how Paul in Galatians 1:8 even expressly includes even "an angel from heaven" in his description of who should be accursed for presenting another gospel.

20. Patton, 2008

21. Mark Oppenheimer, "The Church of Oprah Winfrey and a Theology of Suffering," *New York Times*, May 27, 2011, https://www.nytimes.com/2011/05/28/us/28beliefs.html.

Let me be clear: anytime anyone proclaims to have a "new revelation" from God, we must immediately label that individual a false prophet. God gave us the only revelation of Himself that we would ever need through His word. Why would He need to provide a new revelation when the present revelation has still yet to be completely fulfilled?

LeMay outlined these "new revelations" from Helen Schucman that Oprah and Williamson included in their "A Course in Miracles."[22] Incidentally, millions consumed this garbage, including Christians. Schucman's new revelations included that there is no sin, the slain Christ has no meaning, the journey to the cross should be the last useless journey, one should not make the pathetic error of clinging to the old rugged cross, the name of Jesus is just a symbol or placeholder for the many names by which men pray to access God, the recognition of God is a recognition of self, the oneness of the Creator and creation is your wholeness and is the substance of your limitless power, and man has never sinned and does not need atonement.

While worship of false gods like Mohammed, Buddha, and the ten thousand Hindu gods may not be your cup of tea and while we may wholeheartedly agree that Jesus Christ is the only way, we are not entirely out of the woods when it comes to a pluralistic worldview. There are many, even within the church and who genuinely strive to live right, who may fall into the trap of pluralism by means of a perspective that may not even be on the radar.

This is the "me" generation. Indeed, worship of the self is idolatry and representative of a pluralistic worldview. Remember, God said in Exodus 20:3-5 that He would not accept any other gods before Him. Should we place ourselves; our wishes, dreams, and desires, above that of God's, we are, in effect, worshipping ourselves rather than the Creator. In fact, this perspective is quite prevalent in the modern church movement known as "Word of Faith." Speakers from this movement even go so far as to proclaim we are, in essence, "little gods." They pervert Psalms 82:6 and then cherry-pick other verses like John 10:34, Hebrews 1:3, John 14:12 to support their misinterpretation.

Isaiah 43:10 makes it abundantly clear that there is but one God. There have been none before Him and there shall be none after. Word of Faith speakers have bought into this message in order to propagate their prosperity doctrine. It is an anathema to the Scriptures and is a stench in the nostrils of God Almighty.

---

22. LeMay, 2012.

7. EQUIVOCATING COMMAND: PLURALISM

LeMay recounted a story once told, in public, by one of the founders of the Word of Faith movement. The Word of Faith speaker once iterated he dreamed he was speaking with Jesus when a demon jumped up and began trying to shout them down. He claimed he took authority over the demon and made him stop speaking. This guy then suggested Jesus looked at him and said, "I am glad you took control of that because I do not think I could have."[23] This story was so farcical I almost thought perhaps it was a joke. In fact, the Word of Faith movement is so invested in themselves that they truly believe their own superiority.

We are not little gods. In fact, we are nothing but dirt who God formed Himself. What we are, however, is the very image of God. He has breathed His own Spirit into our bodies; investing Himself in us so that one day He will come back to claim His investment. There is nothing special about us. The only special component is the blood of Jesus Christ that covers our lives. It is His Spirit that dwells within us that is special. It is God's image that He sees in us that is special. When we gather to worship Him, we must never allow the worship service to be about us. It is always about Him. Our worship styles, preaching styles, preferences about the color of the carpet, fondness of the setup on stage, proclivities for where the pulpit is located, and other nonsense makes no difference in the grand scheme. What does God want? Is worship centered on Him? Does the music lift up Jesus? Does the preacher proclaim the truth? Is the Holy Ghost allowed to move and operate as He desires? Those are the pertinent questions one should pose about the effectiveness of worship.

Word of Faith preachers who claim we are little gods are very reminiscent of the words spoken by the serpent in the garden of Eden. The serpent told Eve that if they ate of the tree, they would not surely die but would be like God.[24] Of course, the serpent was lying. So, with such similarities that exist between the serpent's message and that of the Word of Faith speakers, can the reader draw the conclusions? If not, I will be glad to help. Word of Faith speakers are liars straight from the pits of hell and should be labeled as charlatans, thieves, snake-oil salesmen, and false prophets. To be clear: this Word of Faith message is exactly the same as the New Age philosophy and witchcraft peddled by Oprah Winfrey and her minions.

Clearly, "the church of Oprah" and similar Word of Faith messages are antithetical to the primary message of Jesus Christ that is inherent to

23. Ibid.
24. Genesis 3:5.

the Scriptures. In fact, Oprah's "A Course in Miracles" is a training guide to witchcraft. Central to witchcraft is the belief that God is in other earthly objects including the self. Wiccans believe there is limitless power in the creation. How about the teaching that there is no sin? If one were to be a parishioner of ministers who refuse to teach about sin and judgment, this teaching would resonate with them. Is it any wonder such non-committal, politically correct, spineless jellyfish motivational speakers like these are fully acceptable in Oprah's world?

There have been many books and articles written about the anti-Christian teachings of Oprah Winfrey. Christians must be vigilant concerning those they allow to present standard of living guidance to them. They must also be careful of those whose message they allow their children to consume. Children are easily influenced. True to the Adamic nature of humanity, they will gravitate most often toward the sensational, nonconfrontational, emotional, and inherently wrong. As Alan Wimberley posited, we, who should be the more discerning consumers of information, must train the proceeding generation, who is perhaps the most digitally and informationally enhanced generation in history, how to discern between what is correct and incorrect.[25]

No Shout without Roots

While the enemy is successfully deceiving millions with the emotion-inducing tripe of pluralism and religious syncretism, we must be wary of his tactics and resist them at every juncture. As a Pentecostal, I love the emotional responses the Holy Ghost elicits through those who will allow it. Throughout my life, I have witnessed people shout, dance, worship, run the aisles, run the backs of the pews, and yes, even roll in the floor under the awesome power of the Holy Ghost. I will continue to allow the Holy Ghost to use me in such supernatural feats of His power whenever He chooses.

Too many Pentecostals are getting wrapped up in the emotion of worship without having any roots in the Word of God. What will we do when the lights are turned off, the music is no longer pumping, and the preacher is no longer shouting? Will we still be able to shout the victory when the enemy is coming against us? Those moved solely by the emotion of the shout with no foundation in the Word of God and no lifestyle of holiness

25. Alan D. Wimberley, *Designed for Learning: Transferring Wisdom to Digital Generations* (Lanham, MD: Rowman & Littlefield, 2018).

will wilt and crumble at the first sign of trouble. It is by the Word of God that Satan is defeated.[26] It was the powerful, inerrant, infallible, immutable Word of God whereby Jesus resisted Satan in the wilderness.

When we find ourselves in the wilderness, it will not be the shout that brings us out. It will not be the smoke machines and light boards that end our wandering. It will not be the most cutting-edge worship music that ends our suffering. It will not be the diluted motivational messages of charlatans that lead us to victory. It will be our knowledge and proclamation of the omnipotent Word of God that has lasted for eons and will remain for eternity. On His Word, we must stand in order to challenge a satanic attack in our lives. By His Word, we must resist overt and covert tactics like pluralism and religious syncretism because when compared with His Word, they cannot be effective.

---

26. Matthew 4.

8. THE FRONT LINES: PUBLIC EDUCATION OR PUBLIC INDOCTRINATION

I LOVE THE PUBLIC schools. I am an advocate for the public schools. I am a product of public schools. However, I feel the mission of public schools in the last ten to twenty years has changed drastically and that mission is, by and large, more nefarious than innocent. Again, allow me to be crystal clear: there are excellent teachers in our public schools; many of whom love Christ and believe their assignment is a personal mission. There are also those who are utilizing the classroom as a pulpit to preach secularism, relativism, atheism, revisionist curricula, and social activism. Too often, school lessons are either covertly laced or overtly goal-oriented toward activating students to embrace Leftist ideology and to personally attack or blatantly bash objective, reasoned thought that may be contrary to their own ideas. These tactics are often masked in the terminology "social justice" and "multiculturalism."

Separation of Church and State and the Establishment Clause

While the progressive ideologues are provided carte blanche to evangelize and proselytize an entire generation to a damnable doctrine of hate, liberalism, guilt, shame, and compromise of convictions, Christian teachers feel as though they cannot even publicly live their lives in accordance with the Word of God for fear of reprisal, such as job termination or hostile intolerance for their beliefs. Therefore, Christian teachers, with little thought, have been conditioned to willingly leave their faith at the schoolhouse doors. They have resigned themselves to a perceived fact that faith is not welcome in the school, therefore, they willingly leave a component of their very being outside. This is not intended to be an indictment against those

8. THE FRONT LINES: PUBLIC EDUCATION OR PUBLIC INDOCTRINATION

teachers. On the contrary, it is an indictment against a system that is rife with leftist indoctrination.

The public has routinely been indoctrinated with a message of "separation of church and state." It must be noted that this clause does not appear in the federal documents of the United States whereby we are governed. Rather, a more appropriate investigation of the actions in which a teacher or student may engage related to his or her faith should concentrate on the establishment clause in light of the First Amendment.

The establishment clause reads, "Congress shall make no law respecting the establishment of a religion, or prohibiting the free exercise thereof." Proponents of a complete divorce between faith and school often cite the antecedent of that clause, "Congress shall make no law respecting the establishment of a religion." However, there is a subsequent phrase that is just as critical but often ignored, "or prohibiting the free exercise thereof." While the U.S. government cannot make laws respecting a specific religion, the government equally has no authority, according to the Constitution, to prohibit an individual's right to exercise his or her faith practice.

So, where does the controversy originate when it comes to religious practice in schools? Can students and teachers publicly express their faith? What, exactly, can students and teachers say and do with respect to faith practice? These are questions that plague Christians who hold public vocations, particularly in the public school. Has anyone ever considered why there is so much consternation when it comes to faith practice in public schools specifically? Typically, one does not hear of a major outcry when faith is practiced at, say, the sheriff's department, tax office, or prison. In fact, detention center officials, by and large, welcome jail and prison ministries. However, jails and prisons are public institutions. Why is there not the same outrage from anti-religious activists when it comes to jail and prison ministries as there are about relatively minor "infractions" of the church and state separation edict in public schools?

Let me be clear: this is in no way a statement of value on jail and prison ministries. They are incredibly important and, in reality, we, as Christians, do not do enough in this area of ministry. In fact, practitioners of Islam are outpacing Christian conversions in public detention centers by eighty percent.[1] Much of this conversion strategy originates in the highly

---

1. Besheer Mohamed and Elizabeth Podrebarac Sciupac, "The share of Americans who leave Islam is offset by those who become muslim," *Pew Research Center,* January 26, 2018, https://www.pewresearch.org/fact-tank/2018/01/26/the-share-of-americans-who-leave-islam-is-offset-by-those-who-become-muslim/.

progressive, ultra-liberal ideologies associated with social justice. In short, Christians must take jail and prison ministries more seriously because Muslims certainly do.

Getting Control as Early as Possible

Satan has learned that to destroy entire future generations, he must control the daily narrative as early as possible. Research indicates that the age at which most Americans accept salvation is between four and fourteen at a rate of an astounding eighty-five percent.[2] This was the age bracket in which I, myself, came to the saving knowledge of Christ Jesus. From there, the rates of salvation worsen as the age increases with individuals age fifteen to thirty at ten percent and thirty years or more at four percent. Ages four to fourteen encompass the vast majority of a child's educational trajectory. This is pre-kindergarten to ninth grade: the most impressionable years of a child's life.

Satan understands that if he can eradicate the good news of the gospel of Jesus Christ from these most impressionable educational years and virtually silence the Word of Almighty God from reaching these children, he has a vastly improved opportunity to ultimately destroy entire generations. Silencing the gospel from reaching children, while sufficiently destructive in and of itself, the enemy does not stop there. In our modern culture, he has not only succeeded in eradicating the Word of God from the public school, but he has also succeeded in replacing it with a doctrine of secularism, postmodernism, relativism, pluralism, and humanism. Make no mistake: there is still a religion being propagated and disseminated in public school and it is incubated in the pits of hell and delivered through a radical progressive agenda bent on destroying the family, the church, the nation, and the next generations. Vladimir Lenin often stated, "Give us a child for eight years and it will be a Bolshevik forever[3]"

---

2. Nazarene Church Growth Research, "Evangelism statistics: At what age is outreach most effective?" *When Americans Become Christian,* May 1, 2019, http://home.snu.edu/~hculbert/ages.htm.

3. Quotes.net, STANDS4 LLC, 2019. *"Vladimir Lenin Quotes."* Accessed September 28, 2019. https://www.quotes.net/quote/49098.

8. THE FRONT LINES: PUBLIC EDUCATION OR PUBLIC INDOCTRINATION

Sacred Silence

Unfortunately, the scenario only worsens. Not only has the enemy succeeded in silencing the gospel in our schools and replacing it with a radical progressive gospel, but he has also been very successful in silencing the Christian and the church. The church, who has stood for generations as the guardians of morality and values in the community has abdicated that responsibility to the disciples of hedonism, immorality, and atheism. The church has effectively stood silent as the enemy continues to ravage the public schools with violence, drug abuse, sexual promiscuity, homosexuality, hatred, disrespect for authority, and no knowledge of God.

Furthermore, the church has failed to teach parents how to rear their children to counteract such attacks from the enemy. Our modern churches are too concerned with filling the pews and filling the coffers. In order to do both, the modern church has traded the power and anointing of the Holy Spirit for an instant coffee and doughnut religion that is just as diluted as the instant coffee they serve in the lobbies. The church is full of gimmicks but devoid of any substance. The church is full of ear-tickling sermonettes but completely lacking in holiness. The church has relaxed its standards to the point in which the world views it as a sideshow and a pointless waste of time. Too many preachers have traded the impassioned, sweat-soaked, tearful pleas from the pulpit to accept Christ or be eternally lost for a more seeker-sensitive, socially and politically correct motivational speech on how one can be the best he or she can be. Insert that million-dollar smile complete with nice skin products here. Oh, and by the way, buy the books that say the same thing and nothing at the same time.

The world is burning from the foundation while the church continues to play social gathering games. Satan is wreaking havoc on the future of the church while the current modern church is more concerned about trying to appear tolerant and socially acceptable. I have news for those churches and pastors who choose social and political correctness over truth: you will stand before God with hands dripping with the blood of the damned because you refused to preach the unadulterated, unfiltered, unabashed Word of Almighty God in order to earn an extra Sunday morning statistic. The world will never accept the church, no matter how nice she may want to play.

A Little Psychology

The enemy is aware that humans are more receptive to the gospel when they are between the ages of four and fourteen. Psychological research indicates children will begin to make behavior decisions between middle childhood and early adolescence as well as develop social relationships easier, build a sense of self-esteem and individuality, and notice their peers more often.[4] Children begin to move beyond pre-operational, egocentric cognitive processes into more abstract, logical, and social thought.[5] Similarly, Vygotsky hypothesized children will grow into the intellectual life of those around them[6] while Bandura stressed children learn through social imitation and modeling.[7] The apostle Paul also understood the critical importance of surrounding oneself and one's children with good influences and models when he wrote, "Be not deceived, evil communications corrupt good manners."[8] Furthermore, Paul cautioned believers to not be "unequally yoked together with unbelievers: for what fellowship hath righteousness with unrighteousness? and what communion hath light with darkness?"[9]

This is one of the reasons parents with the means to do so choose to enroll children in alternative educational opportunities other than public school. The assumption is that if the child is enrolled in a private Christian school, other children with compatible faith experiences will surround and influence their own children. Some parents take it one step further and home school their children in order to better regulate the influences that their children encounter. Of course, social interaction and influence regulation are not the only reasons parents choose alternate educational opportunities but are among the most often cited.

---

4. J. S. Eccles, "The Development of Children Ages 6 to 14," *Future Child*, 9, no. 2 (1999), 30-44.

5. W. Huitt and J. Hummel, "Piaget's Theory of Cognitive Development," *Educational Psychology*

Interactive, http://www.edpsycinteractive.org/topics/cognition/piaget.html.

6. Lev S. Vygotsky, *Mind in Society: The Development of Higher Psychological Process* (Cambridge, Mass.: Harvard University Press, 1978).

7. Albert Bandura, *Social Learning Theory* (Englewood Cliffs, NJ: Prentice-Hall, 1977).

8. Corinthians 15:33.

9. Corinthians 6:14.

8. THE FRONT LINES: PUBLIC EDUCATION OR PUBLIC INDOCTRINATION

Discerning in a Digital World

The trouble is, however, that no matter how strictly regulated the potential influences on children, some evil influences will infiltrate. The age in which we live is the most digitally and technologically advanced than any other time in history. Daniel prophesized "knowledge shall be increased" in the "time of the end."[10] As a researcher, I am grateful I do not have to perform searches in the method that was most common in the recent past. In order to obtain a key piece of research, one had to search physical databases, endless streams of microfiche, and patiently await an interlibrary loan of a book or journal only to find that the piece of literature really was not necessary.

I grew up in what I like to refer to as the "tech tweener" era. I remember typing on an Apple IIe computer (the one with the stunningly beautiful green and black graphics) in the school library, dying from dysentery on the "Oregon Trail" game, burning the midnight oil playing "Asteroid" on the Atari system and later, "Super Mario Brothers" on Nintendo and "Sonic the Hedgehog" on Sega. It was enthralling to use my dad's bag phone that was larger than the few landline phones that still exist today with reception that was abysmal at best. For home use, my parents finally bought a Tandy computer. In reality, it was only useful for playing games at which we indulged often and thoroughly enjoyed. To say my peers were enamored with the one Macintosh computer the school finally purchased and locked in a specially dedicated room is an understatement. "Oregon Trail" gave way to "Where in the World is Carmen Sandiego" and we were off to the races.

I did not even own a personal cell phone until I was twenty-three years old and I thought it was cool to have the thinnest flip phone possible. The internet, while in existence, was not universal, was clunky at best, consisted of little practical information, and was frustratingly slow. Youth today have never experienced the sensation of "dial-up" internet with all the chirps, chatters, and squealing that accompanied that special experience. Technology was certainly advancing but not nearly at the pace in which we began to experience in the late 1990s to the present. My generation was truly the "first adopters" of some of the newest technology the planet had ever seen. Now, it seems as though children are born with the natural ability to manipulate technology for their own benefit.

The digital age has brought many exceptionally useful tools to the marketplace. Now, instead of having to scan endless streams of microfiche and

10. Daniel 12:4.

wait for interlibrary loans, I can find most any piece of information I need on any device. How many people twenty-five years ago would have believed a phone would possess the capability to provide any piece of information in less than a second, take pictures, send instant messages to someone on the other side of the planet, allow one to read a book or have it read it aloud, tell how to get home or anywhere else, and, oh yeah, still make calls? Who would have dreamed that with the advent of 2019, driverless vehicles are serious concepts for automakers? Who would have imagined virtual reality is now a reality and is utilized in the classroom where an art teacher can project students into the Louvre without actually going to Paris? Twenty-five years ago, I would have discounted these advancements and so much more as mere science fiction. The reality is that Daniel 12:4 is being fulfilled.

With this ever-increasing and fast-paced knowledge stream continuing to develop at such a rapid pace that even new technological advances this year will be obsolete before the end of the year, insulating children from all manner of influences is simply impossible in today's society. I would contend that restricting children from the immense technological explosion happening before our eyes is the incorrect path for parents to undertake. In this digital age, our children will need technological skills to perform even menial tasks. The digital boom is not disappearing but will continue to evolve and children need to be adequately prepared.

Rather, children need to be taught how to become responsible consumers of digital material—to be conscientious engagers.[11] Much of the readily available information in the world today is not entirely true. The enemy is sly and will utilize a tool that is and will be necessary for children to survive in a digital age to deceive an already impressionable mind. Children must be taught to be skeptical and judicious. This is an area in which I fault many of my fundamentalist brothers and sisters in Christ; of which, I am proudly numbered. Too often, we teach our children to accept a teaching without question. While I am certain no Christian parent intentionally misleads his or her children, blind acceptance of doctrine is not advisable and I contend is leading our future generations into apostasy. Allow me to explain.

---

11. Alan D. Wimberley, *Designed for Learning: Transferring Wisdom to Digital Generations* (Lanham, MD: Rowman & Littlefield, 2018).

8. THE FRONT LINES: PUBLIC EDUCATION OR PUBLIC INDOCTRINATION

"Don't Question God!"

How often have we heard the phrase, "Don't question God?" While I understand the spirit of the phrase, I propose that in our effort to ensure that our children accept the Word of God as immutable and inerrant, we have unintentionally caused them to fail at working out their own salvation with fear and trembling.[12] This passage of Scripture is often misapplied in an effort to appease one's own desire to engage in lifestyle activities that are clearly in violation of the commandments in God's Word. In reality, the passage should be considered a call to fully apprehend one's faith in God. Why not ask God, "Why?"

Are we afraid God is not powerful enough to weather such a question from a mere human being? Do we not believe God encourages the active research of His Word in order to answer life's most challenging questions? For millennia, the Word of God has weathered individuals, groups, and governments who have tried to eradicate it, disprove it, challenge it, and destroy it. All attempts have failed miserably. Jesus stated in Matthew 24:35 that even "Heaven and earth shall pass away, but [His] words shall not pass away." Isaiah, when writing about the Word of God, penned, "The grass withereth, the flower fadeth: but the word of our God shall stand for ever."[13]

Our children must learn they are allowed to pose questions of God. They must be allowed to even question their own faith. Many children reared in Christian homes and attending church weekly cannot fully explain why they believe what they believe. How can we "earnestly contend for the faith"[14] when we have no concept of why we believe what we believe? This is why so many wither when an unbeliever mounts a serious challenge to our faith. The theological study of apologetics is an area in which all Christians should engage. In the study of apologetics, one is trained to present reasoned arguments in favor of a specific topic that is generally religious or doctrinal in nature. Certainly, the unfaithful will present cogent, reasoned, and seemingly logical arguments against our faith. Unfortunately, there are not enough faithful apologists who have studied to show him- or herself approved to be able to rightly divide the word of truth in order to challenge the false doctrine of the progressive secularists permeating our culture.[15]

---

12. Philippians 2:12.
13. Isaiah 40:8.
14. Jude 1:3.
15.. Timothy 2:15.

If our children are taught to work out their own salvation and understand why our faith is reasoned and logical, then when the enemy floods their devices, schools, and peers with false teaching designed to indoctrinate them in preparation for anti-Christian and humanist evangelism, they will comprehend enough of their own faith to withstand the onslaught. Then when they sanctify the LORD God in their hearts, "[they will] be ready always to give an answer to every man that asketh [them] a reason of the hope that is in [them] with meekness and fear."[16]

A Personal Experience of Questioning

There was a time when I even questioned the veracity of the resurrection of Jesus Christ. I share this because the work I accomplished with myself resulted in a firmer and more substantive faith than I had previously. I questioned how it was logical or possible for someone to die on a cross and then come back to life three days later. Common science would dictate the body would not withstand such punishment and revive on its own. Was it possible some naysayers were correct and Jesus did not actually die on the cross but passed out and was revived in the cool tomb? Is it possible Jesus lived out the rest of His life in India, married to Mary Magdalene?

These questions began to bother me until the Lord began to speak to me through His Word. When studying the Gospels, one will read multiple occasions when Jesus explained to His disciples that He would die but be resurrected on the third day. Some believe the disciples just did not understand the words of Jesus. I submit that the disciples did not *believe* Jesus would rise again. Had they truly believed, they would have been standing at the tomb on the third day, waiting for Him to come forth. Simple curiosity should have resulted in at least one follower being present the morning of the third day. Furthermore, because Jesus was such a high-profile convict, the disciples, with a few exceptions, scattered and hid during Jesus's death and burial.

As for the guards at the tomb, most dramatic Easter productions depict two guards at the tomb. One must consider that Jesus was a highly important criminal in the eyes of the Jews and Romans; One Whose arrest and trial were very public and contentious. The Romans never would have allowed just two guards to monitor the tomb of Jesus. Additionally, they also knew the predictions that Jesus would rise again on the third day. It

16.. Peter 3:15.

8. THE FRONT LINES: PUBLIC EDUCATION OR PUBLIC INDOCTRINATION

is highly likely the Romans *increased* surveillance on the third day amid suspicions that the disciples would steal the body.

While these two considerations were very powerful to me, it was the third that thoroughly increased my faith. God impressed upon my spirit with, "Would you die for something you knew was an outrageous lie?" My thought was, "No, Lord, I would not." God further impressed upon my spirit, "Not only did the disciples die for the truth, but they suffered unspeakable torture leading to their deaths." This revelation to me, which was really common knowledge all along but revelatory to me at the time, impressed me.

Following Jesus's resurrection, the disciples physically witnessed Jesus, touched Him, and spoke with Him. They witnessed His transfiguration and ascension. Life is too precious to waste on something that is a known lie. Nobody would suffer great persecution for something that was understood to be false. For me, this strengthened my belief and erased all doubt. My questions led to a personal revelation of God's Word, resulting in an experience I could share with others to strengthen their faith. When confronted with naysayers who express skepticism of Jesus's resurrection, I am ready to give an answer.[17]

Fulfilling the Great Commission in Public Schools

The Lord has called us to fulfill the Great Commission.[18] We are to go into all the world and preach the gospel to every creature.[19] However, how do Christian students and teachers fulfill this commandment when it is contrary to the nation's laws? Are we not also commanded to obey the laws of our government?[20] These are, indeed, what I like to call very "pregnant" questions. Many of the answers may begin with "it depends."

A Cursory Analysis of the Law

As a public-school district administrator, I often find myself considering the state of public education and how I may display the love of Christ to a lost

17. Ibid.
18. Matthew 28:16-20.
19. Mark 16:15.
20. Romans 13:1-3.

and dying generation but also remain within the parameters of the law. We, as Christians, must resign ourselves to the fact the prayer and Scripture reading were removed from the public school and it is highly unlikely that will change. The Supreme Court of the United States ruled in the landmark case *Engel v. Vitale* that state-composed, non-denominational prayer in school violated the establishment clause of the Constitution.[21] In another landmark court case, *School District of Abington Township, Pennsylvania v. Schempp*, the Supreme Court ruled that requiring students to read biblical Scripture was also a violation of the establishment clause and the Free Exercise Clause.[22] In 1971, the Supreme Court, in a landmark case decision, implemented a three-pronged test of constitutionality that many in the field of education refer to as the "Lemon test."[23] Named for the plaintiff in the case *Lemon v. Kurtzman*, the court determined a statute is constitutional if:

- It primarily has a secular purpose;
- Its principal effect neither aids or inhibits religion;
- Government and religion are not excessively entangled.

The Lemon test has been uniformly applied to most religious-based complaints related to public school in the United States so it is critical we fully understand it. While the first two prongs of the test are fairly uncomplicated, the third is still considered rather nebulous without a quantifiable definition. How much, exactly, is "excessive?" Generally speaking, the Supreme Court will uphold lower courts' interpretation of this term.

While the elimination of prayer and Scripture in public schools may seem defeatist, the converse is actually true. We must understand that the rulings in the aforementioned landmark court cases are generally concerned with public-school initiated, required, and led religious activity and does not apply to student-initiated religious activity. In fact, the Supreme Court in *Westside Community Schools Board of Education v. Mergens* ruled student-initiated activity must be allowed as long as it does not interfere with or disrupt instructional time.[24] So, rather than concentrate on the activities we cannot do in the public schools, what activities may occur within the walls of the schoolhouse?

21. Engel v. Vitale, 370 U.S. 421 (1962).
22. Abington School District v. Schempp, 374 U.S. 203 (1963).
23. Lemon v. Kurtzman, 403 U.S. 602 (1971).
24. Westside Community Board of Education v. Mergens, 496 U.S. 226 (1990).

8. THE FRONT LINES: PUBLIC EDUCATION OR PUBLIC INDOCTRINATION

What Can Students Say and Do?

For students, the pathway is generally less murky. Students, essentially, may read the Bible, pray, hold religiously related groups, and pass out literature. There is one element that must be considered, however. Students may not engage in these activities during direct instructional time and they may not engage in these activities with a captive audience.

For example, a student who is sitting in his or her desk in the classroom while the teacher is delivering content may not begin to pray aloud. This would be a violation of the rules. That same student may pray silently during this time though. If a student wishes to pray aloud in the hallways during class change or at lunch, this is permissible as it is not occurring during direct instructional time. If a student wishes to hold a Bible study, Fellowship of Christian Athletes huddle, Good News Club, or some such organized meeting, it is permissible as long as it is not implemented during direct instructional time. Disallowing students to engage in such activities is a violation of their First Amendment rights.

What Can Teachers Say and Do?

For teachers, engaging in religiously related activities is somewhat less clear. Unfortunately, too many teachers have incorrectly assumed their faith is unequivocally and categorically restricted and they willingly, without question, shed their faith at the door. Let me be clear: my faith is not a religion—it is my lifestyle. It is who I am. Leaving my faith outside the school while I enter would be tantamount to me leaving my heart, mind, or breath outside the door. In short, it is impossible for a Christian teacher to willingly leave the Lord outside his or her place of work. Again, we unfortunately do so willingly but often because we think there are no recourses.

One method for teachers to share the gospel of Jesus Christ in the public school is, simply, to do so when they are asked. It is legal for teachers to honestly answer students' questions about their own personal faith. In fact, this relates directly to encouraging children's questioning of religious tenets and faith. Some teachers fear engaging students in such potentially contentious discussions. Their fear leads to missed opportunities to share the gospel and provide an answer to every man who asks, as underscored in 1 Peter 3:15. If one is living his or her life as a devout Christian, there are no doubts that others will be able to witness that something is different.

Teachers simply responding with such responses as "praise God," "thank the Lord," or "hallelujah" may make students, consciously or subconsciously, realize that there is something different about this teacher.

An Analysis of an Example

There are also methods for potentially steering lessons and conversations in the appropriate direction whereby questions about faith are even solicited. Christian teachers should never shy away from injecting faith into a lesson as a means of achieving an educational goal. For example, consider a lesson or unit on the Civil War. When discussing slavery, a teacher could ask this question: "Considering that the South was, and still is to some degree, referred to as the Bible Belt, how do you think the South justified slavery? Doesn't the New Testament indicate Jesus came to save the world from slavery to sin?" This question is an exceptional example of what is referred to as *higher order* or *critical thinking*.

According to *Bloom's Taxonomy*, there are six levels of cognition that can be accessed through specific and critically crafted teacher questioning techniques: remember, understand, apply, analyze, evaluate, and create (in lowest to highest order).[25] Such a question on the Civil War would challenge students to think deeply about the perspective of individuals over 150 years ago, utilize their knowledge about the Civil War as well as religious and social thought of the time, and analyze how slavery was justified in the eyes of relatively devout Christians. Is it potentially controversial? Yes. Is it potentially contentious? Absolutely. Does it skirt the line? No. How can that be?

Let us revisit the Lemon test and apply this question. Does such a question primarily have a secular purpose? If I were teaching this subject, my response to that question would be, "I am teaching my students to apply twenty-first century hindsight to nineteen century perspective while incorporating knowledge of the events and contexts encompassing the Civil War to make a reasoned, logical argument for how self-confessed devout Christians could arrive at justification for slavery." In short, the primary purpose of this question is to engage students in analysis—Lemon test prong one, check. At this point with one prong satisfied, the question passes the Lemon test; however, let us continue to apply the test.

---

25. Benjamin S. Bloom, *Taxonomy of Educational Objectives: The Classification of Educational Goals* (New York: Longmans, Green, 1956).

8. THE FRONT LINES: PUBLIC EDUCATION OR PUBLIC INDOCTRINATION

Does the question aid or inhibit religion? Considering the question is primarily posed as a cognitive exercise, the short answer is no. In fact, it could be argued that secularists may incorrectly view the question as an indictment against Christianity and would not have a problem with the question at all.

As for the third prong of the Lemon test, it would be my view as an administrator that government and religion are not excessively entangled. Conversely, the inclusion of this line of questioning is highly analytical and cognitively appropriate for students. It is a great question!

How can such a question be effective for faith reasons? Let me restate the question and this time, include emphasis on the pertinent components of the question.

Considering that the South was, and still is to some degree, referred to as the *Bible Belt*, how do you think the South justified slavery, considering that the *New Testament indicates that Jesus came to save the world from slavery to sin*?

First, I included the term "Bible Belt" when referencing the southern United States. It encourages students to consider why this term is applied to this section of the nation. Historically, the southern United States has been fundamentalist when it comes to faith. "What does it mean to be fundamental?" Well, I am glad you asked, little Johnny! A fundamentalist believes the Word of God is inerrant and immutable. This means the Word of God is true and consists of no errors. That means, whatever the Bible says, fundamentalists believe it is true.

Let us pause here just a moment. Teachers must, admittedly, exercise caution. Notice how in this exchange, I was careful to state, "Fundamentalists believe . . ." Teachers, as actors of the state, must take precaution not to make statements that would not be reflective of the state's perceived religious-neutral stance. Religious neutrality is an important concept that is indeed a two-way street. When prefacing the explanation of the Bible Belt with "fundamentalists believe," teachers are taking precautions to effectively state, "In my capacity with the state, I am not expressing this as the opinion of the state."

Icing on the cake, so to speak, would be for little Johnny to then ask the teacher, "Ms. Teacher, what do you believe?" I referenced this earlier when stating that conversations, lessons, and discussions can sometimes be steered in a potentially evangelistic direction. If little Johnny asks this question, Christian teachers have every right to and should answer honestly. If a teacher wants to make it abundantly clear that this is his or her own opinion and not that of the state, then he or she could state that.[26]

Second, the last phrase in the question posed about the Civil War is filled with potentialities. This phrase could lead to discussions simply about how Jesus came to the world. Other possibilities include referencing slavery to sin and how the Bible defines that, what Jesus did to save the world, what it means to be saved from sin, and what is the New Testament and why is it referred to as such. Indeed, this terrain would be rather dangerous; however, one must consistently keep the focus of the lesson as primarily educational in nature. Most importantly, we must never underestimate the inherent power in the Word of God.[27] These words give life.[28] The Word of God is quick and powerful; sharper than any two-edged sword[29] and will accomplish that which God pleases.[30]

My Public-School Gospel Choir

Can this kind of covert ministry work? The best answer I can provide is by iterating a personal experience that will forever remain with me. In my first teaching position as a high school choral director, I began an after-school gospel choir. There was really no issue with this action as it did not meet during instructional time and it is legal to hold those types of "clubs" or organizations during non-instructional time. That first year, sixty students joined the gospel choir and we traveled all over the area, singing in churches and at other functions. In fact, I included them in the formal concerts that opened up several other possibilities for covert ministry.

The following year, the guidance counselor approached me about making the gospel choir a part of normal school hours and enrolling students in the class. My reaction was what you probably imagined: is that legal? The guidance counselor responded that it was legal because the

---

26. Religious Freedom Center, *A Teacher's Guide to Religion in the Public Schools*, August 2014, https://www.religiousfreedomcenter.org/wp-content/uploads/2014/08/teachersguide.pdf.

27. Nathan L. Street, "Witnessing for Christ in Public Schools: What can teachers and students say and do?" *Church of God Evangel*, November 2017, http://www.evangel-magazine.com/2017/11/witnessing-christ-public-schools/.

28. Proverbs 4:22.

29. Hebrews 4:12.

30. Isaiah 55:11.

8. THE FRONT LINES: PUBLIC EDUCATION OR PUBLIC INDOCTRINATION

students choose to be enrolled in the class. That was enough for me and the gospel choir class became a reality.

This was a miraculous door that God opened and I am thankful He provided me with the courage to walk through. I taught students to sing and perform, utilizing songs with lyrics that praised and honored Jesus Christ. Those wishing to challenge the use of Christian music in the classroom find lyrics about God perfectly acceptable. It is when the lyrics begin to honor the name of Jesus Christ that legal challenges often arise.

The choir became the most popular class in the history of the school as well as the most popular performing ensemble. Organizations, including churches, were calling from all over the area, seeking the choir to perform. The choir grew from sixty students after-school to well over 100 students during normal school hours. The growth was so substantial that I split the choir into two separate traveling choirs because so many churches simply did not possess the capacity to host the entire ensemble. Furthermore, I implemented a smaller seven-member vocal ensemble with a band that would travel to extra functions that neither choir could make.

As a minister of music, I understood the inherent power in the Word of God whether spoken or sung. Let me be clear: I never overtly proselytized any students. I never stood and preached to them about how they should be saved. I never had to because I trusted the Word of God to never return void and God did not fail.[31] Through this ensemble, I was blessed to lead students to the redemptive side of Jesus Christ. There were students who were raised in church and still attended church who rededicated their lives to Christ because of this choir. Clearly, God was at work, changing lives.

There was a young lady who I will refer to as "Hannah." She approached me about joining the choir. The choir was clearly open to all students with no prerequisites or auditions (with the exception of the band that accompanied them). Hannah asked for a meeting, during which she said, "I am an atheist. I do not believe in the lyrics of the songs, do not believe in Jesus, and do not believe God exists or ever existed. I want to join this choir because I like the music and want to learn this style of singing. I thought it was important for me to obtain your permission, given my beliefs. May I join?" I smiled and said, "Of course you can, Hannah. The choir is open to everyone, regardless of race, creed, or beliefs. Indeed, this is an exciting group and I think you will learn much." Of course, I knew even an

---

31. Ibid.

atheist, when bombarded with anointed lyrics that praised God every day could not withstand the awesome power of Jesus Christ.

Indeed, not long after Hannah joined the choir, she approached me, wanting to speak with me privately. Of course, I agreed. Hannah began the conversation by stating, "Clearly, you are a Christian." I affirmed this assumption, as was my right. "Clearly, you believe the lyrics we sing." Again, I confirmed the assumption. "Why do you believe what you believe?" This was the opening I needed. I responded with, "Hannah, why do you believe what *you* believe?" Hannah then proceeded to explain to me all the typical atheistic propaganda that generally leads back to the Creation. I listened intently to her and I did not demean her for her beliefs. In fact, I often stated, "I understand why you believe the way you believe." She made a fairly logical, reasoned argument.

Then, I proceeded to explain that Scripture has stood for millennia and has yet to be disproved. History records that Christ lived, died, and His body has never been recovered. Since Christ endured a very high-profile crucifixion, would not the government have ensured His body would not have been stolen? Finally, I explained that the big bang could not have occurred due to the simple fact of first origin. If two molecules or kinds of gases exploded into the other, where did the molecules and the gases originate? Simple cause and effect dictated that an effect must have a cause. For every action, there is an equal and opposite reaction.[32]

At the conclusion of my explanation, I invited Hannah to my church. A week or two went by and, to my surprise, Hannah appeared at my church one Sunday morning. It was obvious that the immense power of God was at work in her life. That morning, my pastor gave an altar call and, to God be the glory, Hannah accepted Christ as her Lord and Savior. However, the story does not end there. Hannah led her parents, who were also avowed atheists, to the Lord, as well. I will reiterate: I never once proselytized to Hannah. I never needed to. The convicting power of the Holy Spirit moved in that classroom and over the lives of those young people simply through the singing of the Word of God. However, God was nowhere near finished.

Later in my tenure at this school, I invited the Lee University Campus Choir to stop by while on their tour that spring because we sang many of the songs the choir performed. The late Dr. David Horton was still the choir director. This was actually two months just prior to his home-going. Dr. Horton accepted the invitation and we arranged for the performance. I obtained

---

32. Isaac Newton, *Philosophiae Naturalis Principia Mathematica* (1687).

8. THE FRONT LINES: PUBLIC EDUCATION OR PUBLIC INDOCTRINATION

permission for all my choral students, gospel choir, and other ensembles (which, at the time, numbered approximately 200), to convene in the auditorium for the performance. After Dr. Horton led all his and my students in vocal warm-up and technique, he led the Campus Choir in a short performance. As they were singing, more non-music classes began filing into the auditorium. The principal and assistant principal eventually attended, as well. Everything was going smoothly and all the students seemed to enjoy the worship. I call it worship because the Campus Choir students were not ashamed to worship the Lord, even at 1:30 p.m. in a public school.

When the audience in the auditorium was at its peak, Dr. Horton took control of the microphone. He stood flat-footed, unashamed, and confident while he declared the Word of God. Yes, he stood on a public-school stage at 1:30 p.m. during a school day and preached to the audience. If I'm being honest, my heart sank. I thought I'd be fired. As I was languishing in the five stages of grief, I had not yet arrived at acceptance. That's when Dr. Horton took one more step forward and gave an altar call. Let me remind you, the principal and assistant principal of the school are in the same room that happens to be a public-school building.

At this point, my five stages of grief finally ended at acceptance. I had accepted my fate—my career was over. Well, it had been a good run—albeit short! We might as well make this good. To my surprise, several of my students answered the altar call, went to the stage, and Lee University students prayed with my high school students that afternoon; many of whom accepted Christ as their Savior that day.

After the worship service (see, I had accepted what it really was), I bid farewell to Dr. Horton and the choir, ended the day, bid farewell to my students (because I truly believed I would not be returning), and reported to the office without being summoned. The principal was in his office. I knocked on the door and entered. Before he could even say anything, I looked him in the eye, smiled, and said, "I'll gather my belongings this afternoon and resign tomorrow. I know I'm fired." He paused, continued to look at me, and maintained an excellent poker face. After what seemed like an eternity, he broke the silence with one simple question, "When can they come back?"

I think I was in shock at that point. It was not shock at the question because I knew the principal was a Christian but shock at the serious miracle God had just performed. It cannot be overstated—a Pentecostal church service, complete with tongues, had just occurred in the auditorium of a public school during a normal school day. Not only did I not lose my job, but I did not even receive a reprimand. In fact, the assistant principal also commented on her sheer joy at the outcome of the event. After I picked up my bottom jaw, I slowly turned and said, "I'll contact them and see if I can arrange it."

As I left school that afternoon, I heard the Word of God reverberating in my mind, "Why are ye fearful? O ye of little faith."[33] On my long drive home, I asked the Lord to forgive me for doubting Him. Are we not much better than the sparrows that are fed by God? Are we not much better than the lilies of the field that are arrayed by God?[34] While my faith grew due to this miraculous moment, it would soon be tested like never before.

The following school year, the gospel choir's popularity and renown had spread beyond the state and was beginning to attract considerable attention. One morning, I received a phone call from a reporter with a notable newspaper. The reporter was interested in writing a story on the gospel choir. Such an ensemble in the public school was quite an anomaly. Ultimately, I approved his entreaty and we arranged a time for him to attend. The day arrived and the reporter attended a normal class with the gospel choir. He took pictures, interviewed students, cross-examined the principal, and finally conferenced with me.

In the course of the interviews, several students expressed how amazing it was that they were able to "sing about God right here in the classroom." The principal extolled the virtues of the class and how it was the primary catalyst for easing turbulent racial tensions prior to its inception. In my interview, I discussed how I was a licensed minister with the Church of God (Cleveland, Tennessee) and served as a minister of music in my church. When the article appeared in the newspaper, it had been written well, reflected all comments fairly, and underscored the uniqueness of the class, given its existence in public school. All seemed well but the storm was quickly approaching.

A few weeks following the release of the newspaper article, I received a letter in the school mail. Upon opening and reading it, I realized an intense struggle was upon us. The American Civil Liberties Union (ACLU) had issued a letter regarding the gospel choir. The ACLU is notorious for opposing all matters Christian and supporting all matters secular. They are also notorious for advancing lawsuits with a unique rabidity unlike other

---

33. Matthew 8:26.
34. Matthew 6:26-30.

8. THE FRONT LINES: PUBLIC EDUCATION OR PUBLIC INDOCTRINATION

organizations. Once again, my heart sank. I thought this was the end of the gospel choir, especially when I realized the ACLU had carbon-copied my principal and the school district superintendent. School districts' aversions to lawsuits are legendary. I was certain that if the principal did not require me to disband, the superintendent would. It should be noted that one of the primary concerns addressed in the letter was my employment in this capacity as a minister, given the ease of evangelism associated with the content of the musical study.

Later that same day, I met with the principal in his office. We discussed the letter. Because I had respect for him, I asked him how he would like to proceed. He informed me he had spoken with the superintendent earlier in the day and they had decided to resist and support the choir. Once again, I had a jaw-dropping moment. At this point, he asked me to devise a response to the ACLU and develop a plan for future investigations. As I slowly left his office, in a state of shock, I gathered my senses and immediately crafted a response letter. It must have been Holy Ghost boldness that swelled within my spirit because not only did I communicate that we would not disband the ensemble but I challenged the ACLU to "leave their ivory tower and rather than blindly issue edicts, they should attend a class to see what our ensemble was about." I then proceeded to dig in a little deeper with, "Better yet, please accept my invitation to be my special guest at our fall concert. I will leave several tickets in the lobby for you."

Each Christmas, I hired a symphony orchestra and combined all my choirs to produce a full-scale musical work. Just the previous year, I had produced Lanny Wolfe's *The Greatest Story*—yes, *that* greatest story—complete with the nativity scene and baby Jesus. The year of the ACLU challenge, I had planned a show titled *The History of the American Song*, complete with many hymns and gospel songs. I began to worry that perhaps I had bitten off more than I could chew.

Throughout the semester, word began to spread like wildfire that the ACLU had challenged the choir and me. Churches and community organizations began to flood my office phone and email inbox with a desire to "fight back." Several churches had planned a protest to resist the ACLU on the night of the concert. I issued a statement to the general public that while I sincerely appreciate the love and support for my students and me, that I respectfully requested no one protest the ACLU on the night of the concert and that I had specifically invited them as my special guests. Still, as the concert date approached, no one was truly certain what would happen.

The night of the concert was upon us. I stationed a choir mother at the ticket desk. It was her sole responsibility to greet the ACLU members and escort them to their seats. It was my intention to demonstrate the love of Christ to them. Nervously, I awaited the signal from her that they had arrived. By the start of the show, she had not provided that signal. Confused, I took the podium and dropped the baton to begin the opening number. The house was packed and was standing room only. The community demonstrated their support in a mighty way that evening. Before the end of the show, I addressed the audience, thanking them for their support and love. No one protested, no one demanded the show end, and the concert was beautiful. At the end of the show, I asked the choir mother if the ACLU members had attended. She indicated that no one specifically indicated they were in attendance for that purpose but she did see a few people she did not recognize (this was a small town, tight-knit community with a choir mother who knew everyone) and thought they perhaps attended incognito.

In the weeks and months that followed, we received no further letters from the ACLU. They had, effectively, relented. In the years that followed while reminiscing about those moments, I became increasingly impressed with how God moved. Not only did God lead us into a battle with a seemingly impregnable enemy, but He turned around what the enemy had intended for evil and made it good.[35] That night, we raised more money than we had at any concert previously. Not only did God put the enemy to flight,[36] but he used the notoriety of the enemy's challenge to us to provide an increase.[37] I am reminded of how Goliath, who had not been previously defeated, called out the army of Israel. David, a lowly shepherd boy, answered the call and slew a seemingly impregnable foe. The ACLU was our choir's Goliath and God rode in on the wings of praise, built a hedge of protection around His work, and slew the enemy. To God be the glory for the great things He has done!

Religious Texts in Public Schools

This specific experience relates to the oft-challenged Christmas carol or religious music played or sung in school. The law is clear, if the primary purpose of the music is to teach an educational skill or concept, it is allowable. One

---

35. Genesis 50:20.
36. Joshua 23:10.
37. 1 Corinthians 3:6.

8. THE FRONT LINES: PUBLIC EDUCATION OR PUBLIC INDOCTRINATION

must remember, ninety percent of classical choral music from the sixteenth to early twentieth centuries was composed exclusively for the use in the church. To completely eradicate all religious music would eliminate classical standards of which all humanity should know and appreciate. Furthermore, the National Association for Music Education supports the use of sacred music in the classroom when utilized for educative purposes.[38]

This also directly relates to the use of the Bible in school. Christians should not resist the inclusion of "Bible as Literature" classes. While such classes do often negate the authority of Scripture as a spiritual text and make attempts at classifying it as a work of fiction, we must be reminded of the inherent power in the Word of God. Again, it will not return void.

The Proscription of Prayer

Perhaps the most virulently sanctioned activity in the public school for Christians is prayer. While students may pray aloud at non-instructional times and silently whenever they please, teachers do not necessarily possess such luxuries. Teachers often wonder about the legality of praying in school, whether with students or alone. While the law is unclear, it has been the opinion of courts that when in the confines of the normal school day, expressive prayer is not allowed. Restrictions on prayer with students extend even to those moments when students may ask for prayer. However, if a student asks for prayer, a teacher may indicate that he or she will pray for the student. In fact, a teacher may generally indicate that he or she prays for students even without prompting. There are, however, no restrictions on praying silently or privately for teachers.

While restrictions on the Bible are serious, they are not as deeply pertinacious as those on prayer. This begs the question of why there are such strenuous restrictions on prayer. In fact, the majority of the most high-profile landmark court cases center on prayer with the majority of those resulting in restricted prayer. Even today, one will often read of controversies surrounding student-led prayer at school sporting events, graduations, and in other public arenas such as county commissioner, board of education, and city council meetings. At least the Bible can maintain a curricular

---

38. National Association for Music Education, "Sacred Music in Schools (Position Statement)," NAfME.org, https://nafme.org/my-classroom/music-selection/sacred-music/sacred-music-in-schools-position-statement/.

function. What is it about prayer that results in the most acrimonious resistance from secularists?

The enemy knows there is dynamic power in prayer. Now, it must be noted, this is not just any prayer but the prayer of a righteous man or woman.[39] In fact, Scripture reveals to us that whatever we ask *in His name*, that will He do.[40] The qualifier to this passage of Scripture is that our petitions must be made in the name of the Lord. The Lord promised our needs would be met and not necessarily our wants;[41] although, He will, at times, supply those, as well.[42] Wants, when supplied, however, are likely according to the will of God and are meant for a greater purpose. Because as children of the Almighty God, we have the privilege to call unto God whenever we wish. Notice I utilized the word "privilege." Too often we exalt ourselves in declaring we have a "right" to call on God.

God is not our butler, secretary, or governmental representative. He does not exist to be at our beck and call. Because Jesus Christ, God's only Son, has covered us with His precious blood, we have been made heirs and joint-heirs with Jesus,[43] thus we have been granted the privilege to approach the throne of the God Who was, is, and is to come. God is faithful to *hear* our prayers.[44] There are times when God answers with "yes," times when the answer is "no," times when the answer is "wait," and times when He does not answer until much later. I, personally, have known God not answer prayers for saints until long after their deaths. How amazing it is to know the effectual fervent prayers of righteous men and women linger even after they enter their reward!

The effectual, fervent prayer of saints for millennia has captured the attention of God and moved Him to action. The enemy thinks that if he can extinguish the illuminating power of prayer from the public schools, he can fulfill his mission of dominating the narrative delivered to students and promulgating his evil agenda of destroying generations. Not only is it imperative for Christians in the school to conquer Satan's plan to create bastions of wickedness that will bleed out into the communities;

---

39. James 5:16.
40. John 14:13-14.
41. Philippians 4:19.
42. Genesis 18:16-33; John 15:7.
43. Romans 8:16-18.
44. 1 John 5:14.

8. THE FRONT LINES: PUBLIC EDUCATION OR PUBLIC INDOCTRINATION

Christians outside school, even those with no children in the system, must answer the call to battle, as well.

It is every American Christian's right to walk onto a campus and declare the ground on which he or she stands as belonging to Christ. It is every American Christian's right to even walk into the school, during non-instructional time, and anoint the hallways with oil and pray for the convicting power of the Holy Spirit to permeate the building. Where are the warriors? The American public-school system is a mission field white unto harvest but the laborers are few.[45]

A Call from the Mission Field

It is time for we, the people of God and of America, to rededicate our lives *exclusively* unto God; generate a modern spiritual awakening in our homes, churches, and communities; rouse our bodies and minds from the spiritual slumber Satan has inflicted upon God's people; be filled with the dynamic power of the Holy Ghost; put on the whole armor of God;[46] and march into battle against the blasphemous, iniquitous soul-destroying agenda being perpetrated on our culture through public indoctrination of our children. It is our right as Christians and tax-paying Americans to fully understand what is included in the curriculum being administered to our children. If this curriculum is filled with sacrilegious dogma, it is codified in the establishment clause of the First Amendment of the Constitution that this is government support of religious defamation and we have the right to demand its cessation. Christians can utilize the establishment clause to their advantage, as well!

If a teacher is publicly proselytizing to a doctrine of atheism and profanity, it is our right to demand an injunction. Indeed, we must understand the modern practice. Faith in the faithless and secular is, in and of itself, a religious movement. Promulgating the tenets of this faith in the public arena is tantamount to a violation of the establishment clause and we must reveal this practice whenever it is encountered.

Christians must research and study once again to fully comprehend the methods of attack against our public institutions. Unfortunately, too many Christians have allowed themselves to succumb to mental and

---

45. Luke 10:2.
46. Ephesians 6:10-18.

spiritual atrophy whereby we can no longer discern evil even when we are positioned in the center of it.

As a Christian public school administrator, I am crying in the wilderness, imploring the faithful to turn their attention to the foundational destruction of the future that is occurring in real time right at the center of the community in public schools. The agenda of the progressive, secular, liberal Left in this nation is nothing short of a faith movement. They should be subject to the same restrictions on faith practice and evangelism in public institutions as any other faith. This requires us to be sober and vigilant because Satan is walking about as a roaring lion seeking his next meal.[47] I can, beyond a shadow of a doubt, reveal his menu to the world: it is our children, served hot and without hedges of protection, on the buffet of public schools. He is moving about our hallways with reckless abandon, completely unshackled, wreaking havoc and destruction as he sees fit.

I have surveyed the land. I am bearing witness to destruction like no other. In some instances, the destruction is subversive and silent; other times, it is blatant and boisterous. The roaring lion's teeth are dripping with the ruined lives of our children while we, as Christians, sleep. The hallways of our public schools are flowing red with innocent blood, calling out for someone to tell them the truth and provide a way of escape. The church stands idly by watching while the future burns. The darkness that has permeated the once hallowed halls of learning spreads unimpeded while the church socializes. Where is the church? Where are God's people? Where are the warriors? "And I sought for a man among them, that should make up the hedge, and stand in the gap before me in the land, that I should not destroy it: but I found none."[48]

---

47. 1 Peter 5:8.
48. Ezekiel 22:30.

9. THE SECRET WEAPON: PRAYER

As long as I live, I will never forget the night I took a portion of my public-school gospel choir to lead worship in a Pentecostal church a few towns over from our school. This ensemble was a smaller, more portable group because the whole choir had grown too large for easy transport. Furthermore, many of the churches were of insufficient size to hold the full choir. The ensemble was comprised of seven singers, a drummer, bassist, and I played the piano. Unbeknownst to me at the time, one of the singers, a sixteen-year-old boy, had been struggling with homosexuality. For the record, the auditioned singers in this ensemble had been reared in a strict Pentecostal tradition.

The service that night was one of the most powerful services I can remember. The Holy Ghost moved on the congregation as well as my students. A few of them were even slain in the Spirit. Near the end of the service, I noticed all the students converging on the one student who was struggling with homosexuality. They began some of the most earnest and forceful prayers I had ever heard. Their petitions to the Lord continued even after the service ended. Little did I know at the time, they were casting out an evil spirit that had been afflicting this young man.

Once they were satisfied the Lord had heard their prayers, the young man was drained to the point in which we carried him back to the bus to go home. This was an act initiated by these students for one of their own. It was not something that required pumping and priming to get them there. I will reiterate: I was completely unaware of the young man's struggle and, for a while, was unaware of the content of their prayers. The Lord miraculously delivered the young man that night. To this day, he is married with children and is serving the Lord. The Lord still answers prayer. He still delivers from sin. He will deliver from the spirit of homosexuality if allowed.

I titled this chapter "The Secret Weapon" for a specific reason. Research indicates that the average Christian spends less than ten minutes per day in prayer.[1] The average pastor spends less than thirty-nine minutes a day in

---

1. Daniel Henderson, "No Time to pray," *Praying Pastor* (blog), February 5, 2009, http://prayingpastorblog.blogspot.com/2009/02/no-time-to-pray-no-time-to-pray.html.

prayer. Fifty-five percent of adults in America indicated they pray.[2] Pew Research statistics also highlight a disturbing trend. The younger the generation, the less prayer is performed. Only sixteen percent of young adults ages eighteen to twenty-nine reported daily prayer while thirty-three percent reportedly seldom or never prayed. Among those with increasing levels of education, they seldom or never pray when compared with those who possess a high school diploma or less. This obviously relates to the liberal, progressive ideology taught in American colleges and universities.

The research also indicated that the more people pray, the more they believe in absolute standards of right and wrong. The more ideologically liberal one may be, the less they pray. The less people pray, the more accepting of sin they become. Prayer is a secret weapon because, apparently, there are not many who have realized how life-altering it can be for them and their families. God is not intentionally concealing the power of prayer so humankind will not find out some mysterious secret of the universe that God wants hidden. In fact, the Lord encouraged constant prayer[3] while extolling the benefits and virtues of a robust prayer life.[4]

With all the benefits to prayer the Lord has rehearsed in His word, why are the statistics for prayer so abysmal? The reader should recall: these were statistics related to professed Christians. Could it be that people simply believe they do not have the time to pray? Do people believe prayer is unimportant? Are they not witnessing the benefits of prayer, causing them to relegate it? Frankly, it could be any of these possibilities and more. Ultimately, Satan will concoct methods to distract us from prayer and keep our emaciated prayer life in a constant state of ineffectiveness.

Satan is aware his time on earth is quickly coming to an end. His primary mission is to destroy as much of God's creation as he can. He despises humankind because, unlike him, we have a chance to be redeemed. God created humankind in His image and since Satan could not usurp the authority of God, he has settled on destroying the next best thing: we who are the image of God.[5] He understands that prayerlessness equals weakness. If he can keep people in a constant state of flux, he can keep them from praying, thus he has a better chance at destroying the image of God. It is a

---

2. Pew Research Forum, "Frequency of Prayer," *Religious Landscape Study*, 2018, http://www.pewforum.org/religious-landscape-study/frequency-of-prayer/.

3. 1 Thessalonians 5:17.

4. Jeremiah 33:3; Psalms 17:6; 145:18; James 5:16; 1 John 1:9.

5. Genesis 1:27.

vicious cycle: maintaining the status quo on prayerlessness preserves our weakness in which Satan can then utilize our weakness to further perpetuate prayerlessness, thus sustaining our constant state of defeat. He is very cognizant that a praying person is a victorious person. One is victorious even when, to the outside world, it looks like he or she has lost.

I will never forget how my grandmother, while dying in the hospital for a month, lost much of her mind but never lost knowledge of Jesus. As she was dying, I remember her clearly saying, "Oh look at that city! How beautiful it is." There was no doubt that she was seeing the city of God. She began to reach out to it. To the world, she had lost a health battle but in the spiritual realm, she had fought the good fight, finished her course, and kept the faith. She had a crown of righteousness laid up for her that the Lord would place on her head.[6] It is that crown that, no doubt for my grandmother, is so large and heavy that it will take some effort to cast it at Jesus's feet.

The saint who may be dying from cancer looks like he or she has lost the battle. In reality, he or she is gaining a city not made with hands.[7] The dying saint can pass away peacefully because he or she knows that when he or she closes his or her eyes in death, he or she will open them in glory.[8] All of the pain and suffering will be worth it once we see Jesus and hear Him say, "Well done, thou good and faithful servant: thou hast been faithful over a few things, I will make thee ruler over many things: enter thou into the joy of thy Lord."[9] It was Paul who clearly stated, "For me to live is Christ, and to die is gain."[10]

One of my favorite topics of research is the brain. I witnessed one video in a psychology of music course in which a patient was featured who was near death due to Alzheimer's disease. This patient was a piano teacher who also played for her church. Once the staff sat her at the piano, she began to play the songs of Zion as if she had never stopped. This was someone, by all scientific and medical accounts, should not have had the brain matter remaining to do such. It reminded me that Alzheimer's may be able to ransack the brain of every memory, but for the children of the Most High God, it can never remove Jesus from the mind.

6. 2 Timothy 4:7-8.
7. 2 Corinthians 5:1.
8. Luke 16:19-31.
9. Matthew 25:21.
10. Philippians 1:21.

A dear saint of God from my church suffered from dementia and was confined to a rehabilitation facility. Speaking often with his daughter, she would recount how he often had trouble remembering the names of his closest loved ones. However, she often spoke of how, when she would visit him, she would find him reading his Bible and praying. He never forgot those spiritual aspects of his life that he made invaluable. It was something dementia could not pillage from his mind. Even in the process of death and dying, prayer and the Word of God still accomplishes exactly what it sets forth to accomplish.[11]

Prayer opens the heart and mind to God. It is a method by which we can communicate directly with the throne room of heaven and God can communicate with us. Prayer does not have to occur on one's knees in his or her closet; although, prayer on one's knees is symbolic of humbleness. I pray in my car more than anywhere else. My pastor emeritus indicated he prefers to pray prostrate. Everyone has his or her preferred method of prayer. The key to prayer is not in *where* one prays or the physical position *in which* one prays but in the act of praying.

How can Christians defeat the attacks of the enemy outlined in this book? By prayer. I worry when Christians who have an honest concern about not doing enough state that all they can do is pray while a loved one is experiencing difficulty. To be fair, the human mind seeks to control sometimes uncontrollable situations and when that is impossible, one feels powerless. But this is exactly where God wishes to bring His people—to a place of powerlessness in themselves. The apostle Paul wrote in 2 Corinthians 12:7-10 that the Lord's strength is made perfect in weakness and that we should glory in those weaknesses because the power of Christ may work through us. This is exactly the position in which Christ Jesus wishes us to assume. When we admit we have no power within ourselves, that's when His awesome power may work. Prayer is not all we can do, it is the *best* anyone can do.

One thing of which we should be sure: when we begin praying for divine intervention into the issues outlined in this book, Satan will send a buffer.[12] We must understand that Satan has a major foothold in the public arena, particularly in our nation's schools and universities. Leftist ideologies espoused and publicly proclaimed are nothing more than demonically influenced propaganda designed to confuse our children and

---

11. Isaiah 55:11.
12. 2 Corinthians 12:7.

young people. Curriculum written from a revisionist position designed to eliminate the work of God in the founding of the nation, the mathematical impossibilities of a non-existent God,[13] the beauty of holiness in literature, the empirical scientific evidence that points to the God of Creation, and the lifestyle of sanctification in which we should live, is designed to destroy the innate sensibilities, logic, and rationality of moral law written on the hearts of humankind by the Author of the universe.

Territorial spirits exist in our world. The writer of Daniel 10:13 recounted such an encounter by what appeared to an angel who, while on his way to Daniel as a result of prayer, was delayed by the "Prince of Persia" and had to be assisted by Michael, the Archangel. Not only do I believe there are territorial spirits controlling cities, governments, states, and nations; I believe there are strong territorial spirits governing institutions like schools, universities, and political parties. An "asleep in Zion," "Laodicean" church will not possess the spiritual stamina to overcome such highly concentrated powers. The churches of "being the best you can be" will not have the knowledge necessary to entreat heavenly intervention. It will take an on-fire, Holy Ghost-filled, prayed-up church body to break those powers. But where is that church body?

A Final Entreaty

"Put on the whole armor of God, that ye may be able to stand against the wiles of the devil. For we wrestle not against flesh and blood, but against principalities, against powers, against the rulers of darkness of this world, against spiritual wickedness in high places. Wherefore take unto you the whole armor of God, that ye may be able to withstand in the evil day, and having done all, to stand. Stand therefore . . ."[14] It is a constant battle for the Christian in our nation's public arenas and it will wax worse.[15] We should never be so naïve as to think that the Christian life will be a bed of roses. We should never be so ignorant that we cannot see the fight we have before us. Indeed, it is a fight. Jude wrote that we must "earnestly contend for the faith which was once delivered unto the saints."[16]

---

13. Norman L. Geisler, *Christian Apologetics* (Grand Rapids, MI: Baker Academic, 2013).
14. Ephesians 6:11-14.
15. 2 Timothy 3:13.
16. Jude 1:3.

Our fight, however, it not with other people, even though it appears as such. Our fight is not with a political party. It is not with the government. It is not with school and university leadership. It is not with heretical and hireling preachers. It is not with the Leftist, liberal mainstream media. It is not with ourselves, our families, or our children. Our fight is not even with a damnable leftist, socialist, communist ideology. These are all consequences of a weak church, the imminent end of time, and a public satanic agenda at work. We have to remember: Satan's days are short. He has read the Bible; ultimately, he knows what is going to happen to him. There is nothing he can do to stop this. It has been written and will be fulfilled. He is working overtime to destroy as many lives as he can and ensure hell as a final, eternal prison.

But given the imminent return of Christ for His church, why should we earnestly contend? We know what is going to happen. The Bible is clear that evil men are going to wax worse. We know that in the last days, good shall be called evil and evil good. What is the point? Should we not simply abide as best as we can until Jesus comes?

For certain, this attitude would make last-days life simpler. It would be nice to keep our heads down, go about our daily lives, keep to ourselves, refrain from speaking out, and simply live out the last days until Christ's return. But this is not what the Lord called us to do. In fact, He commanded us to "Go ye therefore, and teach all nations, baptizing them in the name of the Father, and of the Son, and of the Holy Ghost: Teaching them to observe all things whatsoever I have commanded you."[17] We *must* earnestly contend for the faith. If we wish to obey the Lord, we have no other choice.

There is a field white unto harvest.[18] I have seen no greater harvest field than in our public schools and universities but the laborers are few. The work will not be easy. In fact, there will be times when it seems impossible. Satan will buffet at every step. He will work diligently to wear down the laborer. The Christian will be met with severe resistance and possible outright persecution.

We need revival in our public institutions. We need the church to reclaim its rightful position as the compass for a community's conscience. We need prayer warriors who are sufficiently bold enough to come to a school each day and anoint the door frames and lockers. We need Holy Ghost-filled Christians to call school principals and ask if they may come in

---

17. Matthew 28:19-20.
18. John 4:35.

9. THE SECRET WEAPON: PRAYER

and pray for them daily. We need Christian teachers to assume positions of authority over the nation's classrooms and refrain from retreating to private schools where your voice is likely blended with several like voices. We need the voices crying in the wilderness. We need Christians who work and assume positions of authority over entire school districts who will cry out to the Lord on behalf of their students. We need Holy Ghost-filled students who will boldly proclaim, "Thus saith the Lord" when they are taught lies contrary to the Word of God. We need bold students who will lead one another to the saving grace of Christ Jesus.

We need the church to rise up and face down the enemy when organizations like the ACLU come in and try to eradicate the public square of God. We need Christians to pray for the nation; not just a simple "lay me down to sleep" prayer but one in which we earnestly contend with the enemy for the souls of our families and nation. We need to demand that our legislators place Christian chancellors and presidents in our colleges and universities who will weed out the leftist ideology of Satan and will stand against the powers of darkness when they try to impede free speech.

We need the laborers. I stand on the front lines of the battle in our public schools. Make no mistake: our public schools are indeed the front lines. I see the destruction Satan is rendering. I see the leftist, socialistic agenda propagated on a daily basis. The curriculum is rife with socialist, anti-Christian propaganda. The leftists have organized themselves to hold positions of authority in schools and universities with the expressed mission of fundamentally changing America. They preach pluralism, secularism, socialism, communism, social justice, relativism, the homosexual agenda, gender confusion, postmodernism, progressivism, and atheism.

We have the truth and we should always share it. Let me be clear: these "isms" are nothing short of religions. Separation of church and state can and should be a two-way street. We should never allow tax-funded organizations to promote these religious ideologies on our watch. But again, where is the church? For far too long, she has been silent. It is time to wake up. Our children are at stake. It is time we, as the body of Christ, shake ourselves once again, find our moral center, get back to holiness as God's standard for living, seek the face of God, and allow Him to lead us into battle.

BIBLIOGRAPHY

A Common Word, "Loving God and Neighbor Together: A Christian Response to a Common Word Between Us and You," *Yale Faith,* https://www.acommonword.com/wp-content/uploads/2018/05/Response_300_leading_Christian_scholars.pdf.

Abington School District v. Schempp, 374 U.S. 203 (1963).

Adams, D. L. "Saul Alinsky and the Rise of Amorality in American Politics." *New English Review.* (January 2010). https://www.newenglishreview.org/DL_Adams/Saul_Alinsky_and_the_Rise_of_Amorality_in_American_Politics/.

Alinsky, Saul D. *Rules for Radicals: A Pragmatic Primer for Realistic Radicals.*

Bandura, Albert. *Social Learning Theory.*

Bell, Larry. "Blood and Gore: Making a Killing on Anti-Carbon Investment Hike." *Forbes.* (November 3, 2013). https://www.forbes.com/sites/larrybell/2013/11/03/blood-and-gore-making-a-killing-on-anti-carbon-investment-hype/#dbc64ee32dc9.

Benedict, Ruth. "Anthropology and the Abnormal." *The Journal of General Psychology,* 10, 1934.

Bloom, Benjamin S. *Taxonomy of Educational Objectives: The Classification of Educational Goals.*

Brett, R. "Turn and Face the Strange – Occultist Aleister Crowley's Influence on Popular Music. *Louder Than War.* (November 17, 2017). https://louderthanwar.com/aleister-crowley-influence-on-popular-music/.

Burgess, J. W. *Political Science and Comparative Constitutional Law.*

Carmody, R. "Trans young people at alarmingly high risk of suicide and depression, report reveals." *ABC News.* (September 1, 2017). http://www.abc.net.au/news/2017-09-01/young-trans-people-at-higher-risk-of-suicide-report-finds/8861156.

Cillizza, Chris. "Harry Reid lied about Mitt Romney's taxes. *The Washington Post.* (September 15, 2016), https://www.washingtonpost.com/news/the-fix/wp/2016/09/15/harry-reid-lied-about-mitt-romneys-taxes-hes-still-not-sorry/?noredirect=on&utm_term=.bc8b14ce5cf1.

Clemens, C. "What We Mean When We Say 'Toxic Masculinity.'" Tolerance.org. (December 11, 2017). https://www.tolerance.org/magazine/what-we-mean-when-we-say-toxic-masculinity.

Colb, S. F. "Withdrawing Consent During Intercourse: California's Highest Court Clarifies the Definition of Rape." FindLaw. (March 1, 2019). https://supreme.findlaw.com/legal-commentary/withdrawing-consent-during-intercourse.html.

Conley, J. J. "Margaret Sanger was a eugenicist: Why are we still celebrating her?" *America: The Jesuit Review.* (November 27, 2017). https://www.americamagazine.org/politics-society/2017/11/27/margaret-sanger-was-eugenicist-why-are-we-still-celebrating-her.

Council for Secular Humanism. "What is Secular Humanism?" SecularHumanism.org. (2018). https://www.secularhumanism.org/.

BIBLIOGRAPHY

Crowley, Aleister. *The Book of the Law (Centennial ed.). (2004).*

———. *Magick: Liber ABA, Book 4.* Parts 1 to 4, 2nd rev. ed. (1997).

Darwin, Charles. *On the Origin of Species by Means of Natural Selection, or, the Preservation of Favoured Races in the Struggle for Life.*

Davis, M. "Why humanity owes a lot to Jupiter." *Big Think.* (November 9, 2018). https://bigthink.com/surprising-science/how-jupiter-protects-earth?rebelltitem=1#rebellitem1.

Dewey, John. *Liberalism and Social Action.*

Eccles, J. S. "The Development of Children Ages 6 to 14." *Future Child,* 9, no. 2 (1999), 30-44.

Edmonson, C. "Sonia Sotomayor Delivers Sharp Defense in Travel Ban Case." *The New York Times.* June 26, 2018.

Engel v. Vitale, 370 U.S. 421 (1962).

Fard, M. F. "Sandra Fluke, Georgetown student called a 'slut' by Rush Limbaugh, speaks out." *The Washington Post,* (March 2, 2012). https://www.washingtonpost.com/blogs/the-buzz/post/rush-limbaugh-calls-georgetown student-sandra-fluke-a-slut-for-advocating-contraception/2012/03/02/gIQAvjfSmR_blog.html?utm_term=.ef46964718f4.

Foucault, M. (1988). *Foucault Live (Interviews 1961-1984).*

Freud, Sigmund. *The Ego and the Id.* In J. Strachey (Ed. and Trans.), *The Standard Edition of the Complete Psychological Works of Sigmund Freud,* vol. 19, 3-66.

Frost, J. J., L. Frohwirth, and M.R. Zolna. *Contraceptive Needs and Services, 2014 Update,* (2014).

Gandhi, Mahatma. *Collected Works of Mahatma Gandhi.*

Geisler, Norman L. *Christian Apologetics.*

Geisler, Norman and Frank Turek. *I Don't Have Enough Faith to Be an Atheist.*

Glum, J. "Bernie Sanders. "Who is Rich, Complains That Wealthy People Always Want 'More, More and More.'" *Newsweek.* (November 13, 2017). http://www.newsweek.com/bernie-sanders-net-worth-assets-cnn-column-oligarchy-709692.

Gray, R. "Star's song captured by scientists." *The Telegraph,* (2010), https://www.telegraph.co.uk/news/science/space/8114694/Stars-song-captured-by-scientists.html.

Griffin, David Ray. *Process Theology: On Postmodernism, Morality, Pluralism, Eschatology, and Demonic Evil.*

Hanson, Victor Davis. "Obama: Transforming America. *National Review.* (October 1, 2013). https://www.nationalreview.com/2013/10/obama-transforming-america-victor-davis-hanson/.

Hegel, G. *General Introduction to the Philosophy of History by Hegel.* [online], 1837.

Henderson, Daniel. "No Time to Pray." *Praying Pastor.*

Hick, John. *A Christian Theology of Religious: The Rainbow of Faiths.*

Hicks, Stephen. *Explaining Postmodernism: Skepticism and Socialism from Rousseau to Foucault.*

Hill, C. "Almost half of Americans won't pay federal income tax." *New York Post.* (April 18, 2017). https://nypost.com/2017/04/18/almost-half-of-americans-wont-pay-federal-income-tax/.

Hodges, M. "CDC: 35% of aborted babies are black." *Life Site.* (December 5, 2016). https://www.lifesitenews.com/news/cdc-statistics-indicate-abortion-rate-continues-to-be-higher-among-minoriti.

BIBLIOGRAPHY

Huitt, W. and J. Hummel. "Piaget's Theory of Cognitive Development." *Educational Psychology Interactive.* (2003). http://www.edpsycinteractive.org/topics/cognition/piaget.html.

Hull, G. G. "Biblical Feminism: A Christian Response to Sexism. *Priscilla Papers: The Academic Journal of CBE International.* (1990).

Hutcheson, Francis. *Reflections on the Common Systems of Morality.* In *Francis Hutcheson: On Human Nature,* ed. Thomas Mautner. (1993).

Jennings, S. "Ralph Northam should be remembered for advocating the slaughtering of deformed babies." *USA Today.* (February 5, 2019). https://www.usatoday.com/story/opinion/2019/02/05/ralph-northam-advocating-abortion-infanticide-worse-than-blackface-column/2776498002/.

Johnson, D. "Al Gore's Personal Energy Use Is His Own 'Inconvenient Truth.'" *The Chattanoogan.* (February 26, 2007). http://www.chattanoogan.com/2007/2/26/102512/Al-Gores-Personal-Energy-Use-Is-His.aspx.

Koehne, Samuel. "Hitler's Faith: The debate over Nazism and religion. *ABCNews.com.* (April 18, 2012). http://www.abc.net.au/religion/hitlers-faith-the-debate-over-nazism-and-religion/10100614.

Kranz, J. "Which Old Testament Book Did Jesus Quote Most?" *Biblia.* http://blog.biblia.com/2014/04/which-old-testament-book-did-jesus-quote-most.

LeMay, Michael D. *The Suicide of American Christianity: Drinking the "Cool"-Aid of Secular Humanism.* Bloomington, IN: WestBow Press, 2012.

Lemon v. Kurtzman, 403 U.S. 602 (1971).

Lyotard, Jean-Francois. *Postmodern Fables.*

Mac Donald, Heather. *The Diversity Delusion: How Race and Gender Pandering Corrupt the University and Undermine Our Culture.* New York: St. Martin's Press, 2018.

Marx, Karl and Friedrich Engels. *The Communist Manifesto.*

Mattera, Joseph. "8 Signs of 'Hypergrace' Churches." *CharismaNews.* (June 28, 2013). https://www.charismanews.com/opinion/40060-eight-signs-of-hyper-grace-churches.

McGinnis, B. "Who is Lucy Flores? Nevada politician has accused Joe Biden of unwanted kiss on back of her head." *USA Today.* (March 30, 2019). https://www.usatoday.com/story/news/politics/2019/03/30/who-lucy-flores-who-has-accused-joe-biden-sexual-harassment/3319322002/.

Miller, E. M. "What Does the Bible Say About Ghosts?" *Relevant Magazine.* (October 21, 2017). https://relevantmagazine.com/god/worldview/what-does-bible-say-about-ghosts2.

Mohamed, Besheer and Elizabeth Podrebarac Sciupac. "The share of Americans who leave Islam is offset by those who become Muslim. *Pew Research Center.* (January 26, 2018). https://www.pewresearch.org/fact-tank/2018/01/26/the-share-of-americans-who-leave-islam-is-offset-by-those-who-become-muslim/.

Moore, A. "Al Gore Busted About Private Jet Use." *DCStatesman.* (2017). https://www.dcstatesman.com/al-gore-busted-private-jet-use/.

Moore, G. E. *Principia Ethica.*

Moreland, J. P. *Scientism and Secularism.*

National Association for Music Education. "Sacred Music in Schools (Position Statement)." (1996). https://nafme.org/my-classroom/music-selection/sacred-music/sacred-music-in-schools-position-statement/.

Nazarene Church Growth Research. "Evangelism statistics: At what age is outreach most effective?" *When Americans Become Christian*. (2015). http://home.snu.edu/~hculbert/ages.htm.

Newton, Isaac. *Newton's Principia: The Mathematical Principles of Natural Philosophy*.

O'Kane, C. "New York passes law allowing abortions at any time if the mother's health is at risk." *CBS News*. (January 24, 2019). https://www.cbsnews.com/news/new-york-passes-abortion-bill-late-term-if-mothers-health-is-at-risk-today-2019-01-23/.

Oppenheimer, Mark. "The Church of Oprah Winfrey and a Theology of Suffering." *New York Times*. (May 27, 2011). https://www.nytimes.com/2011/05/28/us/28beliefs.html.

Patton, C. M. "Oprah's Millions of Paths to God: Dealing with Religious Diversity." *CredoHouse.org*. (May 20, 2008). https://credohouse.org/blog/oprahs-millions-of-paths-to-god-dealing-with-religious-diversity.

Patton, Judd. "The Pilgrim Story: Vital Insights and Lessons for Today." Bellevue University Economics Department. (2000). http://jpatton.bellevue.edu/biblical_economics/pilgrimstory.html.

Perkins, Tony. "Late-Term Abortions: A Tough Fact to Follow." Tony Perkins' Washington Update. (February 7, 2019). https://www.frc.org/updatearticle/20190207/tough-fact.

Pew Research Forum. "Frequency of Prayer." *Religious Landscape Study*. (2018). http://www.pewforum.org/religious-landscape-study/frequency-of-prayer/.

Piaget, Jean. *The Moral Judgment of the Child*.

Planned Parenthood. "PPFA Margaret Sanger Award Winners." Planned Parenthood. (2018). https://www.plannedparenthood.org/about-us/newsroom/campaigns/ppfa-margaret-sanger-award-winners.

Pojman, Louis. "A Defense of Ethical Objectivism." *Moral Philosophy, Fourth Edition*.

Post Editorial Board. "Why is CNN avoiding the truth about Lanny Davis' lies?" *New York Post*. (August 29, 2018). https://nypost.com/2018/08/29/why-is-cnn-avoiding-the-truth-about-lanny-davis-lies/.

Raico, R. "What is Classical Liberalism?" Mises Daily Articles. (November 1, 2018). https://mises.org/library/what-classical-liberalism.

Rectenwald, Michael. *Springtime for Snowflakes: "Social Justice" and Its Postmodern Parentage*. Nashville, TN: New English Review Press, 2018.

Reilly, P. J. "Bernie Sanders and the 90% Income Tax Rate That He Does Not Call For." *Forbes*. (December 18, 2015). https://www.forbes.com/sites/peterjreilly/2015/12/18/bernie-sanders-and-the-90-income-tax-rate-that-he-does-not-call-for/#7e3a44bc69dc.

Religious Freedom Center. *A Teacher's Guide to Religion in the Public Schools*. (2014). https://www.religiousfreedomcenter.org/wp-content/uploads/2014/08/teachersguide.pdf.

Roberts, W. R., I. Bywater, F. Solmsen, & Aristotle. *Rhetoric*.

Samenow, Jason. "Debunking the claim 'they' changed 'global warming' to 'climate change' because warming stopped." *The Washington Post*. (January 29, 2018). https://www.washingtonpost.com/news/capital-weather-gang/wp/2018/01/29/debunking-the-claim-they-changed-global-warming-to-climate-change-because-its-cooling/?utm_term=.48be66b92f9c.

Sanger, M. "My Way for Peace." MSM Margaret Sanger Papers. Library of Congress: Washington, DC.

Sanger, Margaret and Paul Avrich Collection (Library of Congress). *Margaret Sanger: An Autobiography*.

BIBLIOGRAPHY

Schambra, William and Thomas West. "The Progressive Movement and the Transformation of American Politics." The Heritage Foundation. (July 18, 2007). https://www.heritage.org/political-process/report/the-progressive-movement-and-the-transformation-american-politics.
Serena, Katie. "How Aleister Crowley Inspired Led Zeppelin – and Terrified Most Everyone Else." *ATI*. (February 12, 2018). https://www.allthatsinteresting.com/aleister-crowley.
Sharot, Tali. *The Influential Mind: What the Brain Reveals About Our Power to Change Others.*
Shermer, M. "The Unfortunate Fallout of Campus Postmodernism: The Roots of the Current Campus Madness." *Scientific American,* 317, no. 3, 90 (2017).
Smith, A. "Bernie Sanders' income tax brackets: How much would you owe?" *The Motley Fool*. (May 12, 2016). https://www.usatoday.com/story/sponsor-story/motley-fool/2016/05/12/motley-fool-bernie-sanders-income-tax-brackets/32607881/.
Smith, Wilfred Cantwell. "Idolatry in Comparative Perspective." In Hick and Knitter, eds. *Myth of Christian Uniqueness.*
Sonfield, A., K. Hasstedt, and R.B. Gold. *Moving Forward: Family Planning in the Era of Health Reform.* 2014.
Street, Nathan L. "Witnessing for Christ in Public Schools: What can teachers and students say and do?" *Church of God Evangel*. (November 2017). http://www.evangelmagazine.com/2017/11/witnessing-christ-public-schools/.
Thomas. *The Summa Theologica of St. Thomas Aquinas.* 1912.
Trotsky, L. *Their Morals and Ours.* New York: Pioneer Publishers, 1939.
University of Minnesota. *Sociology: Understanding and Changing the Social World.*
Van Biema, David. "Christians: No One Path to Salvation." *Time*. (June 23, 2008). http://content.time.com/time/nation/article/0,8599,1817217,00.html.
Vygotsky, L. S. *Mind in Society: The development of higher psychological processes.* 1978.
Wade, N. "The Editorial Notebook: How Old Is Man?" *The New York Times*. (October 4, 1982). https://www.nytimes.com/1982/10/04/opinion/the-editorial-notebook-how-old-is-man.html.
Warren, Mary Ann. "The Personhood Argument in Favor of Abortion Rights." *The Monist,* 57, no. 1 (1973).
Watson, L. "The Water People." *Science Digest,* 90, 44 (1982).
Westside Community Board of Education v. Mergens, 496 U.S. 226 (1990).
Will, George. "George Will: Barbara Boxer's Position on Abortion." *Newsweek*.
Wilson, R. A. "The Enigma: Beyond the Legend of Infamy." Introduction to Israel Regardie, *The Eye in the Triangle,* (2018). http://www.aleistercrowley666.co.uk/content/bookextracts_content_text.html.
Wimberley, Alan D. *Designed for Learning: Transferring Wisdom to Digital Generations.*
———. *Reshaping the Paradigms of Teaching and Learning.*
Zacharias, Ravi. *Deliver Us from Evil: Restoring the Soul in a Disintegrating Culture.* Nashville, TN: W Publishing Group, 1997.
———. Zacharias, Ravi. *The End of Reason: A Response to the New Atheists.* Grand Rapids, MI: Zondervan, 2008.

www.ingramcontent.com/pod-product-compliance
Lightning Source LLC
Chambersburg PA
CBHW050806160426
43192CB00010B/1658